The *Sams Teach Yourself in 24 Hours* !

Sams Teach Yourself in 24 Hours books provide quick and easy ;
proven step-by-step approach that works for you. In just 24 se:
hour or less, you will tackle every task you need to get the resu
Let our experienced authors present the most accurate informa:
reliable answers—quickly!

Works Suite 99 Quick Reference

Works Shortcut Keys

KEY COMBINATION	FUNCTION
Ctrl+N	Opens a new file
Ctrl+O	Opens an existing file
Ctrl+W	Closes the active file
Ctrl+S	Saves the file
Ctrl+P	Prints the file
Ctrl+X	Cuts the selected data and places it on the Windows Clipboard
Ctrl+C	Copies the selected data and puts it on the Clipboard
Ctrl+V	Pastes the cut or copied data from the Clipboard into the file
Ctrl+A	Selects all the data in the file
Ctrl+F	Opens the Find dialog box to search for data
Ctrl+H	Opens the Replace dialog box to search and replace data
Ctrl+G	Opens the Go To dialog box to move to a specific area in the file
Ctrl+Enter	Inserts a page break in the file
F7	Opens the spelling checker tool
Shift+F7	Opens the thesaurus tool

Works Calendar Shortcut Keys

KEY COMBINATION	FUNCTION
Ctrl+N	Opens the New Appointment dialog box
Ctrl+P	Prints the Calendar
Ctrl+Z	Undoes your last action
Ctrl+X	Cuts the selected data and places it on the Windows Clipboard
Ctrl+C	Copies the selected data and puts it on the Clipboard
Ctrl+V	Pastes the cut or copied data from the Clipboard into the file
Ctrl+F	Opens the Find dialog box to search for data
Alt+1	Opens the Calendar in Day view
Alt+-	Opens the Calendar in Week view
Alt+=	Opens the Calendar in Month view
Ctrl+R	Go to previous day
Ctrl+T	Go to next day

Word 97 Shortcut Keys

KEY COMBINATION	FUNCTION
Ctrl+N	Opens a new file
Ctrl+O	Opens an existing file
Ctrl+S	Saves the file
Ctrl+P	Prints the file
Ctrl+X	Cuts the selected data and places it on the Windows Clipboard
Ctrl+C	Copies the selected data and puts it on the Clipboard

continues

Word 97 Shortcut Keys (continued)

KEY COMBINATION	FUNCTION
Ctrl+V	Pastes the cut or copied data from the Clipboard into the file
Ctrl+A	Selects all the data in the file
Ctrl+F	Opens the Find dialog box to search for data
Ctrl+H	Opens the Replace dialog box to search and replace data
Ctrl+Enter	Inserts a page break in the file
Ctrl+K	Inserts a hyperlink
F7	Opens the spelling checker tool
Shift+F7	Opens the thesaurus tool
F1	Opens Office Assistant for help
Ctrl+Z	Undoes your last action
Ctrl+I	Italicizes text
Ctrl+B	Makes text bold
Ctrl+U	Underlines text
Ctrl+Shift+W	Underlines words but not spaces between words

Internet Explorer Shortcut Keys

KEY COMBINATION	FUNCTION
Ctrl+N	Opens a new browser window
Ctrl+O	Opens a Web page or folder
Ctrl+P	Prints the Web page
Ctrl+X	Cuts the selected data and places it on the Windows Clipboard
Ctrl+C	Copies the selected data and puts it on the Clipboard
Ctrl+V	Pastes the cut or copied data from the Clipboard into the file
Ctrl+A	Selects all the data in the file
Ctrl+F	Opens the Find dialog box to search for data on a page
Esc	Stops a Web page from loading
F5	Refreshes the current page
F11	Views the Web page in full screen mode, without menu bar and toolbars

Money 99 Shortcut Keys

KEY COMBINATION	FUNCTION
Ctrl+N	Opens a new account
Ctrl+O	Opens an existing account file
Alt+F4	Closes the program
Ctrl+X	Cuts the selected data and places it on the Windows Clipboard
Ctrl+C	Copies the selected data and puts it on the Clipboard
Ctrl+V	Pastes the cut or copied data from the Clipboard into the file
Ctrl+Z	Undoes the last action
Ctrl+F	Opens the Find dialog box to search for data
Ctrl+Shift+H	Opens the Money home page window
Ctrl+Shift+A	Opens the Accounts window
Ctrl+Shift+B	Opens the Bills & Deposits window
Ctrl+Shift+O	Opens the Online Finances window
Ctrl+Shift+I	Opens the Investments window
Ctrl+Shift+P	Opens the Planner window
Ctrl+Shift+R	Opens the Reports & Charts window
Ctrl+Shift+N	Opens the Decision Center window
Ctrl+Shift+C	Opens the Categories & Payees window
Ctrl+Shift+W	Opens the Web window

Lisa Bucki

SAMS
Teach Yourself
Microsoft®
Works Suite 99
in 24 Hours

SAMS

A Division of Macmillan Computer Publishing
201 West 103rd St., Indianapolis, Indiana, 46290 USA

Copyright © 1999 by Sams Publishing

International Standard Book Number: 0-672-31368-5

Library of Congress Catalog Card Number: 98-85626

Printed in the United States of America

First Printing: November 1998

01   00   99   98   4   3   2   1

Trademarks

EXECUTIVE EDITOR:
Angela Wethington

ACQUISITIONS EDITOR
Stephanie J. McComb

DEVELOPMENT EDITOR
Rob Tidrow

TECHNICAL EDITOR
Mark Hall

MANAGING EDITOR
Thomas F. Hayes

PROJECT EDITOR
Karen A. Walsh

COPY EDITOR
Sydney Jones

INDEXER
Larry Sweazy

LAYOUT
Cynthia Davis-Hubler

PROOFREADING
Sheri Replin

Overview

Contents

About the Author

Lisa Bucki has been involved in the computer book business for more than eight years, both as an author and a publishing consultant. She wrote *PCs 6-in-1* (Que), *Easy Microsoft Home Essentials 98* (Que), *Que's Guide to WordPerfect Presentations 3.0 for Windows* (Que), *Managing with Microsoft Project 98* (Prima Computer Books), and *Excel 97 Power Toolkit* (Ventana). She also was the lead author for the recently released *SmartSuite Millennium Edition Bible* (IDG Books Worldwide). For Que, she was a contributing author for *Special Edition Using Microsoft Office 97*, *Special Edition Using SmartSuite 97*, *The Big Basics Book of PCs* (both editions) and *The Big Basics Book of Excel for Windows 95*. For Alpha Books, a former Macmillan imprint, she wrote *10 Minute Guide to Harvard Graphics*, *10 Minute Guide to Harvard Graphics for Windows*, and *One Minute Reference to Windows 3.1*. She has contributed chapters dealing with online communications, presentation graphics, multimedia, and numerous computer subjects for other books, as well as spearheading or developing more than 100 computer and trade titles during her association with Macmillan. For Que Education & Training, Bucki created the Virtual Tutor CD-ROM companions for the *Essentials* series of books, as well as provided consulting services to a number of publishing clients.

Tell Us What You Think!

As the reader of this book, *you* are our most important critic and commentator. We value your opinion and want to know what we're doing right, what we could do better, what areas you'd like to see us publish in, and any other words of wisdom you're willing to pass our way.

As the Executive Editor for the General Desktop Applications team at Macmillan Computer Publishing, I welcome your comments. You can fax, email, or write me directly to let me know what you did or didn't like about this book—as well as what we can do to make our books stronger.

Please note that I cannot help you with technical problems related to the topic of this book, and that due to the high volume of mail I receive, I might not be able to reply to every message.

When you write, please be sure to include this book's title and author as well as your name and phone or fax number. I will carefully review your comments and share them with the author and editors who worked on the book.

Fax: 317-817-7448

Email: office@mcp.com

Mail: Executive Editor
           General Desktop Applications
           Macmillan Computer Publishing
           201 West 103rd Street
           Indianapolis, IN 46290 USA

Introduction

Firing up a new software program for the first time can cause both a jolt of enthusiasm and a pang of frustration. You're exited about the new possibilities the program offers and want to experience instant results—but you might not know how to get started with the program's features to accomplish the task you want.

Sams Teach Yourself Microsoft Works Suite 99 can help you get up and running with the Works Suite software in 24 hours or less. This book teaches the most important skills you need to use the software, providing enough background information without bogging you down in computer babble. This book leads you through the most important tasks, with To Do steps to help you practice how to accomplish a task.

What's in Works Suite 99?

Works Suite, a group of software applications packaged together for you, enables you to tackle work for home, school, or business, and even to entertain yourself. If you purchased Works Suite on your own, you may already know about what it offers. If, on the other hand, Works Suite came preinstalled on your new computer, you may not know how many applications you've really received. Here's a rundown of the software included in Works Suite, which you'll learn about in this book:

- Works 4.5   Offering Word Processor, Spreadsheet, Database, and Communications tools, Works can help you create documents, perform calculations, and perform other home and business tasks.

- Word 97   As the leading word processor in the world, Word enables you to create and published powerful, well-designed documents.

- Money 99 Basic   Whip your household finances and investments into shape with this financial management package. Track your investments, and even set a budget so you can better plan for the future.

- Internet Explorer 4.0   If you don't have Windows 98, which includes this Web browser installed, you can get it with Works Suite. Use the Internet Explorer 4.0 browser to go online and view graphical World Wide Web information on the Internet.

- Encarta Encyclopedia   To resolve a dispute about a trivia question or complete a homework assignment, consult this online encyclopedia. It not only includes article text, but also includes photos, timelines, and other graphics; sound and movies; and many more exciting media to enhance your learning experience.

- Graphics Studio Greetings   Make and print your own cards, announcements, invitations, and more with the design ideas and graphics provided in this tool.

- Calendar   Schedule your family's or small business' time more effectively with this planning software, new in this version of the Works Suite group of products.

- Expedia Streets 98 (U.S.) or Trip Planner (Canada)   If you're traveling by car, bus, plane, or train, you'll find getting there just got easier with Streets 98. Expedia Streets 98, which comes with the U.S. version of Works Suite 99, is a detailed electronic road atlas that maps more than 5 million miles of U.S. roads. Trip Planner 98, which comes with the Canadian version of Works Suite, is a planning tool to help you plan a trip anywhere in the U.S., Canada, or Mexico.

Conventions Used in This Book

In addition to including a Q&A question-and-answer session at the end of each chapter to help you reinforce what you learned, this book uses conventions to highlight information and help you pick out the high points. Here is a summary of the conventions you'll find in this book:

- New terms appear in *italic*.
- Words you need to type appear in `mono`.
- If a task requires you to select a command from a menu, a vertical bar appears to separate the menu name and command name. For example, "Choose File|Print" means to open the File menu and choose the Print command.
- To Do steps lead you through essential operations, one action at a time.

Tips offer shortcuts to save time and advice so you can achieve more professional results.

Notes provide supplemental details that can shed further light on a tricky issue. You don't have to read them, but they can really soup up your skills.

Most computer users learn through experience—sometimes disastrous experiences. In Caution boxes, I highlight traps and mistakes you can avoid so you don't have any disasters.

PART I

Kicking Off Your Day with Works 4.5a

Hour

HOUR 1

Introducing Works 4.5a

Getting the right software for the task you want to tackle can become an expensive proposition if you have to buy a new program for each new task. Fortunately, Microsoft Works 4.5a equips you to create letters, calculate numbers, organize lists of information, and more.

In this hour, you'll learn these key skills, which you'll need no matter what you're trying to accomplish in Works:

- Understand what software tools Works includes and what each tool does.
- Start and exit Works.
- Use the Works Task Launcher to open Works tools and files.
- Save, close, and open the files you create in Works.
- Display another Works tool.
- Print your Works file.

Reviewing What Works Offers

You can think of Microsoft Works 4.5a as a "Swiss Army" program—it actually includes different tools for accomplishing different types of tasks. Because Works really combines a group of applications, it's sometimes called an integrated program. Works does refer to each of its applications as a tool.

The following list introduces you to the Works tools and describes which tool to use to perform a particular type of activity:

- Word Processor   Use the Works word processor to type documents such as letters, memos, your résumé, brochures, newsletters, and so on. The word processor enables you to check your spelling and then apply formatting to make your documents more attractive and readable.

- Spreadsheet   When you want to calculate numbers, create a spreadsheet with the Spreadsheet tool. You enter the values to work with and then build a formula using mathematical operators and functions (predefined calculations) to calculate a result.

- Database   To organize a list of addresses, vendors, inventory items, or anything else, use the Database tool. After you enter information into a database file, you can sort the information, find a particular item in the list, or display only matching items.

- Communications   This tool communicates with your computer's modem so you can connect with another user's computer or a computer bulletin board system (BBS).

This book won't cover the Works Communications tool, because the Internet now provides superior online resources and most people use the Internet as their primary online venue. This book forgoes coverage of the Communications tool in favor of covering the Internet in more detail. See Part III, "Late Afternoon Online—Internet Explorer and Outlook Express," to learn more about Works Suite's other methods of going online.

Starting Works

To begin using any of the individual Works tools, you must first start the Works program. From there, you can select the tool to use or the type of document to create.

Depending on how you installed Works, you can use one of two methods to start the Works program:

- If you see a desktop shortcut for Works, you can double-click that shortcut icon (see Figure 1.1).

FIGURE 1.1

Double-click this desk-top shortcut to start Works.

- If you don't see the shortcut, click Start on the taskbar, point to Programs, and click Microsoft Works.

In Windows applications, you select commands from menus. Most applications, including Works, offer a menu bar at the top of the application window; the menu bar lists the menu names. Click the menu name to open the menu bar. To point *to* a command on the menu, drag the mouse pointer down to the command, so a highlight appears behind the command name. (When you point to a command with a triangle beside its name, a submenu of additional commands appears.) To choose a command from a menu or submenu, click it with the mouse. If you see a shortcut key combination such as Ctrl+N listed beside a command on a menu, you can press that key combination to choose the command without opening the menu.

You can create your own desktop shortcut to launch Works, if needed. Double-click the My Computer icon on the desktop; then open the C:\Program Files\MSWorks folder (or the folder you specified for Works during installation). Drag the MSWorks icon onto the desktop and release the mouse to drop the shortcut.

Working with the Task Launcher

When you start many applications, a blank document file appears, and you can get to work. In contrast, Works presents its Task Launcher, so you can choose how to begin working (see Figure 1.2).

FIGURE 1.2

Use the Works Task Launcher to create a file or choose a Works tool.

The three tabs in the Task Launcher enable you to choose what to do in Works. Here's what you can do with each tab:

- TaskWizards   The Works TaskWizards create particular kinds of files for you, such as a letter in the word processor or a job bid in the spreadsheet. The TaskWizard prompts you to make choices about the look and starter contents for the file you're creating, and then displays the new file in the applicable Works tool. From there, you enter additional information for the file to supplement the predefined content that the TaskWizard provides. Figure 1.2 shows some of the available TaskWizards. When you learn more about the Works tools later in this book, you'll see how to use a TaskWizard to create an example in each.

- Existing Documents   If you want to open a Works File you've previously created and saved, do so in this tab. See "Opening a File Using the Task Launcher" later in this hour to learn how to use this tab.

- Works Tools   Use this tab to start a Works tool, creating a blank document, spreadsheet, or database file in the process. See "Choosing a Works Tool (Starting a Blank File)," next, to learn how to use the Works Tools tab.

Because it's the key jumping-off point for using any Works tool, next you learn to master key techniques for using the Task Launcher.

Choosing a Works Tool (Starting a Blank File)

If you don't want to use a TaskWizard or open an existing file, you can simply start one of the Works tools, instead. Doing so creates a blank file in the Works tool, so that you can develop your own file content from the ground up.

The more formatting (fancy decoration), graphics, and other contents a file contains, the more space it takes up on your hard disk after you save it. If you're just intending to jot down a few notes in the word processor or use the spreadsheet as an electronic calculator, don't waste your disk space (or time) by using a TaskWizard to create a fancy file. Launch the Works tool and make a blank file, instead.

No matter which Works tool you want to use, the process for selecting and starting the tool is roughly the same. Follow these steps to select and open a Works tool and blank file:

To Do: Creating a Blank File from the Task Launcher

1. Display the Works Task Launcher, if needed. (See "Redisplaying the Task Launcher," next, to learn how.)
2. Click the Works Tools tab in the Works Task Launcher to display buttons for launching the tools (see Figure 1.3).

FIGURE 1.3

Click the button for the Works tool of your choice to open that tool and create a blank file in it.

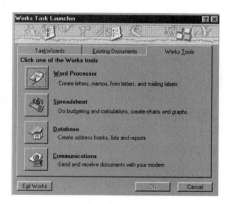

3. Click the button for the tool you want to use. If you click Word Processor, the word processor opens and a blank document file appears. Similarly, clicking Spreadsheet opens the Spreadsheet tool and a blank spreadsheet file. In contrast, if you click Database, the Database tool prompts you to provide further information for creating the blank database. To learn how to proceed, see "Creating a Blank Database" in Hour 7, "Capturing Lists in a Database."

Redisplaying the Task Launcher

After you open a new file, open an existing file, or use a TaskWizard to create a file, you'll be working in one of the individual Works tools. From there, you might decide that you want to create another file in another Works tool. You can return to the Task Launcher at any time, without closing the document you're presently using. After you've redisplayed the Task Launcher, you can use it as described elsewhere to start another Works tool (and blank file) or use a TaskWizard to create another file.

You can use either of the following methods from any Works tool to redisplay the Works Task Launcher:

- Choose File | New (Ctrl+N).
- Click the Task Launcher button (see Figure 1.4) on the Works toolbar, which appears in each of the Works tools.

FIGURE 1.4

To redisplay the Task Launcher, click the Task Launcher button on the toolbar in any Works tool.

If you start Works and don't open a Works file or tool and you then click the Cancel button to close the Task Launcher, the blank Works window remains open. It does offer a File menu, from which you can redisplay the Task Launcher or open a file, as described later in this hour.

After you choose a command that has an ellipsis (...) beside the command name (such as File | New), a dialog box appears so that you can provide more details about how the command executes. (Yes, the Task Launcher is a dialog box.) It's easy to use most dialog box options. Click a tab to display its options. Click to check or uncheck a check box. Click to select an option button, a small round button that's one in a group. Click scroll arrows to display more choices in a list box; or, click a drop-down list arrow to open a drop-down list. After you see the list choice you want, click it. Type a choice in a text box. Click a command button to select it and execute the command; for example, click the OK button to close the dialog box and accept the choices you've made in it.

Using the Works Help Window

No matter which Works tool you're using, the Works window looks about the same and resembles the windows you see in other Windows applications. For example, the Works window includes a title bar listing the name of the program (Microsoft Works), a menu bar listing the available menus, and a toolbar presenting buttons you can click to perform commands. The Works window generally also displays a file window for each open Works file.

 By default, the individual file windows aren't maximized. That is, the file window appears as a smaller window within the Microsoft Works window. The name of the file appears in the file window title bar.

The Help window that appears at the right side of the Works window (see Figure 1.5) might look unfamiliar to you. This window lists a menu of Help topics that apply to the Works tool you're using. You can use the Help window to display steps for performing a Works operation. Or, you can shrink the Help window if you want to be able to see and work with more of the open file onscreen. The Help window supplements the Help menu, which (like its counterparts in other Windows applications) offers commands for getting help.

FIGURE 1.5

You can use the Help window at the right side of the Works screen to get information about the tool that you're using.

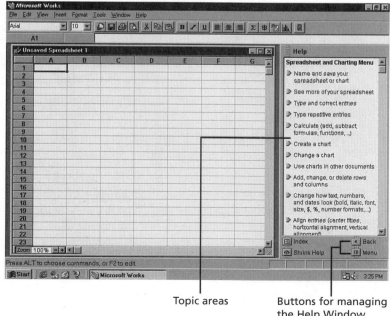

Topic areas

Buttons for managing the Help Window

The following steps explain how to navigate Works' onscreen Help window:

To Do: Finding the Help You Need

1. Click the button beside the topic area you want help about.

2. In the list of tasks that appears, click the button beside the task you want to learn.

3. After you review the instructions on the Step-by-Step tab that appears, click the More Info tab to display it (see Figure 1.6).

FIGURE 1.6

The Works Help window presents a Step-by-Step help option about the topic you select or a More Info option.

4. Click the button beside the topic you want to review. The Help window displays either more step-by-step help or a separate window with information about the topic that you selected. (The window name varies depending on the topic you select, but it's usually named Overview or What if....)

5. After you review the information in the window that appears, click Done to close the window.

6. At any time, you can click the Back button at the bottom of the Help window to redisplay the previous Help window contents.

7. To search for help about a topic or find help about another Works tool, click the Index button to display a Help Topics window that has Index and Contents tabs. To find help about a particular topic, type the topic in the text box at the top of the Index tab, and then double-click the matching topic in the scrolling list below the text box. Alternatively, click the Contents tab; click the Works tool you need help with; click to open the folder icon, and then click a specific topic (denoted by a page icon) to display it in the Help window at the right side of the screen. Click the Close button to close the Help Topics window.

▼ 8. To redisplay the initial menu of Help topics, click the Menu button at the bottom of
        the Help window.

    9. To reduce the Help window to a narrow bar at the right side of the screen, click the
        Shrink Help button.

   10. To redisplay the Help window, click (again) the Shrink Help button at the lower-
▲   right corner of the screen.

> If you don't need to work with it at all, you can hide the Help window by
> choosing Help | Hide Help. Choose Help | Show Help to redisplay the Help
> window.

> To further help you, Works offers a First-time Help feature, which appears
> when you start certain tougher Works operations. The First-time Help dialog
> box that appears offers you the choice of taking a Quick tour to see a
> demonstration of how the feature works or choosing to immediately start
> the operation. To turn off First-time Help, click the Don't Display This
> Message in the Future check box to place a check in it.

Saving a Works File

No matter which tool you use, you use the same process to save and name the file in all
the Works tools. By default, Works assigns a working name with a number to each new
file you create, as in *Unsaved Spreadsheet 1*, *Unsaved Spreadsheet 2*, and so on. When
you save a file the first time, you give it a unique filename.

Works also assigns a filename extension to the file to identify which kind of file it is:
word processor, spreadsheet, or database. You won't always see and use these filename
extensions, but Table 1.1 lists them so you'll be familiar with them, if you need them.

TABLE 1.1 EXTENSIONS FOR WORKS FILENAMES

Extension	Type	Description
.WPS	Works WP	Works word processor file
.WKS	Works SS	Works spreadsheet file
.WDB	Works DB	Works database file
.WCM	Works CM	Works communications file
.W*	Works Files	Any Works file

Saving a file stores it on disk, so that you can later retrieve it, make changes to it, or print it. By default, Works prompts you to store files in the \Program Files\MSWorks \Documents folder on your hard disk. However, you can save the document to another folder if, for example, you've created a separate folder for each family member's files.

Don't make the common beginner mistake of saving an important file directly to a floppy disk, Zip disk, or other type of removable disk. Although these media are more reliable than ever, they're more subject to human error because they're outside the computer. For example, you could pull a disk out of the floppy drive before the drive stops spinning, thus corrupting your files. Or, your child might slide open the metal protector on the end of a disk, stick in a paper clip, and (you guessed it) destroy your file. If a file really matters, save it to your hard disk first, and then use My Computer or the Windows Explorer to copy it to a floppy.

Use these steps to save (and name) a file for the first time:

To Do: Saving a File the First Time

1. Choose File | Save, press the Ctrl+S shortcut, or click the Save button on the Works toolbar. The Save As dialog box appears (see Figure 1.7).

FIGURE 1.7

After you choose File | Save, the Save As dialog box appears to enable you to name your file and specify the folder that will hold it.

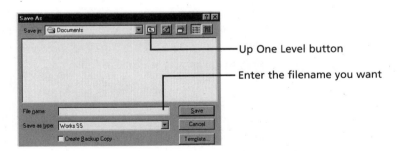

2. To save to a folder other than the default one, click the Up One Level button on the Save As dialog box's toolbar once or twice. This is called moving up a level in the folder tree. (You also can click to open the Save In drop-down list and click a folder higher on the tree to select it.) Then, double-click the folder you want to select in the list of folders that appears in the dialog box.

▼

3. Click to place the insertion point in the File Name text box, and then type the name you want for the file. Your filenames can be very descriptive because they can include more than 200 characters, spaces, and special capitalization.

4. If you want Works to create a backup copy of your file (and update the backup copy each time you subsequently save), click to check the Create Backup Copy check box. Then, you can open the backup file if you need it. (Works assigns a BPS extension to word processor backup files, BKS to spreadsheet backup files, and BDP to database files.)

5. Click the Save button. After you save and name the file, its name appears in the file window title bar.

> After you save a file the first time, you can choose File I Save As to redisplay the Save As dialog box. If you enter a new filename and then click Save, Works saves a copy of the file under the new name. Also note that any folder you selected previously appears in the Save In text box in the redisplayed Save As dialog box. To save to another folder, use the Up One Level button or Save In drop-down list to select it.

▲

After you save your file the first time, resaving it adds your recent changes to the file without renaming the file. You should save it every 10 minutes or so to ensure that you won't lose any work if your system reboots due to power fluctuations. To resave a Works file, choose the File I Save command (Ctrl+S) again or click the Save button on the Works toolbar.

Closing a Works File

After you finish working with a particular file in Works, you can close it to reduce onscreen clutter or prevent others from seeing it.

To close a Works file, follow these steps:

To Do: Closing a File

1. Choose File I Close (Ctrl+W) or click the Close button (X) on the right side of the file window title bar.

2. If you made changes that you haven't saved to the file, a message box prompts you to save the file (see Figure 1.8). Click Yes to save your changes and finish closing the file. Works displays the next open file (and the Works tool for working with that file).

FIGURE **1.8**

*When you try to close
a file that holds
unsaved changes,
Works reminds you to
save them.*

When you save or close a file, it needs to be the current *or* active file.
Commands you perform apply to the current file only. (See "Switching
Between Works Files (and Tools)" later in this hour to learn how to select
the current file and Works tool.)

Opening an Existing File in Works

Opening a file redisplays it in a file window and activates the Works tool for working
with that file. The newly opened file becomes the active file and remains active until you
open or create another file or choose to make another open file active. Depending on
your starting point, you use slightly different steps to open the file, as described next.

Opening a File Using the File Menu

If you've already been busy with another Works file, you can use the File menu to open
another Works file, as follows:

Opening a File

1. Choose File | Open (Ctrl+O). The Open dialog box appears and lists the files
   stored in the default folder (\Program Files\MSWorks\Documents), as shown in
   Figure 1.9. The icon beside each filename identifies what type of Works file it is.

Also check the bottom of the File menu. If the file you want to open
appears there, click its filename to open it and skip the lengthier process
covered here.

FIGURE 1.9

Select a file to open in the Open dialog box.

Database file icon   Spreadsheet file icon

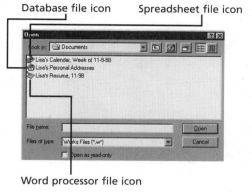

Word processor file icon

> If you want to list only files of a particular type (Works WP, Works SS, and so on), select the type from the Files of Type drop-down list.

2. To open a file stored in a folder other than the default one, click the Up One Level button on the Open dialog box's toolbar once or twice. (You also can click to open the Look In drop-down list, and click a folder higher on the tree to select it.) Then, double-click the folder you want to select in the list of folders that appears in the dialog box.

3. In the list of files shown in the dialog box, click the file to open it.

4. Click the Open button to open the file and display the Works tool for using it.

Opening a File Using the Task Launcher

If you've just started Works, you need to use the Task Launcher to open an existing file. Click the Existing Documents tab in the Task Launcher. As shown in Figure 1.10, the tab displays a list of files. These are files you recently created or opened; you don't have to save a file to the default folder for it to appear on the list. If you see the file you want to open, click its name in the Click the Document That You Want to Open list, and then click the OK button to close the Task Launcher and open the file.

If the tab doesn't display the name of the file you want to open, click the Open a Document Not Listed Here button to display the Open dialog box. Then, follow steps 2-4 under the previous section titled, "Opening a File Using the File Menu," to find and open the file.

FIGURE **1.10**

The Existing Documents tab in the Works Task Launcher lists files you can open.

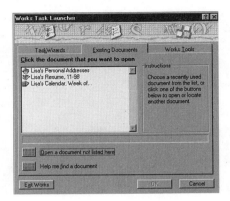

Switching Between Works Files (and Tools)

If you have started creating files in more than one Works tool (leaving each file open), you can switch between the open files and the tools used to create them. When you change to a file created with another Works tool, the menu bar changes to list the menus for that tool. The file you switch to becomes the current or active file; that is, if you switch to a spreadsheet file, the window for that file moves to the front of the other open files, so you can start working with the spreadsheet.

To display another file (and its Works tool), open the Window menu (see Figure 1.11), and choose the name of the file you want to display from the bottom of the menu. Works displays the file in the Works tool you used to create it.

FIGURE **1.11**

To display another open Works file, choose the filename from the bottom of the Window menu.

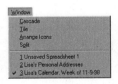

If you can see the file window title bar for the Works file you want to use, you can click the file window title bar to select the file (make it active).

Printing a File

The Print dialog box in Works offers the settings you can use to control how your Works file prints. The available settings differ slightly, depending on the type of Works file you want to print. However, for word processor, spreadsheet, and database files, you can select another printer from the Name drop-down list. You can print the entire file by clicking the All option button, or specify a range of Pages to print using the From and To text boxes. You also can enter a Number of Copies to print in the text box of that name. If you print multiple copies, you can ensure that the Collate check box is clicked to collate them.

Beyond those choices, the Print dialog box offers additional choices based on the file type:

- For a word processor file, you can print the Main Document or an Envelope (if you've created one) by clicking the appropriate option button under What to Print. For a mail merge (which inserts information from a database file into unique copies of a word processor file), you can click to clear the Print Merge check box if you want to print only a single copy of the merge document, without database information. If you're printing mailing labels, enter a number in the First Label Row to Print text box to specify the top row of labels on the label sheet.

- For word processor or spreadsheet file, you can check the Draft Quality Printing check box to print a draft, for faster printing.

- For a database, you can print All Records or the Current Record Only by clicking the appropriate option button under What to Print.

When you're ready to print, use these steps:

To Do: Printing in Works

1. Display the file you want to print.

2. Choose File | Print (Ctrl+P). The Print dialog box appears. (Figure 1.12 shows an example.)

3. If you can print to more than one printer, open the Name drop-down list and select the printer you want to use.

4. To print only a range of pages rather than the entire document, click Pages; then enter the number of the first and last page to print in the From and To text boxes.

5. To print multiple copies, change the Number of Copies text box entry. If you print more than one copy, keep the Collate check box checked to print all the pages of the first copy and then all the pages of the second copy, and so on.

6. Change any other settings, as described previously.

7. Click OK to print.

FIGURE 1.12

The Print dialog box for a Works word processor file offers the settings that are common for all Works files, as well as those available only for word processor files.

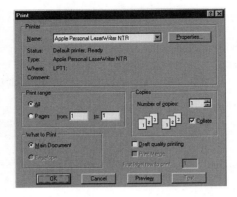

But there are also other ways to find help while using UnInstaller. UnInstaller's online Help feature can help you out in any jam. But there are also other ways to find help while using UnInstaller.

If you've done a lot of fancy formatting or have changed the page setup for a file as described later in this section, you can preview the file before printing it to make sure it has the overall appearance you want. To display the preview, choose File|Print Preview or click the Print Preview button on the toolbar. If the preview looks all right, click the Print button to send it to the printer. Alternatively, click the Cancel button, and then display the Print dialog box and specify the printing options you want.

Exiting Works

Shutting down or exiting Works removes it from your computer's working memory. You need to save your work and properly exit Works before you shut down windows, or you risk losing some changes or even corrupting a file. The fastest way to close Works is to click the Close button (X) on the right side of the Works title bar, but you also can choose File | Exit Works. If an open file contains changes that you haven't saved, Works prompts you to save it (refer to Figure 1.8). Click Yes to do so (repeating if prompted to save additional files) and finish closing Works.

The Works Task Launcher also offers an Exit Works button. You can click it to close the program from the Task Launcher.

Summary

The skills you learned in this hour might have seemed a little basic, but you wouldn't be able to survive your morning in Works without them. To navigate in Works, you need to understand what tools Works offers and how to display different files. And, if you don't stop now and learn how to save, close, and open files, you'll be doomed to repeat your keystrokes over and over again. The next several hours reveal how to manipulate the information you capture in various kinds of Works files. You can skip directly to the hours that cover the Works tool you need—word processor, spreadsheet, or database.

Q&A

Q. How do I start Works or close it when I'm finished working?

A. To open Works, double-click the Shortcut to Microsoft Works shortcut icon on the desktop or click the Start button on the taskbar, point to Programs, and click Microsoft Works. The fastest way to close Works is to click the Close button (X) on the right side of the Works title bar, but you also can choose File | Exit Works.

Q. What is the Task Launcher, and how do I redisplay it?

A. The Works Task Launcher enables you to create files and open any Works tool or file. After you create or open a file, you need to redisplay the Task Launcher to create a new file or launch another Works tool. Choose File | New (Ctrl+N) or click the Task Launcher button on the Works toolbar to redisplay the Task Launcher.

Q. How do I open a Works tool and a blank document?

A. Click the Works Tools tab in the Task Launcher; then click the button for the tool you want to use. If you open the Database tool, it prompts you for information to set up the new database file.

Q. How do I display another Works tool?

A. That's almost a trick question, because it has more than one answer. If you've only opened one Works file, you'll need to create or open another file to display another tool. Redisplay the Task Launcher (File | New). Then create a new file with another tool. (Click the Works Tools tab and then click the button for the tool you want to use.) Alternatively, click the Existing Documents tab and click the name of a file you want to open from another tool. (You also can use a TaskWizard as described in later hours to create another file.) If you've already opened multiple Works tools and just want to redisplay an open file in another tool, open the Window menu, and click a filename to redisplay that filename and the Works tool used to create it.

Q. How do I save a file?

A. Choose File | Save (Ctrl+S) or click the Save button on the Works toolbar. To save to a folder other than the default one, use the Up One Level button and Save In list to display a list of folders, and double-click the folder you want. Type the filename in the File Name text box; then click the Save button.

Q. How do I open a file?

A. When you have another Works file open, choose File | Open (Ctrl+O). Click the name of the file you want to open; then click Open.

Q. Can I print my file without wading through a bunch of settings?

A. Yes. Click the Print button on the Works toolbar to print one copy of the current Works file.

HOUR 2

Building Documents with the Word Processor

All of us have loads of experience creating documents—by hand writing them, using a typewriter, or maybe even a basic word processor. When you start using a new word processor, your thoughts will probably flow as quickly as ever, but you might get a bit hung up on the word processor's new features and commands.

This hour shows you how to get off the hook and return your attention to your writing. Learn to tackle the following with the Works Word Processor tool:

- Make a new document that already has some content and a nice design.
- Enter your unique content for the document.
- Make changes to a few characters, a sentence, or even an entire paragraph.
- Move or copy information with commands or drag and drop.
- Check your document's spelling.

Creating a Document with a TaskWizard

A Works document TaskWizard helps you create a new document. The TaskWizard enables you to choose a design for the document you create. Even better, it enters standard document text for you, so you don't have to type that text at all. For example, if you use a TaskWizard to create a memo, you don't have to enter the document title (Interoffice Memorandum), or the Date, To, and other labels. You supply the unique text for each new memo you create.

You select a document TaskWizard from the TaskWizards tab of the Works Task Launcher. The TaskWizards tab organizes different TaskWizards (including those for the Spreadsheet, Database, and Communications tools) into both business and home-oriented categories.

 To improve your odds of finding the TaskWizard you need, some TaskWizards appear in more than one category.

Although the individual word processor TaskWizards create different types of documents, the TaskWizards all present the same steps and choices to you. To create a word processor document using a TaskWizard, follow these steps:

To Do: Create a Document Using a TaskWizard

1. Click the Task Launcher button on the Works toolbar or choose File | New (Ctrl+N).
2. Click the TaskWizards tab, if needed.
3. Click the button for the category you want to open. The Task Launcher categories display all the TaskWizards, including those for tools other than the Word Processor tool (see Figure 2.1). A pencil and paper icon appears beside each document TaskWizard.
4. Double-click the icon for the TaskWizard you want to use, or click it and then click OK.
5. Click the Yes, Run the TaskWizard button to tell Works that you want it to create the document for you.
6. Click the button representing the document design you want to use, and then click the Create It button. Works displays the new document, which appears with its standard text and the design you selected. Figure 2.2 shows a sample document created from a TaskWizard.

▼

FIGURE 2.1

The Works Task Launcher organizes TaskWizards in categories to make it easier for you to create the type of document you need.

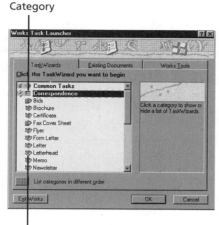

2

Icon for a document TaskWizard

FIGURE 2.2

Each TaskWizard supplies a neat design and standard text for a new document, like the memo document shown here.

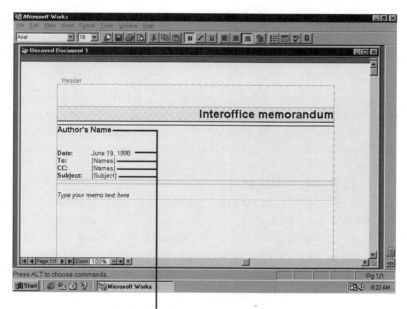

Placeholders for your unique text

7. You can then enter additional text to complete the new document. The rest of this hour covers the numerous techniques you can use to enter and edit text in a blank file or one you created using a TaskWizard. Don't forget to save the new file periodically to preserve your work.

▲

After you create a document with a TaskWizard, it appears in Page Layout view, which shows all the design features of the document. In contrast, plain new documents (created by clicking the Word Processor button on the Works Tools tab of the Task Launcher) appear in Normal view, where some of the design elements are hidden. Most of the figures in this book show the Normal view. To learn to switch views, see the section, "Changing Between Page Layout and Normal Views" in Hour 3, "Formatting Characters and Paragraphs."

Entering Text

When it comes to entering your text in a document, most word processors work about the same, including the Works Word Processor tool.

Look for the blinking vertical *insertion point* onscreen. As you type, each keyboard character you press appears at the insertion point, moving the insertion point to the right. When you type enough text to fill the current line all the way to the right margin (*margins* are the white spaces around the page), the insertion point moves (or *wraps*) automatically to the next line. So, you can type without pause until you reach the end of the paragraph.

Press the Enter key to start a new paragraph; this action is called inserting a *paragraph break*. You have to press Enter for every paragraph. In contrast, you don't have to do anything to start a new page. After you type a page's worth of information, the word processor inserts a *soft page break* (an automatic page break) to start a new page for you.

Typing Hints

When you're creating a short, simple document, you can survive on the skills described in the previous section. As you gain confidence or encounter situations where you need more control, you can use the following tricks while typing text:

- Press the Spacebar only once after each sentence. Although your typing teacher might have instructed you to add a second space after each sentence, that's not necessary with today's word processors. The lettering your computer displays and prints has been optimized to close up spacing within words and leave ample spacing between words and sentences. So, one Spacebar press does the job and looks more professional.

- To wrap text to a new line without starting a new paragraph (called a *soft return*), press Shift+Enter. Try this technique if you want to create a compact list of short items.

- Press Enter twice to insert a blank line between paragraphs.

- Press Tab to move the insertion point to the next *tab stop*, the location to which the insertion point jumps when you press the Tab key. Tab sets are preset every .5 inches in a document and help you vertically align text. After you move the insertion point to a tab stop, the text you type next starts at the tab stop. If you used a TaskWizard to create a document, the tab stops might be set to locations other than the default.

> Don't press Tab at the beginning of each paragraph. If you later need to combine paragraphs, you might forget to delete the Tab and leave an unsightly gap in your text. Instead, adjust the indention for the paragraph. See "Changing Paragraph Alignment" in Hour 3 to learn how to combine paragraphs, as well as how to add space between paragraphs without inserting a blank line.

Using Easy Text

You'll find that you type certain blocks of text frequently, such as your name, title, company, company address, and phone number. Or, you might have a mission statement for your business, club, or volunteer group that you insert in a variety of documents. It can be tedious to type such entries over and over—not to mention the fact that you might have to look up information before you can type it, consuming even more of your time.

You can use the Easy Text feature to save a block of text and assign a name to that block, so you can later insert the block into the document just by choosing its name. Follow these steps to create an Easy Text entry:

To Do: Create an Easy Text Entry

1. Choose Insert | Easy Text | New Easy Text. The New Easy Text dialog box appears.

2. Enter a brief, one-word name for the Easy Text entry in the Type a Name for the Easy Text Below text box.

3. Click in the Easy Text Contents text box, and then type the block of text for your Easy Text entry. You can press Enter to insert paragraph breaks in the text as needed. Figure 2.3 shows sample entries in the New Easy Text dialog box.

4. Click the Done button to finish creating the Easy Text entry and close the dialog box.

FIGURE 2.3

*When you create an
Easy Text entry in the
New Easy Text dialog
box, you can quickly
insert all the text into
a document without
retyping it.*

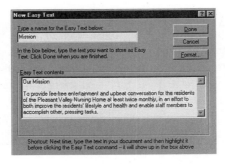

After you've created an Easy Text entry, position the insertion point where you want to
insert the Easy Text entry's contents in the document. (See the later section, "Moving the
Insertion Point.") Then use one of these two methods to insert the Easy Text entry:

- Choose Insert | Easy Text, and then click the name of the Easy Text entry to insert
  in the submenu that appears.
- Type the name of the Easy Text entry where you want it to appear in the document.
  (Do not press the Spacebar after the name.) Then press F3.

Editing Text

Unless you're working on a quick or informal piece of correspondence, you'll need to
come back to the text of your document and make corrections and changes. Also,
because documents you create using TaskWizards already contain sample text, you'll
need to use editing techniques to add your unique text to those documents and replace
the placeholders for that text. This section and the remaining sections in this hour cover
the various techniques you can use to fix and adjust the information in a document.

Moving the Insertion Point

Because anything you type appears at the insertion point, you need to move the insertion
point to the area that you want to change to correct the text there. You can use one of the
following techniques to reposition the insertion point in the document:

- A character at a time   Press an arrow key on the keyboard to move the insertion
  point one character or row in the direction of the arrow.
- A word at a time   Press Ctrl+left arrow or Ctrl+right arrow to move the insertion
  point one word to the left or right.
- To the beginning or end of the current line   Press Home or End.

- To the beginning of a paragraph   Press Ctrl+up arrow or Ctrl+down arrow to move the insertion point to the beginning of the paragraph that holds the insertion point, or to the beginning of the previous or subsequent paragraph.

- To the top or bottom of the current screen   Press Ctrl+Home or Ctrl+End to move the insertion point to the top or bottom of the information currently displayed onscreen.

- To a particular location onscreen   Click to position the insertion point at the location you want, such as within a word or within a sentence.

- Earlier or later in the document   Press PgUp or PgDn or click the area above or below the square scrollbox on the vertical scrollbar at the right side of the document to display the previous or next screen of information. (Repeat either action to move several screens up or down.) Then click to position the insertion point onscreen.

- To the beginning or end of the document   Press Ctrl+Home or Ctrl+End.

Simply displaying another screen of information does not move the insertion point. After you display another screen of information, you must click to reposition the insertion point on that page. If you press a key, instead, the word *scrolls* the display back to the insertion point location.

Making Basic Changes

You can use a few basic keystrokes to fine-tune the words and phrases in your document. Just as text you type appears at the insertion point, edits you make occur to the left or right of the insertion point.

Use one of the techniques described previously to position the insertion point to the left or right of the text you want to delete. Press the Backspace key to remove the character to the left of the insertion point. Pressing Backspace multiple times deletes multiple characters. To delete characters to the right of the insertion point, press the Delete key as many times as needed.

You can undo any edit you make. To do so, choose Edit I Undo (Action) or press Ctrl+Z. (The name of the Undo command changes based on the action you last performed.) If you're typing and you get an unexpected result, you might have accidentally pressed the Ctrl key or Alt key instead of the Shift key. If that happens, click the Cancel button or press Esc once or twice to close any dialog box or menu that appears.

After you delete characters as needed, you can type new text to insert it into the document. Read the next section to learn more about techniques for adding text into a document.

Understanding Insert and Overtype

By default, text you type appears at the insertion point, and existing text moves further right to make room for the new text. Because this method inserts text within the document, it's called *Insert mode*. In other instances, you might want to replace or simply type over the text to the right of the insertion point. For example, if you're working with a list of short entries, you can type over an entry to replace it.

To replace the text to the right of the insertion point, turn on *Overtype mode* by pressing the Insert key and then typing the replacement information. An OVR indicator appears in the Works window status bar to alert you when Overtype mode is on. After you finish working in Overtype mode, press the Insert key again to return to Insert mode. Figure 2.4 illustrates the difference between inserting and typing over text.

FIGURE 2.4

The top example shows the original sentence. The middle example shows inserted text, and the bottom example shows the result of using Overtype mode.

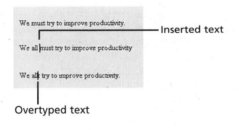

Inserted text

Overtyped text

As the bottom of Figure 2.4 shows, check your work after using Overtype mode. You might have mistakenly typed over text you need to keep, or might not have deleted characters left from words you partially typed over.

Selecting Blocks of Text

You need to *select* (or *highlight*) text before you perform most operations in a document. For example, you need to select text to delete, copy, or move it (see the next section). You also need to select text to apply boldface or other formatting to it. (See Hour 4, "Formatting Pages," to teach yourself different formatting techniques.) Table 2.1 lists the different techniques you can use to select text in a document before you perform an operation on it.

TABLE 2.1 TECHNIQUES FOR SELECTING TEXT

Do this...	To select...
Press and hold the left mouse button while you drag over text	All the text you drag
Double-click a word	The word
Click in the left margin next to a line	The entire line
Press and hold Ctrl; then click a sentence	The entire sentence
Double-click in the left margin next to a paragraph	The entire paragraph
Press Shift+Ctrl+left arrow or Shift+Ctrl+right arrow	The word (or portion of the word) to the left or right of the insertion point
Shift+Ctrl+up arrow or Shift+Ctrl+down arrow	The paragraph (or portion of the paragraph) before or after the insertion point
Shift+left arrow or right arrow	Any amount of text to the left or right of the insertion point; press the applicable arrow key repeatedly to extend the selection
Choose Edit I Select All or press Ctrl+A	The entire document

2

Copying, Moving, and Deleting Text

Using Backspace or Delete to remove a character at a time can consume quite a bit of your time if you need to remove an entire paragraph or significant portion of the document. Instead, you can select a larger block of text, and then press Backspace or Delete to remove the entire selection.

In addition, you can copy or move a selection to a location elsewhere in the document. For example, you might type an introductory paragraph for a report, but decide that the paragraph would better serve as an introduction to a particular section later in the document. Rather than deleting the material at its present location and retyping it, you can move it to the new location. Moving or copying information not only reduces typing time, but also reduces the potential for typos (assuming you typed material correctly the first time).

To place a duplicate of a selection in a new location (create a copy), you copy text and then paste it into the new location. To move it, you cut the text from its present location and paste it into a new one. Windows holds copied or cut text in its Clipboard (a holding area for text in your computer's memory) until you paste the text, or cut or copy another selection.

> When you press Delete or Backspace to remove a selection, Windows does not place the deleted text on the Clipboard. To get the text back, choose Edit I Undo or press Ctrl+Z immediately.

When you need to copy or move text in a document you're editing, follow these steps:

To Do: Copy and Move Text

1. Select the text you want to copy or move.

2. Choose Edit I Copy (Ctrl+C) or Edit I Cut (Ctrl+X). Alternatively, click the Copy or Cut button on the Works toolbar.

3. Move the insertion point to the location where you want to insert the copied or cut text.

4. Choose Edit I Paste (Ctrl+V) or click the Paste button on the Works toolbar. The copied or cut material appears at the insertion point. Figure 12.5 shows an example of copied text.

5. (Optional) Repeat Steps 3 and 4 to paste the text into additional locations.

> You also can move or copy text to another open word processor document. Copy or cut the selection, and then choose the document into which you want to paste it from the Window menu. Then position the insertion point and paste the information into place.

Using Drag-and-Drop

The *drag-and-drop* feature enables you to move or copy a selection using the mouse. You drag a selection from one location and drop it into a new location to move or copy it. For small changes, this technique works much faster than using commands or toolbar buttons.

FIGURE 2.5

Copying or moving text saves you the trouble of retyping it.

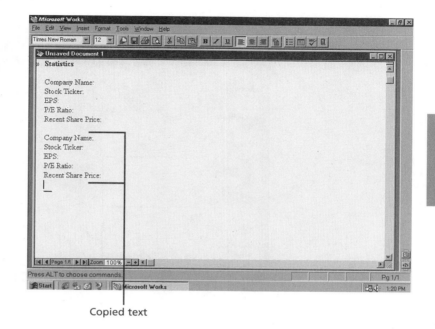

Copied text

I recommend using drag-and-drop only to move or copy information within the same paragraph or screen of information. If you try to drag information to a further location, the screen might scroll, making it more difficult to zero in on the location where you want to drop the selection.

Here's how to use drag-and-drop to move or copy text:

To Do: Drag and Drop Text

1. Select the text you want to move or copy.
2. To move the text, press and hold the left mouse button, and drag the text; a drag pointer appears as you drag. To copy the text, press and hold the Ctrl key and the left mouse button; then drag the text. A copy pointer appears as you drag. (Figure 2.6 shows text being copied via drag-and-drop.)

▲ To Do

FIGURE 2.6

You can drag with the mouse to move or copy text.

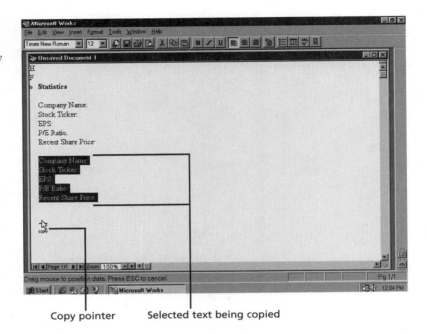

Copy pointer   Selected text being copied

3. Drag until the gray insertion point appears where you want to insert the text. Release the mouse button (and the Ctrl key, if needed) to drop the moved or copied information into place.

> You can click selected text using the right mouse button to display a short-cut menu of commands for copying, cutting, clearing (deleting), and formatting the text.

Correcting Your Spelling

Sloppy spelling typically indicates sloppy work habits and certainly doesn't win good grades in school. You or your family members can improve how others perceive your work by always using the Spell Check feature in Works to help you proofread your documents. While the spelling checker won't catch every mistake, it can catch a good number of them. You should both proofread and spell check a document before you print it to ensure its spelling accuracy.

The spelling checker skips some mistakes because it's not set up to determine whether you've used the right version of a word. For example, it would skip the sentence "I went their yesterday," because "their" is spelled correctly, even though it's the wrong word. So, you still need to proofread your documents to supplement Spell Check's effort.

2

Follow these steps to have the word processor find and correct spelling errors in the current document:

To Do: Correct Spelling Errors

1. Press Ctrl+Home to move the insertion point to the beginning of the document, so you start spell checking from the beginning.

2. Choose Tools | Spelling (F7) or click the Spelling Checker button on the Works toolbar. The spelling check begins. When it finds the first word that might be misspelled, it highlights the word in the document and displays the Spelling dialog box (see Figure 2.7).

Highlighted (misspelled) word   Spelling Checker button

FIGURE 2.7

Works highlights a word that's possibly misspelled and provides you with options for correcting it.

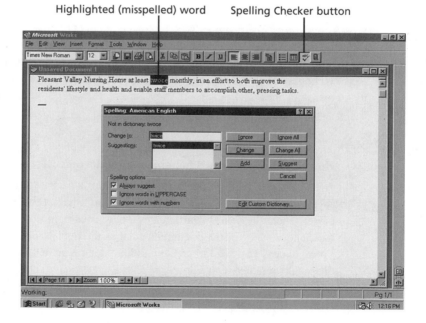

3. Choose one of the following methods to correct or bypass the word:

- Click Ignore if the word isn't misspelled, or Ignore All to leave the word as it is and avoid highlighting it for the rest of the spelling check.
- To correct the word, click the word you want to use in the Suggestions list box or type a correction in the Change To text box. Then, click Change to replace the highlighted word with the correction, or Change All to replace all instances of the highlighted word in the document with the correction.
- If the word is correct as is, you can click Add to include it in the Spelling Checker's dictionary, so the Spelling Checker won't think the word is misspelled in the future.

4. Repeat Step 3 as many times as needed to continue with the spelling check.

5. When the Spelling Checker has checked the entire document and you've told it how to handle all the needed corrections, it displays a message box informing you that the spelling check is finished. Click OK to close the message box and finish.

Summary

In an hour or less, you've taught yourself how to enter and make changes to the text in a Works word processor document, including spell checking the document for typos. You also learned how to create a new document with some of the text entered and most of the formatting already handled for you—by using a TaskWizard to create the document. The next two hours show you how to further improve a document's appearance by formatting its words, sentences, and pages.

Q&A

Q. How does a TaskWizard help me start a document?

A. A TaskWizard helps you create a document of a particular type, such as a fax cover sheet or a letter. The TaskWizard enables you to select the document design you prefer. Then, the TaskWizard creates a new document using that design and enters the standard text for the document, such as the document title or labels like To and From. Unless you need to create a unique document, a TaskWizard saves design time and some text-entry time.

Q. What are the most essential text-entry and editing techniques?

A. When you type text, let the word processor wrap it to the next line. Press Enter only to create a new paragraph. You can click or press an arrow key to reposition the insertion point, and then press Backspace or Delete to delete a character to the left or right. You need to select a larger block of text before you can delete or format it. Drag to select or highlight any block of text. Double-click a single word to select it, or press Ctrl and click a sentence to select the whole sentence.

Q. What is one of the biggest timesavers when creating documents?

A. Copying or moving text to a new location in the document saves you the trouble of retyping that text and reduces typos. To copy or move text, first select it. Then click the Copy button on the toolbar to copy the selection, or the Cut button to remove the selection from its current location. Click to position the insertion point at the location where you want to insert the copied or cut text, and then click the Paste button on the toolbar. To move a selection a short distance in a document, drag the selection using the mouse (hold down the left mouse button while dragging), and then drop it into place.

2

HOUR 3

Formatting Characters and Paragraphs

After you've entered your text and have made changes and corrections to polish it up, you can get a little bolder—literally. Text formatting like boldface or a new *font* (lettering style) helps to call attention to words or headings and can help differentiate your document from dozens of others that a reader might see. Formatting can be functional, as well as decorative. For example, you can increase the size of text or adjust the spacing after each paragraph to help make a document more readable.

This hour presents the most crucial formatting techniques you can use to control the appearance of text and paragraphs. You can work on these skills:

- Choosing a view to better view your work.
- Applying formatting using Toolbar buttons.
- Specifying even more formatting with the Format Font and Style dialog box.
- Adjusting and highlighting paragraphs.
- Letting the Works word processor suggest formatting for you.

Changing Between Page Layout and Normal Views

When you're entering text, you can work quite effectively in the Normal view in the Works word processor. The Normal view doesn't show any graphical elements for the document and doesn't fully illustrate settings like *margins* (the white space around text) and multiple columns. The Normal view hides bells and whistles so you can focus on the text.

On the other hand, the Page Layout view displays your document just as it will print, with graphics, margins, and other formatting fully in place. You should switch to the Page Layout view when you're working with graphics and text and page formatting, so you can see the effects of your formatting changes. (When you perform certain actions, however, Works changes to the Page Layout view for you.) However, because Page Layout view can cause your screen to scroll and refresh more slowly, you might want to limit the amount of time you use Page Layout view.

To display the current document in Page Layout view, choose View | Page Layout. To switch back to the Normal view, choose View | Normal. Figure 3.1 compares a document window, displayed in Page Layout and Normal view.

Using the Toolbar to Format

The Works Word Processor tool enables you to choose a number of different types of formatting for your text. If you only need to make one or two formatting changes to text you've selected (yes, you need to select the text to change its formatting), you can use some of the choices on the Works toolbar. It offers drop-down lists and buttons you can use to apply text formatting, as follows:

- Boldface, Italic, and Underlining (Attributes or Styles)   Click the Bold, Italic, or Underline button on the toolbar to add or remove the attribute of your choice. Figure 3.2 identifies these toolbar buttons and other formatting tools, and also shows some formatting examples. You also can use the keyboard shortcuts Ctrl+B, Ctrl+I, or Ctrl+U to add and remove boldface, italic, and underlining for a selection.

FIGURE 3.1

Page Layout view (top) displays more of the formatting and layout elements in a document than the Normal view (bottom).

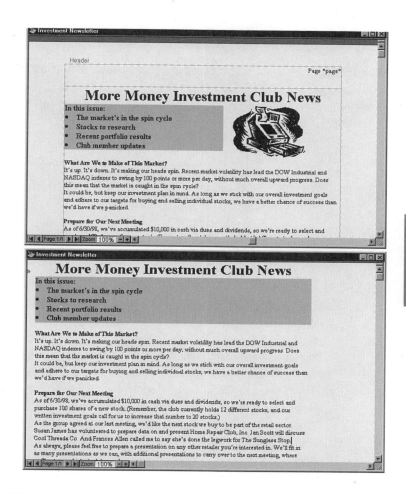

3

The Works word processor refers to boldface, italic, and underlining as "styles." Word 97, which you'll learn more about in Part II of this book, uses "style" in another way. In Word, "style" refers to a collection of formatting settings that you save and name. Refer to Hour 13, "Using Templates and Styles to Save Time," for more information.

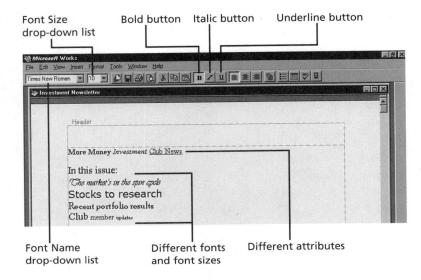

FIGURE 3.2

Use the Works toolbar to apply formatting to text.

- Choosing a Font   The style of lettering you apply to text affects the mood of your document. A script font like ZapfChancery or Brush Script looks formal and works well for invitations. A font with *serifs* (cross-strokes on the end of letters) like Times New Roman, Garamond, or Palatino makes text more readable. And a *sans serif* (without serifs) font like Arial, AvantGarde, or Helvetica looks more casual. To choose a different font for some text you've selected, click the Font Name drop-down list arrow, use the scrollbar to find the font you want; then click the font to close the drop-down list and apply it.

- Choosing a Font Size   Computer applications measure text size in points, with each point equaling 1/72nd of an inch. So, when you change a font the 12 pt. size—a comfortable size for body text—it's about 1/6th of an inch. To choose another size for selected text, click the Font Size drop-down list arrow, scroll to the size you want, and click it. Alternatively, you can click the text box for the Font Size drop-down list, type a new size measurement, and press Enter.

When you select text that has different formatting applied (such as two different fonts or font sizes), the Font Name and Font Size drop-down lists go blank to indicate the mixed formatting. The next font or font size you select applies to all the text, no matter what its previous formatting was. To apply a new attribute to a selection with mixed attribute settings, you might have to click a button, such as the Bold button, more than once.

Using the Format Font and Style Dialog Box

If you know you want to change a few different formatting settings for a selection, the toolbar tools might not be your fastest option. Instead, you can display the Format Font and Style dialog box and use its choices to format your text. As a bonus, the Format Font and Style dialog box displays a Sample preview of how the current settings look, so you can experiment before you settle on the look you want. The dialog box also includes a few additional formatting settings not available via the toolbar; for example it allows you to apply a text color or add strikethrough.

Follow these steps to use the Format Font and Style dialog box:

To Do: Formatting Text

1. Select the text to which you want to apply the new formatting.
2. Choose Format | Font and Style. The Format Font and Style dialog box appears.
3. Choose a new font for the selection from the Font list and a new text size from the Size list.
4. To apply a color to the selected text, choose the color that you want to use from the Color drop-down list.
5. To choose the attributes you want, click the appropriate check boxes in the Style area of the dialog box.
6. If you want to format the text as superscript (aligning higher than other text) or subscript (aligning lower than other text), click the appropriate option button in the Position area of the dialog box.
7. Check the results of your selections in the Sample area of the dialog box (see Figure 3.3). If you aren't satisfied, you can go back and make changes to your choices.
8. (Optional) If you like the formatting settings you've chosen and want to use them as the default text settings for all new documents you create in the Works word processor, click the Set Default button.
9. Click OK to finish and apply the settings to the selected text.

FIGURE 3.3

The sample area displays how the current settings look. As shown here, just a few text formatting changes provide a dramatic impact.

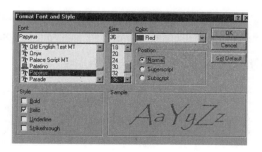

To simultaneously clear a number of formatting settings from selected text and return the text to the default format, press Ctrl+Spacebar.

Using Bullets

You can use a *bullet* (small graphical character inserted to the left) to emphasize any paragraph and set it off from other paragraphs. Many different types of publications— newspapers, magazines, and even this book—use bullets to highlight lists of information.

Adding bullets to a list provides a strong cue to your readers. You can use a bulleted list to do the following:

• Indicate "Slow down; important information here."

• Preview the important points you'll cover in a report or other document.

• Summarize your thoughts at the end of the document.

• Present a number of choices or examples to your readers.

To create a bulleted list, follow these steps:

To Do: Creating a Bulleted List

1. Enter the text you want to format as a bulleted list. Because Works assigns one bullet to each paragraph, press Enter after each list item to place it in its own paragraph.
2. Select all the list text.
3. Click the Bullets button on the Works toolbar to apply the default bullet style.
4. Click outside the list to see the bullets.

By default, Works uses a 12-pt. round bullet. You can choose to apply a different bullet style or size. Works offers two dozen bullet styles, so you can choose one that suits the tone of your document text.

Follow these steps to apply a different type of bullet to your bulleted list:

To Do: Choosing Another Type of Bullet

1. Create your list items and select all the list text. (You also can select a list to which you've previously applied bullets, to change the style of bullets it uses.)
2. Choose Format | Bullets. The Format Bullets dialog box appears, as shown in Figure 3.4.

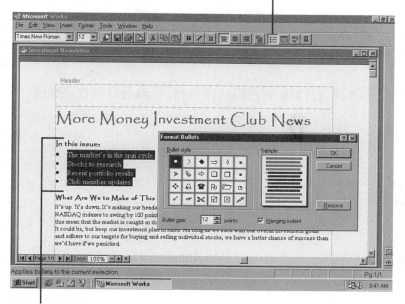

FIGURE 3.4

Works offers a number of bullet styles for your bulleted lists. Choose the style to use here.

List with default bullets

3. Click the new bullet design that you want to use in the Bullet Style list.

4. Adjust the Bullet Size text box setting to increase or decrease the size of the bullets.

5. If you don't want Works to *indent* (add spacing between the text and the margin) all lines in the list paragraphs at the left, clear the Hanging Indent check box. The Sample preview area shows how your list will look, depending on whether or not it's indented.

6. Click OK to close the Format Bullets dialog box and apply the new bullets to the list.

After you select a new bullet style and size using the Format Bullets dialog box, that style becomes the default. Clicking the Bullets button on the toolbar applies the new bullet style. To change back to the original, default bullet style, you have to redisplay the Format Bullets dialog box, choose the settings illustrated in Figure 3.4, and click OK.

To remove bullets from any bulleted list or any single item within a bulleted list, highlight the paragraph(s) from which you want to remove bullets; then click the Bullets button on the toolbar.

Applying bullets also indents the bulleted text at the left to further distinguish the bulleted text from the surrounding text. When you remove the bullets, Works removes the indention for you as well.

Changing Paragraph Alignment

By default, all text you type in the Works word processor aligns along the left margin, with text wrapping irregularly at the right (called *ragged right*). This traditional alignment helps readers keep moving through larger blocks of text. However, you can change the alignment for one or more paragraphs in your document to improve its design, make it more readable, follow a stylistic convention, or add interest. Alignment changes you might make include the following:

- Centering text   You can center a heading to set it off from the following text or center all the information on a title page you create for your document.

- Right-aligning text   For a special effect, you can align a paragraph to the right, so that it has a ragged left edge. Don't use this alignment for large amounts of text, however, because it's more difficult to read.

- Justifying text   Justified text aligns to both the left and right margins, with extra spacing added into each line. You'll often see this type of alignment used in reports and legal documents.

- Indenting the first line of a paragraph   Indenting the first line of a paragraph from the left margin helps the reader distinguish the beginning of the new paragraph, especially when there's no space between paragraphs.

- Indenting either or both sides of the paragraph   Indenting a paragraph from either the left or right margin helps set off that paragraph. For example, it's accepted style to indent lengthy quotes from both the left and right margins.

To change the alignment for any paragraph, click in the paragraph. Alternatively, you can select all the paragraphs for which you'd like to change the alignment. To make a quick alignment change, click the Left Align, Center Align, or Right Align button on the Works toolbar. The selected paragraphs immediately adopt the new alignment.

You can use another method to choose text alignment: displaying the Format Paragraph dialog box. The Format Paragraph dialog box also offers the settings for paragraph indention. Follow these steps to work with the Format Paragraph dialog box to alter alignment and indention:

To Do: Changing Paragraph Alignment

1. Select the paragraph(s) for which you want to change alignment.

2. Choose Format | Paragraph. The Format Paragraph dialog box appears.

3. Click the Indents and Alignment tab, if needed.

4. In the Indention area of the dialog box, enter the indention values you want. The Left entry specifies left side indention for all lines. The Right entry controls right side indention for all lines. The First Line setting changes the indention for the first line of each paragraph only. Figure 3.5 shows an example of first line indention.

FIGURE 3.5

The Indention settings control whether Works indents paragraphs from the left or right. The selected paragraphs illustrate the First Line entry shown here in the Format Paragraph dialog box.

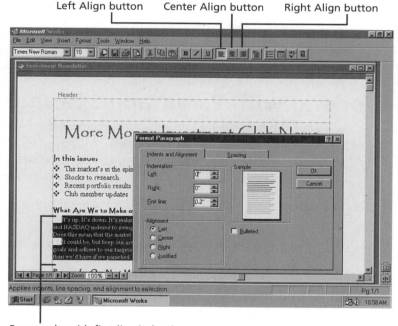

Paragraphs with first line indention

5. Click an option button in the Alignment area of the dialog box to choose an alignment for the selected paragraphs. This area offers the Justified choice, which isn't available on the Works toolbar.

6. (Optional) If you want to add bullet(s) to the selected paragraph(s), click to check the Bulleted check box.

7. Click OK to close the dialog box and finish applying alignment and indention.

If you right-align or center paragraphs to which you've applied bullets, the bullets don't move. You can try to fix the list appearance by adjusting the indention settings, but you might have difficulty achieving a nice appearance for your list.

Works doesn't provide an automatic way to create a numbered list, but you can create your own nicely formatted list. At the beginning of the paragraph for each item in the list, type the number and a period, then press Tab to move the text to the .5" tab stop. Select all the list paragraphs, then choose Format | Paragraph. In the Indention area of the Indents and Alignment tab, enter .5 into the Left text box and -.5 into the First Line text box. Click OK to finish formatting the list.

Working with Paragraph Spacing

The Format Paragraph dialog box also enables you to control spacing before, within, and after paragraphs. You can, for example, change the spacing for selected paragraphs to double-spacing. Rather than pressing Enter to add a line of white space between paragraphs, you can have Works automatically insert one or more lines' worth of spacing before or after a selected paragraph.

It's a standard practice to insert a line of spacing *after* every paragraph in a document (except, perhaps, bulleted lists). Then, to emphasize document headings, you might want to insert a line or so of spacing *before* each heading.

To adjust text spacing, follow these steps:

To Do: Changing the Spacing Between Lines

1. Select the paragraph(s) for which you want to change the spacing.

2. Choose Format | Paragraph. The Format Paragraph dialog box appears.

3. Click the Spacing tab, if needed.

4. In the Spacing area of the tab, you can change the settings by clicking a spinner button to increment a setting by a full line at a time, or by entering a measurement (in decimals) to specify more precise spacing. The Before and After settings control spacing before and after paragraphs, and the Line Spacing setting controls the

▼ spacing between lines in the selected paragraphs. Figure 3.6 shows paragraphs formatted with .5 (one half) line of extra spacing after each paragraph and with Line Spacing of 1.5 (one and one half) lines.

FIGURE 3.6

The paragraphs highlighted in this document use the spacing settings shown in the Format Paragraph dialog box.

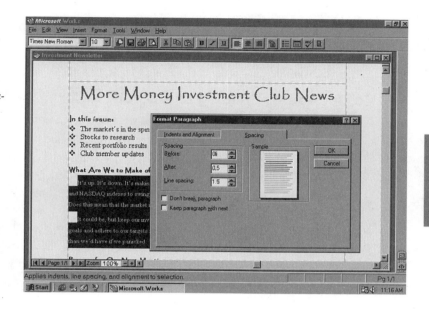

3

5. If you want to prevent an automatic page break from occurring in the selected paragraph(s), click to check the Don't Break Paragraph check box.

6. If you want to prevent Works from inserting an automatic page break between the selected paragraph(s) and the following paragraph, check Keep Paragraph with Next.

 You can still insert your own page breaks within or between paragraphs where you've told Works not to insert an automatic page break. See "Controlling Page Breaks" in Hour 4, "Formatting Pages," to learn how.

▲ 7. Click OK to finish applying the spacing settings.

Adding Borders and Shading to Paragraphs

Indention emerged as the traditional way to emphasize paragraphs because indenting text was within the capabilities of every typewriter. With a word processor, however, you can use graphical treatments to set off paragraphs. In addition to using bullets, you can use *borders* (rule lines) and *shading* (colors and patterns) behind a selected paragraph to call attention to it.

When you want to add borders or shading to text, use this approach:

To Do: Adding Shading or a Border to Text

1. Select the paragraph(s) to which you want to apply a border or shading.

2. Choose Format | Borders and Shading. The Borders and Shading dialog box appears.

3. To apply a border to the selection, click the Borders tab. Click the type of border to use in the Line Style area. Specify a border color by clicking a choice in the Border list. Then, in the Border area, click to place a check beside each side of the paragraph where you'd like the border to appear: Top, Bottom, Outline (all around the paragraph), and so on. The Sample area previews your choices.

4. To apply shading to the selection, click the Shading tab. In the Shading area of the tab, scroll the Pattern list; then click the shading pattern you want to apply. Then, choose the colors you want to use for the pattern by clicking choices in the Foreground Color and Background Color lists. As shown in Figure 3.7, the Sample area previews your choices.

FIGURE 3.7

Shading and border settings like the ones shown here emphasize paragraphs.

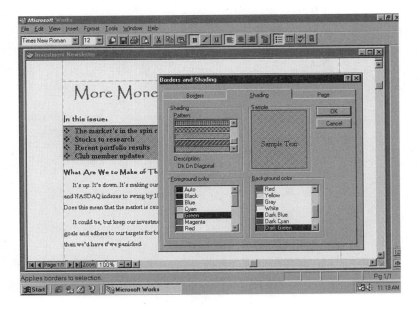

▲ 5. Click OK to close the dialog box and finish applying your formatting choices.

> The borders and shading you add to text span all the way to the margins.

Using Easy Formats

The Works word processor offers paragraph styles called *Easy Formats*. Each Easy Format can specify the font, font size, font color, alignment, indention, spacing, borders, and shading for a paragraph. To apply all the settings specified by the Easy Format, you simply apply the Easy Format to the paragraph(s) that should use the Easy Format's formatting.

To apply an Easy Format, follow these steps:

To Do: Formatting Text with an Easy Format

1. Select the paragraph(s) to which you want to apply the Easy Format.
2. Choose Format | Easy Formats or click the Easy Formats button on the toolbar and then click More Easy Formats. The Easy Formats dialog box appears.
3. Scroll through the list of formats and click the one you might want to apply. The Sample area displays the selected format, as shown in Figure 3.8.

3

FIGURE 3.8

Select an Easy Format to apply its formatting to the paragraph(s) you've selected in a document.

Easy Formats button

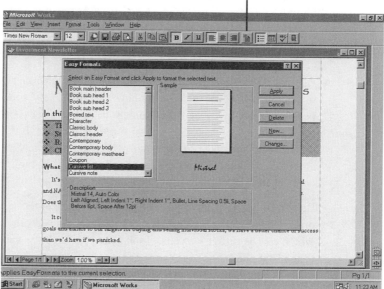
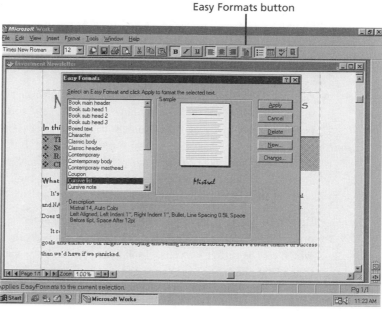

▲   4. Click Apply to apply the Easy Format to your selection and close the dialog box.

To create your own Easy Format, first specify all the formatting settings it should use on a paragraph; then select the paragraph. Click the Easy Formats button on the toolbar and then click Create From Selection in the menu that appears. Type a name for the Easy Format in the text box in the New Easy Format dialog box; then click Done.

Text Design Tips

Although Easy Formats provide a welcome document design shortcut, there's no reason you can't be successful with your own document designs. It takes years of college and experience to train a professional graphic designer, but you can avoid rookie mistakes by following a few basic guidelines:

- When choosing fonts for a document, stick with two or three For a more traditional look, choose a font with serifs for body text, a sans serif font for headings and titles, and a third font for special elements like captions. To give the document a more modern or festive feel, use a sans serif font for body text and a fancy or whimsical font for headings and titles.

- Be smart with font sizes and special formatting Keep your documents readable. In general, a larger text size or special formatting like boldface or lines to set off a paragraph emphasizes text, but too many different sizes just make a mess and slow the reader down. Limit special formatting as much as possible, so that it really stands out when you use it. And, as a rule, the wider the body of text is, the larger the font needs to be to keep it readable. For a standard letter-sized page with 1-inch margins, stick with 12-point text or larger.

- Use color to accent text, not overwhelm it Color inkjet printers have fallen so far in price that if you don't already have one, it's likely you will soon. Limit the number of colors you use in the document to two or three—one for body text, another for titles and headings, and a third for special elements. Generally speaking, use a darker color for body text or smaller text, and a somewhat lighter text for headings and titles. If you add background shading to a paragraph, be sure there's enough contrast between the text and the shading.

- Be careful using color if you'll also print the document using a black-and-white printer, especially an older one The printer converts the colors to shades of gray, which can be difficult to read, look grainy, or lack the variation you were seeking in the first place.

- Study documents that you find attractive   Look at magazines, brochures, annual reports, and even junk mail you receive to see how professional designers use fonts, alignment, and graphics. Even create a file of sample documents you think you might want to copy in look and feel.

Summary

It only took an hour or so for you to teach yourself how to punch up your text using text and paragraph formatting. You can use fun fonts, spicy bullets, shady patterns, and a variety of other settings offered in the Works word processor to set a tone for your document and make it more interesting and readable. Now you can move on to page formatting, which complements the text and paragraph formatting settings you choose.

Q&A

Q. What's the fastest way to apply formatting?

A. Select the text you want to format; then use the Font Name or Font Size drop-down lists on the toolbar. Also, you can use the Bold, Italic, Underline, Left Align, Center Align, Right Align, or Bullets buttons to change formatting, paragraph alignment, and bullets.

Q. How do I select another bullet style?

A. Choose Format | Bullets. In the Format Bullets dialog box, click the new bullet design to use in the Bullet Style list. Adjust the Bullet Size text box setting; then click OK.

Q. Do I have to press Enter at the end of each line to double-space my document?

A. No, and doing so would just make your document more difficult to edit later. Instead, change the line spacing used for your text. To do so, select the paragraphs for which you want to use double-spacing. Choose Format | Paragraph and click the Spacing tab in the Format Paragraph dialog box. Enter 2 in the Line Spacing text box to specify that you want to double-space the text; then click OK. You can use the other settings in the Format Paragraph dialog box to adjust a selection's alignment, indention, and spacing before and after paragraphs.

Q. What are Easy Formats, and how do I use them?

A. An Easy Format stores a collection of formatting settings. Rather than choosing each of those settings individually, you simply apply the Easy Format to one or more paragraphs. To do so, choose Format | Easy Formats. Scroll through the list of formats in the Easy Formats dialog box, and click the one you want to apply. Click Apply to finish and close the dialog box.

3

Hour 4

Formatting Pages

The choices you make in setting up the page design in your Works Word Processor documents should complement the text formatting choices you make. Page design choices not only make your document more attractive, but they also help the reader navigate through the document's information.

The next sixty minutes offer you the opportunity to finalize your document's appearance by adjusting these aspects of the page:

- Add and remove page breaks where needed.
- Display text in two or more columns.
- Insert a graphic to illustrate your point.
- Create a header or footer for each page.
- Use borders, change margins, and more.

Controlling Page Breaks

Although Works does start a new page whenever the current page fills with text, the nature of your document might create situations where you need to determine where a new page starts. This is called inserting a *manual* or *hard* page break. You might need to insert a hard page break, for example, if you want to start a new section of a report on a new page.

To start a new page at a particular location, choose Insert | Page Break or press Ctrl+Enter. Figure 4.1 shows how a hard page break looks in the document in Normal view. In Page Layout view, a hard page break also appears as a dotted line across a page.

FIGURE 4.1

Insert a hard page break when you need to present information on a new page in the document. Here's how a hard page break looks in Normal view.

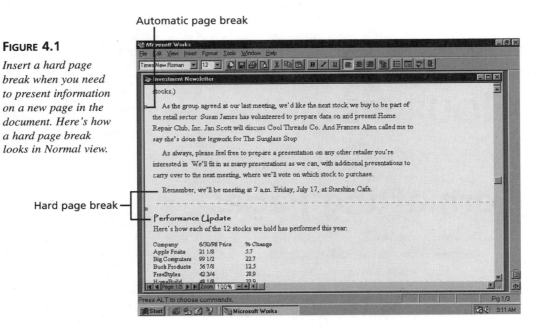

To remove a hard page break, click to position the insertion point at the beginning of the paragraph that follows the page break, and then press Backspace.

Hard page breaks enable you to put less information on a page, such as when you want to create a title page for a document. To squeeze more onto a page, format the text with a smaller font or make the margins smaller. The section "Changing Other Page Settings" later in this hour explains how to adjust page margins, among other changes.

Displaying Text in Multiple Columns

If you have a lot of information that you want to fit on a single printed page, consider formatting the document text in multiple columns, much like a newspaper or magazine. Because columns divide the text into shorter lines, you can format the text in a much smaller font without making the text less readable.

> When you divide a document's text into columns, that change applies to all the pages in the document.

Follow these steps to add and remove columns in a document:

To Do: Dividing a Document's Text into Multiple Columns

1. Choose Format | Columns. The Format Columns dialog box appears.
2. Type a value in the Number of Columns text box to specify the number of columns you want in the document.
3. To adjust the amount of white space between columns, double-click the entry in the Space Between text box, and type a new value, in inches. Use decimals to specify fractions of an inch.
4. If you want to print—but not display onscreen—a vertical line between columns to better separate the column text, click to check the Line Between Columns check box. (Figure 4.2 shows settings specified in the Format Columns dialog box and the resulting document's appearance.)
5. Click OK to close the Format Columns dialog box and apply your choices.
6. If you were working in Normal view before you displayed the Format Columns dialog box, a dialog box asks you to verify that you want to switch to Page Layout view. Click Yes to do so. Otherwise, you'll see your text in the Normal view in one long, thin column, and you won't be able to judge how the document looks with multiple columns.

If you specify, a vertical line appears between
columns when you print the document

FIGURE 4.2

The settings shown here in the Format Columns dialog box have already been applied to the document behind it.

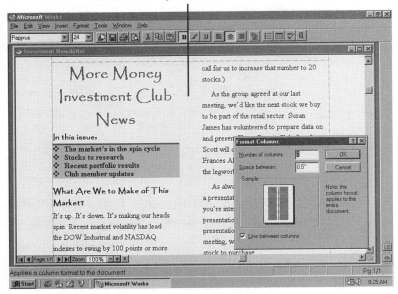

Inserting Graphics

Graphics improve a page's appearance by emphasizing the text's subject matter or by providing interesting decoration. Works enables you to add a number of different kinds of graphics; this section focuses on two: ClipArt and WordArt.

 After you insert a graphic, you can click it to select it. Gray selection handles appear around the graphic. Drag the selected graphic to move it to a new location. Press Delete to remove the selected graphic from the document.

Adding ClipArt

Works provides predrawn images called ClipArt that you can insert into your documents. The Microsoft Clip Gallery that comes with Works organizes the dozens of images into categories to make it easier to find an image that suits your document's contents.

Follow these steps to insert a ClipArt image into the document and adjust it relative to the surrounding text:

To Do: Adding a ClipArt Image to Your Document

▲ To Do

1. Insert the Works Suite CD-ROM that holds the Works program into your CD-ROM drive. Click the button for exiting the Setup program if it starts. You could skip this step, but having the CD-ROM in the drive means you can access hundreds of additional ClipArt images!

2. Click to position the insertion point at the approximate location where you want the ClipArt graphic to appear.

3. Choose Insert | ClipArt. The Microsoft Clip Gallery 3.0 dialog box appears.

4. In the list at the left, click a category to display its images to the right.

5. Click the image you want to insert (see Figure 4.3), and then click Insert. The image appears in the document at the insertion point. Selection handles appear around the image, and the image appears at its default size. Additionally, the text automatically breaks where the image appears, so that the text appears above and below the image but does not flow around it.

FIGURE 4.3

The Clip Gallery orga-nizes the ClipArt. Select a category and then select the image to insert.

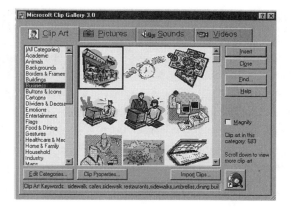

4

6. To adjust the graphic's size, drag one of the gray selection handles.

Drag one of the corner handles to ensure the graphic retains its original proportions.

7. To have more flexibility in moving the graphic or to wrap text around the graphic for a more polished document appearance, right-click the graphic, and then click Format Picture. The Format Picture dialog box appears. Click the Text Wrap tab,

▼

▼ click the Absolute button, and then click OK. You can then drag the graphic to the precise location you need.

▲ 8. Click outside the graphic to deselect it.

 If you want to get even more ClipArt images, click the Connect to Web for Additional Clips button in the lower-right corner of the Microsoft Clip Gallery 3.0 dialog box. (The button has a globe on it.) Clip Gallery launches Internet Explorer and connects to a Web site from which you can download more ClipArt. See Hours 14 and 15 to learn more about going online and browsing the Web.

Adding WordArt

When you create WordArt, you apply a decorative effect to text that you type to create a graphic headline or "pull quote" (a phrase you want to highlight in the document). Follow along now to see how to create a piece of WordArt in your document:

To Do: Designing WordArt in a Document

1. Click to position the insertion point at the approximate location where you want the WordArt graphic to appear.
2. Choose Insert|WordArt. A box for the WordArt graphic appears, with placeholder text inside it. Below that, the Enter Your Text Here dialog box appears. Also, the WordArt toolbar replaces the Word toolbar at the top of the screen.
3. Type the text you want to format as a WordArt graphic. The text automatically appears in the graphic box in the document.

 I recommend sticking with short, punchy phrases for WordArt graphics. Because some of the WordArt designs distort text quite a bit, cramming a lot of text into those designs makes the text virtually unreadable.

4. Click the drop-down list arrow for the far-left drop-down list on the WordArt tool-bar. A pop-up palette of the available WordArt shapes appears (see Figure 4.4). Click the shape you want to use.

▼

FIGURE 4.4

Select a shape for the text in your WordArt graphic from the far-left drop-down list.

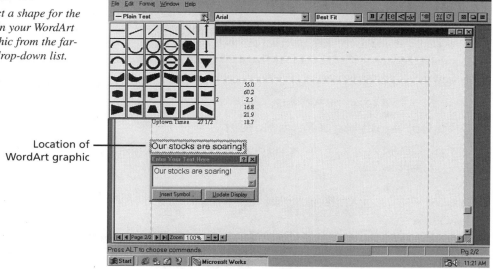

Location of WordArt graphic

5. Use the other buttons and drop-down lists on the WordArt toolbar to enhance the WordArt graphic. For example, open the third drop-down list, which displays Best Fit by default, and click a new font size for the WordArt text. You might be asked whether to resize the WordArt object to accommodate the new text size. Click Yes to do so. Other tools enable you to change the color for the text, apply boldface or italic to it, and so on.

6. Click outside the WordArt graphic to finish formatting it.

7. To adjust the graphic's size, drag one of the gray handles.

8. To have more flexibility in moving the graphic or to wrap text around the graphic for a more polished document appearance, right-click the graphic, and then click Format Picture. The Format Picture dialog box appears. Click the Text Wrap tab; click the Absolute button, and then click OK. You can then drag the graphic to the precise location you need.

9. Click outside the graphic to deselect it.

4

It'll take a little practice, but if you have a color printer, you can use the WordArt feature to create colorful nametags printed on mailing labels or nametag sheets that you can run through your printer. Test how everything lines up by first printing to a piece of paper and then comparing it with the label sheet layout.

Adding a Page Border

You can add a border around the entire page, if you want to decorate the page itself. For example, if you're creating personal or small business letterheads to print with a color printer, adding a page border to define the writing area makes it look like you had your letterhead custom printed.

To decorate a document with a page border, follow these steps:

To Do: Applying a Page Border

1. Choose Format | Borders and Shading. The Borders and Shading dialog box appears.

FIGURE 4.5

Use the choices in this dialog box to create a border around your document pages.

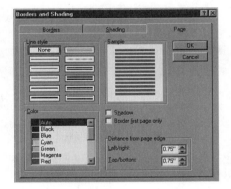

2. Click the Page tab to display it, as shown in Figure 4.5.

3. In the Line Style area, click the type of border you want to use.

4. Scroll the Color list and click the color you want to apply to the border.

5. If you want to include a drop shadow with the border, click to check the Shadow check box.

6. You can add the border only to the first page of the document instead of on all the pages, such as when the document includes a title page that warrants special formatting. To do so, click to check the Border First Page Only check box.

7. Works positions page borders relative to the edge of the page (not the margin). To adjust how far from the page edge the border appears, double-click an entry in the Left/Right or Top/Bottom text boxes, and then type a new measurement in inches, using a decimal value to indicate a fraction of an inch. You can change the measurement in either or both of the text boxes.

▲ 8. Click OK to close the dialog box and display the page border.

Adding Page Headers and Footers

For lengthier or more formal documents, including a *header* or *footer* can remind your reader of key document information or even help the reader navigate in the document. A header or footer can include information such as the document's name or topic, the current page number, your name and phone number, or any other information that you want to be unobtrusive, but readily available to the reader. A header appears at the top every page, whereas a footer appears at the bottom of every page.

> In Works, a header or footer appears on every page of the document by default. You can prevent the header or footer from printing on the first page of the document, but to do so, you need to use the Page Setup dialog box, described in the later section, "Changing Other Page Settings."

You enter a header or footer in the header or footer area of the document. In Normal view, you can see both the header and footer areas at the top of the first page in the document only. An H in the left margin designates the header area, and an F designates the footer area. In Page Layout view, you can find the header area at the top of every page, bounded by a light gray outline and labeled Header. You will find a similarly identified footer area at the bottom of each page.

Follow these steps to add or edit a header or footer for your document:

To Do: Creating or Changing a Header or Footer

1. Click in the header or footer area. Alternately, you can choose View | Header or View | Footer to move the insertion point to the header or footer area.

2. Type the header or footer text, or edit the text it already contains. Note that the header and footer area has three tab stops by default: one flush left, one centered, and one flush right. This helps you attractively align the header or footer contents.

3. To number the pages, position the insertion point in the header or footer to indicate where you want page numbers to appear, and then choose Insert | Page Number. Works inserts a code that updates to correctly number each page. You also can use the Insert | Document Name and Insert | Date and Time commands to insert useful information. (You also can insert a page numbering code, document name, or date and time outside the header or footer area.)

4. Select the header or footer contents, and then choose the text and paragraph formatting settings that you want to adjust the header or footer's appearance. Figure 4.6 shows an example of a footer.

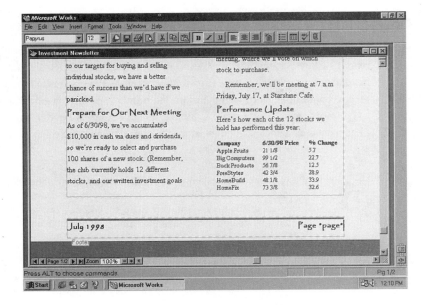

▼ **FIGURE 4.6**

You can use text and paragraph formatting to make your footer (shown here) or header complement other document formatting. Note the page numbering code at the far right.

▲ 5. Click outside the header or footer area to finish working with the header or footer.

> You can insert special symbols from the Windows Character Map into your header, footer, or any other location in a Works word processor document. For example, you might want to add the copyright symbol (©) into the footer for a document that contains an original work of fiction or client proposal. Or, you might want to insert actual Greek characters in a letter to your fraternity or sorority mates. To insert a special symbol, choose Start | Programs | Accessories | System Tools | Character Map. Select the font to use from the Font drop-down list in the Character Map window, and then double-click the symbol you want to insert in the grid of characters below. Click the Copy button, and then the Close button. Back in your Works document, click to position the insertion point where you want to insert the symbol, and then click the Paste button on the toolbar.

Changing Other Page Settings

The *page setup* refers to a collection of remaining settings for designing your page, such as the width of the margins (white space) around the page and its *orientation*. (In *Landscape* orientation, the page is wider than it is tall, and in *Portrait* orientation the page is taller than it is wide.) You can change the page setup settings at any time. Just be aware that doing so can cause pages to break differently, so that you need to double-check that graphics still appear in the correct location.

Change the page setup as follows:

To Do: Adjusting the Page Setup

1. Choose File | Page Setup. The Page Setup dialog box appears.
2. Click the Margins tab to display its choices, if needed. Figure 4.7 shows the Page Setup dialog box, with the Margins tab selected.

FIGURE 4.7

Use the Page Setup dialog box to control white space around the page (margins) and other page layout choices.

3. To change the width of any page margin, double-click the applicable text box entry in the Margins area, and then type a new measurement in inches, using decimals if needed.
4. To adjust the distance between the edge of the page and the document header or footer, double-click either (or both) the Header Margin or Footer Margin text box entry, and then type a new measurement in inches, using decimals if needed.
5. Click the Source, Size & Orientation tab. This tab offers options for controlling the page size and orientation.
6. In the Orientation area, click either the Portrait or Landscape option button.
7. Make your choices in the Paper area. If your printer has more than one paper tray, choose the tray to use from the Source drop-down list. Choose a paper (page) size from the Size drop-down list.
8. To use a nonstandard page size, edit the page dimensions in the Width and Height text boxes. Double-click one of those entries; then type a new measurement, in inches.

▼   9. Click the Other Options tab to display its options.

10. If you're using a page numbering code to automatically number the pages in your document, it numbers the first page of the document as page 1 by default. If you want the first page to use another number, such as page 10, enter the new number to use in the Starting Page Number text box.

11. To prevent the header or footer from printing on the first page of the document, click to check either (or both) the No Header on First Page or No Footer on First Page check box.

12. Although this book doesn't cover creating footnotes, you might have experimented and added them on your own. If so, you can click to check the Print Footnotes at End check box to print the notes in one list at the end of the document, instead of printing each footnote on the page with the footnoted text.

▲   13. Click OK to close the dialog box and apply your page setup settings.

To create a three-panel brochure, set up the page in landscape orientation, and then format the text in three columns.

Page Design Tips

Form follows function is a useful axiom in home and document design. Although some experimentation will lead you to better, more interesting documents, over designing your pages can get in the way of your reader's ability to understand information. Here are a few ideas to help you combine page design choices and document usefulness:

- Give white space as much consideration as other design elements   Cramming every free bit of space on your page with stuff not only makes it look cluttered, but also can reduce its readability. Adding extra white space—between columns or in the margins, for example—makes a document look more elegant and inviting, and less overwhelming.

- Limit the number of graphics you use if you have a slower printer, or be prepared to wait   Even ClipArt graphics can cause your document to consume more printer memory for printing, slowing down the process for each page.

- If you have a black-and-white printer, use color sparingly   Black-and-white printers handle different colors with varying degrees of success. Most black-and-white printers convert colors to shades of gray (as opposed to black and white), so slightly different colors could look identical when printed. Choose a medium color for page accents like borders, or stick with a black and white ClipArt image for better results.

- Insert the filename in the header or footer of a business document or important household documents   This helps you remember the name of the file if you later need to edit or reprint it. It helps others find the correct file when it's needed.

Summary

At this point, you've taught yourself all the key tasks for creating documents with the Works word processor. Your universe of skills now includes controlling page breaks and the number of columns in a document; inserting graphics; changing page margins, borders, and other page settings; and adding a header or footer to every page. From here, you can move on to calculating with the Works Spreadsheet tool.

Q&A

Q. Can I control where pages break?

A. Of course. Press Ctrl+Enter or choose Insert | Page Break to add a break wherever you need one.

Q. How do I add a graphic to my document?

A. To view the greatest number of available images, insert the Work Suite CD-ROM that holds the Works program into your CD-ROM drive. Click the Exit Setup button. Position the insertion point about where you want the graphic to appear, and then choose Insert | ClipArt. Click a category; click the image you want, and then click Insert.

Q. What is the purpose of a header or footer, and how do I add one?

A. A header or footer presents information that your readers need, no matter what page they're reading, such as the publication date for the document. You can use the header or footer to display that information in a standard, unobtrusive location on each page. To create a header or footer, click in the header or footer area and type the text. You also can use the Page Number, Document Name, and Date and Time commands on the Insert menu to insert special information in the header or footer. Click outside the Header or Footer area to finish.

Q. How do I control the layout of the page?

A. Choose File | Page Setup, and then choose the layout settings you want on the three tabs of the Page Setup dialog box.

4

HOUR 5

Calculating with a Spreadsheet

Whether or not you're mathematically challenged, using a spreadsheet to perform calculations improves both speed and accuracy. In this hour, you learn to

- Create a spreadsheet with predefined information and calculations.
- Type your labels and numbers.
- Navigate and select spreadsheet information.
- Tell the spreadsheet what to calculate.
- Make changes to spreadsheet contents.
- Open an Excel worksheet in Works and vice versa.

Creating a Spreadsheet with a TaskWizard

In Hour 2, "Building Documents with the Word Processor," you learned how to use a document TaskWizard to create a new Word Processor document.

Works also offers spreadsheet TaskWizards. Again, the TaskWizard provides a design and creates a spreadsheet with standard cell entries and some calculations (*formulas*) already entered. You simply fill in some label information and enter the numbers you want the new spreadsheet to calculate. The Task Launcher offers a number of useful spreadsheet TaskWizards, including Bids, Invoice, Mortgage and Loan Analysis, and To Do List.

To create a spreadsheet using a TaskWizard, you follow virtually the same steps you use for creating a document TaskWizard:

To Do: Using a Spreadsheet TaskWizard

1. Click the Task Launcher button on the Works toolbar or choose File | New (Ctrl+N).
2. Click the TaskWizards tab, if needed.
3. Click the button for the category you want to open. The Task Launcher categories display all the TaskWizards, including those for tools other than the Spreadsheet tool (see Figure 5.1). A calculator and ledger paper icon appears beside each spreadsheet TaskWizard.
4. Double-click the icon for the TaskWizard to use, or click it, and then click OK.
5. Click the Yes, Run the TaskWizard button to tell Works that you want it to create the spreadsheet for you.

FIGURE 5.1

Choose a spreadsheet TaskWizard from the Works Task Launcher. I created the spreadsheet shown behind the Task Launcher with the highlighted Mortgage and Loan Analysis TaskWizard.

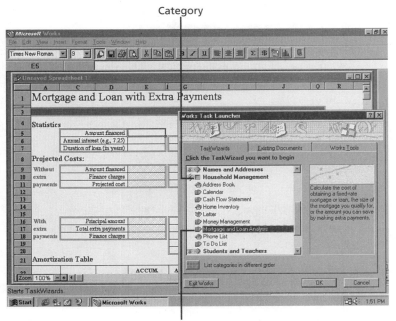

Category

Icon for a spreadsheet TaskWizard

▼ 6. Click the button representing the spreadsheet design you want to use, and then click the Create It button. Works displays the new spreadsheet, and the Works Spreadsheet Tool menu bar and toolbar appear.

7. You can then enter additional text and numbers to complete the new spreadsheet. The rest of this hour covers the numerous techniques you can use to enter and edit entries in a blank spreadsheet or one you created using a TaskWizard. Don't forget

▲ to save the new file periodically to preserve your work.

Entering Spreadsheet Information

Each Works spreadsheet organizes information in a grid of rows and columns that intersect to form *cells*. The spreadsheet displays the number for each row in the row header at the left and the letter for each column in the column header at the top of the spreadsheet. Works identifies each cell by its *cell reference* or *cell address*, which is the column letter and row number for the cell combined, for example, C7 (the cell in row 7 of column C) or F32 (the cell in row 32 of column F).

A black cell selector highlights the *current cell* or *selected cell*—the cell where your entry will appear. The address for the current cell appears to the left of the Entry bar that appears below the toolbar in the Works Spreadsheet tool. (See Figure 5.2 for a look at some of the spreadsheet parts.)

FIGURE 5.2

Works inserts the information you type into the current cell.

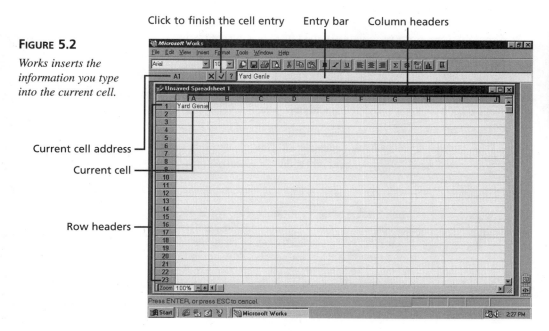

5

Each cell holds a single spreadsheet entry, which can be a *label* (text entry), *value* (number), *date*, or *formula* (calculation instructions). No matter what type of entry you're creating, you type the cell contents, and then use one of the following methods to finish the entry:

- Press Enter, which finishes the entry and leaves the cell selected where you made the entry.
- Click the check mark button (refer to Figure 5.2) that appears on the Entry bar to finish the entry and leave the current cell selected.
- Press Tab or right arrow to finish the entry and select the cell to the right of the cell where you made the entry.
- Press the down arrow to finish the entry and select the cell below the cell where you made the entry.

Although you use the same technique to make different types of spreadsheet entries, the Spreadsheet tool aligns each type of entry differently, as follows:

- Labels   Lines up at the left side of the cell. The spreadsheet automatically inserts a left double prime (") to the left of a label entry to identify the entry as text. If a text entry is too lengthy to fit within the columns current size, it spills over the cell(s) to the right. If the cells to the right already contain entries, the Works truncates (cuts off) the display of the long text entry.
- Values   Numbers line up at the right side of the cell. You can type a dollar sign before an entry to identify the entry as a currency entry. Also be sure to type the decimal point where you want it to appear.
- Dates   Dates align at the right side of the cell. You must use forward slashes (6/6/99) not dashes (6-6-99) when you enter a date. Otherwise, the Spreadsheet tool converts the date to a label or text entry.
- Formulas   A cell holding a formula displays the result the formula calculates to, not the formula itself. Because a formula's result is almost always numeric, the formula result aligns to the right side of the cell.

When a value, date, or formula entry is too wide to fit the current cell, the Spreadsheet tool might display pound signs (###) in the cell. You can make the column wider to display the entry, as described in Hour 6, "Formatting Your Spreadsheet" in the section, "Changing Column Width and Row Height." The Spreadsheet tool also might convert large numbers to scientific notation or round a decimal entry to help the entry display in the cell.

Behind the scenes, the Spreadsheet tool converts each date entry to a *date serial number*. Then, it can more easily perform calculations involving dates, such as the length of time between two dates you enter. If you're worried about the Year 2000 bug or Y2K problem, where programs can't understand dates beyond 12/31/99, don't sweat it. This version of Works has been updated to handle dates from the next millennium.

Selecting Cells

Just as you must select text in a word processor document to format or work with that text, you have to select a cell or cells in a spreadsheet to perform an operation. For example, you select a single cell to make a cell entry or select a *range* (a contiguous group of cells) to apply formatting. Any time you make a selection in the spreadsheet, you move the cell selector, moving yourself around in the spreadsheet. This section describes the various types of selections you can make in a spreadsheet.

The *range address* or *range reference* combines the cell reference for the upper-left cell in the range with the cell reference for the lower-right cell in the range, separated by a colon. If a range spans from cell A3 to cell G10, the range reference is A3:G10.

Going to a Cell

When you need to select a specific cell to enter, edit, or format its contents, you can select that cell. Works gives you a number of different methods for doing so:

- Press an arrow key to move one column or row in the direction of the arrow. You also can press PgDn or PgUp to select a cell that's one screen below or above the current cell.

- Click a scroll arrow or drag a scrollbox on either the vertical or horizontal scrollbar to display the cell you want to select, and then click the cell.

- Press Ctrl+Home to go to cell A1. Press Ctrl+End to display the last cell in the spreadsheet containing data.

- Press Home or End to go to the first cell in the row, or the rightmost cell containing data in the row.

- Use the Go To feature to display and select a particular cell without scrolling around to find it or using multiple key presses. Choose Edit | Go To (Ctrl+G) to display the Go To dialog box. Type the cell reference for the cell you want to select in the Go To text box (see Figure 5.3), and then click OK to select the specified cell.

FIGURE 5.3

Select a specific cell without scrolling or hunting for it by using the Go To dialog box.

Selecting a Range

Selecting or highlighting more than one cell enables you to save time when performing certain operations. For example, you can select a range of cells, copy it, and paste those cell entries into another location. Use one of these techniques to select a range of cells:

- Click the cell in the upper-left corner of the range you want to select. Press and hold the Shift key, and then press one or more arrow keys to extend selection.

- Drag from the upper-left cell to the lower-right cell of the range, as shown in Figure 5.4.

FIGURE 5.4

Drag to select (high-light) a spreadsheet range.

Range reference for the selected range

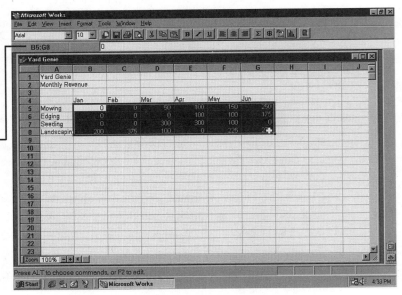

- Choose Edit I Go To (Ctrl+G) to display the Go To dialog box. Type the range reference for the range you want to select in the Go To text box, as in B5:G8 (the range shown in Figure 5.4) or F54:I76, and then click OK to select the specified range.

> In the Spreadsheet tool, the mouse pointer most often looks like a plus sign rather than an arrow, as in Works tools. When you click on a cell to select it or select a range, the mouse pointer looks like a plus.

Selecting a Row or Column

To work with a row or column in the spreadsheet, you need to select the entire row or column. For example, to insert a new column into the spreadsheet you must select a column first. (See "Adding and Deleting Columns and Rows" in Hour 6.)

To select a row or column (or more), use one of the following techniques:

- Click the row number (row header) or column letter (column header) for the row or column you want to select.
- Click a cell in the row or column want to select, and then choose Edit I Select Row or Edit I Select Column.
- Drag over adjoining row or column headers to select multiple rows or columns.
- To select the entire spreadsheet, click the gray button in the upper-left corner of the spreadsheet window, where the row and column headers intersect. Or, choose Edit I Select All (Ctrl+A).

Creating Formulas

A *formula* calculates a result based on the values you've entered into spreadsheet cells, on other numbers you enter into the formula, or even on the results calculated by other formulas. The formulas you create can range from simple math to more sophisticated statistical or logical analysis.

If you can do math, you can enter simple formulas on your own. For example, a formula such as =G10+G11+G12 totals three values, such as your monthly expenditures for groceries, dining out, and lunch money, assuming those values are entered in cells G10, G11, and G12. Or, if you want to calculate how much extra cash you'll have if you cut your expenses by $45 per month for the next year, the formula =45*12 calculates the information in a snap.

5

If you failed in high school trig, business school statistics, or some other form of higher math, don't worry. The Works Spreadsheet tool gives you help with those types of calculations, like calculating monthly interest payments, as you'll learn later in this section.

Understanding Operators and Functions

To enter a formula, you start by typing an equal sign. The Spreadsheet tool then recognizes that it should calculate what comes next. After you create the formula contents, press Enter or use one of the other methods presented earlier to finish entering the formula in the cell. The cell then displays the calculated result of the formula, not the actual formula. If you select a cell that holds a formula, you can see the formula itself in the Entry bar above the spreadsheet.

Every formula can use the mathematical operators + (addition), - (subtraction), * (multiplication), and / (division). It can calculate discrete numbers you enter within the formula, or the contents of a cell you reference in the formula. For example, =F15+100 adds 100 to whatever value you entered in cell F15. Similarly, =C9*D18 multiplies the values contained in two cells.

The Spreadsheet tool performs operator calculations in a particular order. It multiplies and divides first, and then adds and subtracts. It does not work from left to right as you learned in basic math classes. You can, however, include parentheses in a formula to control the calculation order. Works calculates the contents of the innermost pair of parentheses first, and then works outward. For example, Works would calculate the formula =5+7*(3+2) as 40.

The *functions* provided by Works perform more complicated calculations for you and also enable you to perform a calculation on a range. For example, rather than entering a formula to total a number of cells, as in =B5+B6+B7+B8, you can use the SUM function to total that range, as in =SUM(B5:B8). Examples of other functions include the AVG function (averages the values in the specified range) and the NOW function (displays the current date).

Almost every function requires one or more *arguments* to be enclosed in parentheses. The function calculates a result based on the arguments you enter, such as averaging the values in a specified range. If a function requires multiple arguments, you separate each one with a comma (more on this shortly).

To enter a range in a formula, you can simply type the range into the formula. Alternatively, you can type the formula up to the point where you need the reference, drag over the range in the spreadsheet (see an example in Figure 5.5), type the closing parentheses and rest of the formula, and then press Enter to complete it.

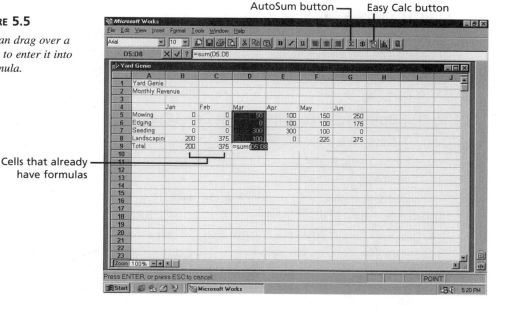

FIGURE 5.5

You can drag over a range to enter it into a formula.

AutoSum button ——   Easy Calc button

Cells that already have formulas

Click the AutoSum button (refer to Figure 5.5) to start a formula that sums the range immediately to the right or above the current cell. Verify that the formula uses the correct range, type the closing parenthesis, and then press Enter.

5

If you press Enter and Works finds an error in your formula, it displays a message box. It either tells you it can correct your formula (in which case you can press Enter to have it do so), or advises you to click OK to return to the formula to correct it yourself.

A formula can include both operators and functions if you use pairs of parentheses to organize or nest the different parts of the formula. For example, in Figure 5.5, cell B9 calculates to a result of 200, and C9 calculates to a result of 375. You can sum those values and add 100 to the result (for a total of 675) with the formula =(SUM(B9:C9))+100.

Using Easy Calc

The spreadsheet's Easy Calc feature presents the most commonly used functions in the spreadsheet and walks you through the steps for entering a formula using that function. It even prompts you to enter the correct arguments for the function.

To use Easy Calc to create a formula with a function, use these steps:

To Do: Building a Formula with Easy Calc

1. (Optional) Select the cell where you want to enter the formula.
2. Choose Tools | Easy Calc or click the Easy Calc button on the toolbar. The Easy Calc dialog box opens.
3. In the Common Calculations area of the dialog box, click the button for the function you want to use.
4. The next Easy Calc dialog box that opens explains how to select the argument(s) for the function you selected. Easy Calc might even guess at the cells(s) to specify for the arguments (see Figure 5.6), depending on the location of the cell you selected in Step 1, if any. You can either drag in the spreadsheet to enter a range or click individual cells, depending on which method Easy Calc specifies. If the Easy Calc dialog box gets in the way of your selections, you can drag it by its title bar to a new location.

Cell that will hold the formula

FIGURE 5.6

Easy Calc explains how to select arguments, displays the currently selected argument contents, and even previews the formula (bottom of the dialog box).

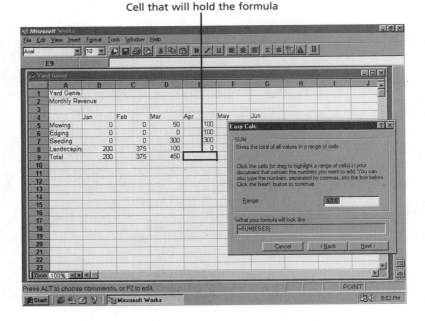

5. After you enter the arguments as directed by Easy Calc and verify that the preview of the formula at the bottom of the dialog box looks correct, click Next.

6. Verify that the Result At text box shows the address for the cell that you want to hold the formula. If you need to correct it, type a new cell address or, in the spreadsheet, click the cell you want to use.

7. Click Finish to close the dialog box and enter the new formula in the spreadsheet.

Using Functions

If you have a lot of free time, you can memorize and type the function you need into a formula, but that requires you to memorize the arguments the function requires in addition to the function. However, it's faster to use the Insert Function dialog box.

The Insert Function dialog box organizes the dozens of spreadsheet functions into categories, so you can more quickly find the function you want. In addition, the Insert Function dialog box provides a description of each function to make the function selection process even easier and reminds you of what arguments to include for each function.

To use the Insert Function dialog box to enter a formula, follow these steps:

To Do: Building a Formula That Uses a Function

1. Click the cell where you want to insert the new formula.

2. Choose Insert | Function. The Insert Function dialog box opens (see Figure 5.7).

FIGURE 5.7

The Insert Function dialog box helps you select the right function and fill in its arguments.

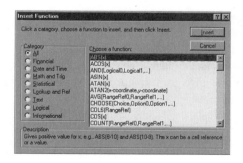

5

3. In the Category list, click the option button for the category that you think holds the function you want. The functions in that category appear in the Choose a Function list at the right.

4. Click the function you think you want. The Description area at the bottom of the dialog box explains what the function calculates and sheds some light on the type of arguments it requires.

▼   5. Click the Insert button to close the dialog box and insert the function you selected
          into the spreadsheet cell you specified in Step 1. The function appears with the first
          (or only) argument placeholder highlighted.

       6. Type the value or cell or range reference for the argument. Alternatively, you can
          click a cell or drag over a range in the spreadsheet to insert the cell or range in
          place of the highlighted argument.

       7. If needed, drag over the next argument to highlight it, and then repeat step 6 to
          enter the argument contents. (Be sure not to drag over any comma between argu-
          ments because you'll accidentally wipe it out when you specify the argument.)
          Repeat this step and the prior one as needed to finish specifying all the arguments.

       8. After you've specified all your arguments, if there are any unused argument place-
          holders left or an ellipsis to the right of the arguments, drag over them and the
          comma just to the left of them, and press Backspace to remove them.

▲   9. Press Enter to finish the formula.

> Pay attention to how Works tells you to enter arguments, and be sure to
> specify the right type of information for the argument. For example, if an
> argument calls for a percentage, be sure to enter a percentage or specify a
> cell that contains one. You also might need to divide a percentage rate by
> 12 (as in 6.5%/12) to yield a monthly rate.

Editing Cells

As you review your spreadsheet contents, you might find that you need to correct a value
or update a label with more current information. To enter completely new contents for a
cell, click the cell, type the new entry, and press Enter.

To change a cell's contents, for example, when you need to change the argument for a
formula, here's the process to use:

To Do: Changing a Cell's Contents

       1. Click the cell to display its contents in the Entry bar, and then click to place the
          insertion point in the Entry bar. Alternatively, double-click the cell or click it and
          press F2 to display the cell contents and the insertion point right in the cell (see
          Figure 5.8).

FIGURE 5.8

*You can edit a cell's
content in the Entry
bar or right in the cell.*

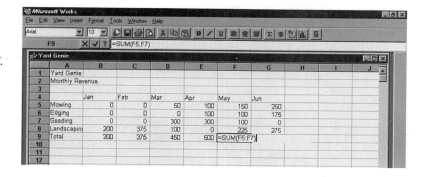

2. Use the Backspace key or Delete key to delete parts of the entry, and then type new contents. You also can drag over part of the entry, and then type new information to replace what you highlighted. If you're changing a label (text entry), you can double-click a word in the entry to select the entire word.

3. To replace a cell or range reference in a formula, drag over the reference you want to replace, and then click or drag in the spreadsheet to specify the replacement reference.

4. Press Enter or click the check mark button on the Entry bar to finish and accept your changes.

> When you're making or editing a cell entry, you can press Esc or click the X button on the Entry bar to cancel it.

5

Copying, Moving, or Clearing a Range

You can select and then copy or move an entire range of information to another location on the spreadsheet. Information you copy or cut stays on the Windows Clipboard until you copy or cut an additional selection. The steps for copying or moving spreadsheet information are virtually identical to copying and moving text in a word processor, as follows:

To Do: Copying or Moving a Range's Contents

1. Select the range to copy or move.

2. Choose Edit | Copy (Ctrl+C) or Edit|Cut (Ctrl+X). Or, click the Copy or Cut button on the Works toolbar.

3. Select the cell in the upper-left corner of the range where you want to insert the copied or cut information.

> You also can right-click the selected range to display a shortcut menu that offers the Copy and Cut commands. Similarly, to paste your selection, right-click the cell you selected in step 3, and then click Paste in the shortcut menu that appears.

4. Choose Edit | Paste (Ctrl+V) or click the Paste button on the toolbar. The copied or cut range appears in the new location in the spreadsheet.

5. (Optional) Repeat Steps 3 and 4 to paste the selection into additional locations.

You also can copy or move information using drag-and-drop. To do so, point to the selection border until the mouse pointer changes to an arrow with the word DRAG attached. To move the selection, drag it—the pointer then reads MOVE—and drop it into place. To copy the selection, press and hold the Ctrl key until you see COPY beside the pointer, and then drag and drop the copy into place.

When you want to remove information from the spreadsheet rather than cut it to place it on the Clipboard, you should *clear* the information. Select the range you want to clear, and then open the Edit menu or right-click the selection. Click Clear in either menu to remove the selection from the spreadsheet.

> To undo a copy or paste operation or a change to a cell, press Ctrl+Z or choose Edit | Undo (Action) immediately. The Undo command undoes the last change you made.

How Moving and Copying Affects Formulas

Before you engage in rampant copying and moving, you need to understand the difference between *relative referencing* and *absolute referencing*.

By default, all cell and range references you enter are relative. If you enter a formula in cell E9, and that formula sums the range E5:E8, what the formula really tells Works to do is to add the contents of the four cells immediately above the cell holding the formula. It tells Works to add the cells positioned in a certain location *relative to* the cell holding the formula. If you then copy the formula from cell E9 to cell E14, the formula automatically changes to sum E10:E13—the four cells immediately above (relative to) the new location.

When you apply absolute referencing in a formula, the formula always refers to the cell or range with the absolute referencing, no matter where you copy the formula. For example, say that you enter a product discount percentage in cell A4 of the spreadsheet. In cell C10, you enter a formula that multiplies the discount percentage by the price of a product in another cell: =A4*C6. If you then copy the formula from C10 to D10 (one cell to the right), the formula changes the cell references in the formula copy to refer to the cell(s) to the right of the cells referenced in the original formula. The copied formula becomes =B4*D6, and because it no longer refers to the correct discount percentage in A4, the calculated result is wrong. So, when you create the original formula in cell C10, you need to use an absolute reference to refer to cell A4, so that no matter where you copy the formula, it always refers to cell A4.

> You need to worry about relative versus absolute references only when you're copying formulas that contain cell and range references. When you move formulas from one cell to another, the cell and range references in the formulas do not change.

Using Absolute Referencing

Works denotes an absolute reference with dollar signs in a formula. The cell reference $A$4 is completely absolute, but you also can create a mixed reference where only the column reference ($A4) or row reference (A$4) is absolute. Similarly, you can make one cell or both cells in a range reference absolute, as in $A$4:$C$8.

There are two ways to make a cell reference in a formula absolute.

The first method is to use the F4 key as you enter the formula. Type the equals sign to start the formula; enter a function and its opening parenthesis if needed, and then click the first cell (or the first cell in the range) you want to reference, such as A4. (You have to click the cell; you can't type its reference.) With the A4 entry still highlighted, press the F4 key to apply absolute referencing; press F4 as many times as needed to make the reference absolute or mixed. Then, finish the formula by typing an operator and specifying another cell or value, or by typing a colon and clicking the second cell in a range reference.

You also can type or edit a cell reference to make it totally absolute or mixed. Just enter one or two dollar signs where needed in a cell reference in a formula.

Using absolute versus relative referencing can take some time to grasp, so look at another example. Say that you're a teacher with 15 students. In the range B1:B15, you enter each student's score on the first test for the semester. Then in cell B16, you enter the formula =AVG(B1:B15) to calculate the average score for all the students. As the year progresses, you'll want to enter scores for subsequent tests in C1:C15, D1:D15, and so on. So, you should stick with relative referencing in cell B16's formula, because you'll want to copy it to average the scores for subsequent tests, too. So, then, when you copy the formula from B16 to C16 after entering the next set of test scores, the cell references update so the formula reads =AVG(C1:C15), correctly averaging the test scores in column C.

Now suppose you want to help improve the average test score by a certain percentage over time, but you're not sure whether to shoot for 5%, 10%, or 15%. You can calculate the average that represents each percentage milestone, using absolute referencing. First, enter 5%, 10%, and 15% in cells B18, B19, and B20. (When you enter those percentages using the percentage sign, Works converts them to the correct decimal value for you, changing 5% to .05, so calculations work correctly.) Then, in cell C18, enter the formula =(B18+1)*$C$16. The formula multiplies the average score from C16 by 105% (B18+1), so the formula result is the score that's 5% higher than the original average in C16. Now put the absolute reference to work. Copy the formula from C18 to C19, then look at the copied formula. It reads =(B19+1)*$C$16, retrieving another percentage from B19, adding 1, and multiplying the result by the same original average score from $C$16. The calculated result is the score that's 10% higher than the original score in C16. You can finish the job by copying the formula once more from C19 to C20, with the result in C20 showing the score that's 20% higher than the original in C16.

Filling a Range

We're running short on time now in this hour, but there's one great data entry trick I'd like to pass along. You can use the Works *Fill* feature to copy an entry or a series from one cell to a group of adjoining cells. To do so, select one or more cells to begin the fill, and then point to the fill handle in the lower-right corner of the selection. The mouse pointer changes to a cross with the word FILL beside it. Drag to the right or down until you highlight all the cells you want to fill, and then release the mouse to complete the fill.

The entries that Works fills depends on what was in the initial cell(s) you selected:

- A cell with a formula   Works copies the formula to the adjoining cells, adjusting all relative cell references.
- One cell holding text or a value   Works repeats the same value in the adjoining cell.
- One cell holding a month name or abbreviation such as Qtr 1   Works recognizes some entries as part of a series and completes the series for you. For example, if a cell holds "January," Works fills the adjoining cells with "February," "March,"

and so on. If you select "Qtr 1," Works fills "Qtr 2," "Qtr 3," and so on into subsequent cells.

- The first few entries in your own series of numbers For example, enter 5 and 10 into two adjoining cells, select them, and drag the fill handle to expand the series with 15, 20, 25, and so on. Figure 5.9 shows how to begin filling this example series.

FIGURE 5.9

Drag the fill handle to create a series of entries based on the selection.

A filled series of months

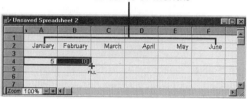

Sharing Spreadsheet Information in Excel

Works provides enough functions and other features to handle the vast majority of calculations you might need, especially if you're using it for home or small business management. Unfortunately, your employer might have chosen to install the even more powerful Microsoft Excel spreadsheet program on your office computer, or you might need to share spreadsheet data with clients who use Excel. Fortunately, you can open a Works spreadsheet in Excel, and vice versa.

Follow these steps to open an Excel file in Works:

To Do: Opening an Excel File

1. If the file is on a floppy disk, insert it into the file, and then choose File | Open (Ctrl+O). The Open dialog box appears.
2. Use the Look In list to navigate to the disk and folder holding the file to open.
3. Open the Files of Type drop-down list, and then click Excel SS (*.xl*). The file you want to open appears in the list.
4. Click the file, and then click Open. The Import Excel Spreadsheet dialog box opens.
5. Because each Excel file contains several different spreadsheets (worksheets), click the name of the sheet you want to open in the Select a Worksheet list.
6. Click OK to finish opening the Excel information.

▲ To Do ▼

5

To enable an Excel user to open your Works file, you can save the Works file as an Excel file. To do so, choose File | Save As with the spreadsheet onscreen in Works. Open the Save As Type drop-down list, and then choose the Excel SS choice. Change any other information you want, such as entering a new File Name; then click Save to save the Excel version of the file. You or another user can then open the file in Excel, using the same process as for any other Excel file.

Summary

Now you know how to build your own Works spreadsheet from the ground up. You can enter and edit cell contents and create formulas—basic ones or fancier ones using functions. You also learned how to select cells, move and copy them, or clear their contents. Finally, I showed you two handy tricks: filling information and sharing cell entries with Excel. Press on to the next hour to learn how to improve the appearance of your spreadsheet information.

Q&A

Q. How do I enter something in a cell?

A. Use the arrow keys to select the cell that you want to hold your entry, type the entry, and press Enter. You can use a variety of other techniques to move around and finish a cell entry; you can survive with the arrow keys and Enter key alone.

Q. How do I create a formula?

A. Start by typing an equals sign, enter values (or references for cells holding values) and mathematical operators to build the formula, and then press Enter. The formula result appears in the cell. You also can click the Easy Calc button on the toolbar and use the Easy Calc dialog box to build a formula using a function.

Q. How do I edit a cell?

A. Click the cell, type a completely new entry, and then press Enter. Or, to change only part of the entry, double-click the cell and make your changes to the existing data. You can edit cell entries just like you edit data in a word processing program; use the Delete and Backspace keys to remove characters.

Hour 6

Formatting Your Spreadsheet

Although the spreadsheet aligns information in an orderly grid, you still
need to ensure that it presents information in the clearest possible way.
Making simple formatting changes can help your reader more easily pick
out the most important entries in a spreadsheet, or can help correct problems
such as when a narrow column can't display a cell's full entry.

Within this hour, you'll be able to use the following techniques to improve
your spreadsheet's appearance and usefulness:

- Change the look of the characters in a cell.
- Adjust how cell contents align.
- Highlight a range with a border or shading.
- Tell the spreadsheet what to calculate.
- Work with row height and column width.
- Add and delete rows and columns.
- Choose another number format.

- Access and use page formatting settings.
- Create a chart.

Formatting Cell Contents

If you start with a blank spreadsheet, the cell entries in your spreadsheet display in plain-vanilla 10 pt. Arial font. Labels (text) align to the left side of the cell, and numbers, dates, and formulas align to the right. In short, there's little to excite your viewer or identify the most important information in your spreadsheet, such as a cell that holds a total. Even if you used a TaskWizard to create a spreadsheet, you might not like the formatting results.

This section covers the key formatting techniques you can use to format the contents within cells (not the cell borders).

> As when you're formatting a document, use restraint in formatting your spreadsheet. Formatting every cell or row with a different look creates a confusing, ransom-note effect. Focus on jazzing up elements like the spreadsheet title, column labels (in the top row of a block of information), row labels (which you enter to identify each row), and cells holding important calculations.

Changing Attributes, Fonts, and Font Sizes

You can change the font and size for the information in any cell, as well as apply the boldface, italic, underline, and strikethrough attributes (or styles). Follow these steps to format spreadsheet cells:

To Do: Choosing Another Look for Cell Contents

1. Select the cell(s) to format.
2. Choose Format | Font and Style. The Format Cells dialog box appears, with its Font tab selected.
3. Choose another Font from the Font list, and another font size from the Size list.
4. If needed, choose another color for the text in the selected cell(s) from the Color drop-down list.

The color red has special meaning when it comes to spreadsheets, especially those that deal with financial calculations. In such spreadsheets, you should apply red only to negative numbers (where you're "in the red" financially) or other values that don't measure up to expectations. In fact, some number formats automatically apply the color red to negative numbers. (See this hour's later section, "Working with Number Formats," to learn how to apply number formats to spreadsheet values.)

5. In the Style area, check any attribute you want to apply. Figure 6.1 shows formatting selections in the Font tab of the Format Cells dialog box.

FIGURE 6.1

Use the Font tab of the Format Cells dialog box to change the appearance of entries within cells.

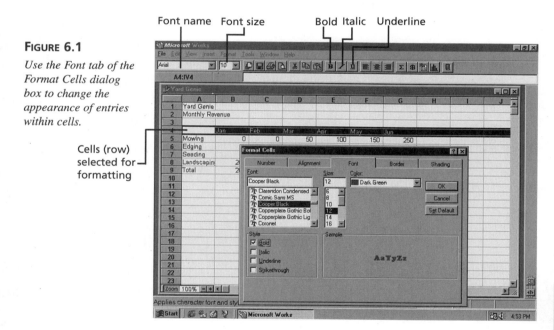

6. Click OK to apply your changes and close the Format Cells dialog box. If you selected a larger or smaller font size, the row height adjusts automatically to reflect the new font size.

7. Click outside your selection to see the result of your formatting changes.

Figure 6.1 also identifies several toolbar buttons you can use to apply one formatting change at a time to a selection. Use the Font Name and Font Size drop-down lists to apply a different font or make the contents of the selected cells larger or smaller. Click the Bold, Italic, or Underline buttons to add or remove boldface, italic, or underlining.

If you click Set Default right before you close the Format Cells dialog box, your formatting settings become the default for new spreadsheets you create during future work sessions with the Works spreadsheet tool.

Aligning Cell Contents

The default alignments (left for text entries and right for numbers, formulas, and dates) work fine for quick and dirty spreadsheets. On the other hand, if you're creating a spreadsheet for an important meeting or to document something like team scores, you may want to spend some time considering how items line up. For example, if column titles you enter line up to the left but the values below line up to the right, centering or right-aligning the titles makes your spreadsheet look more consistent.

In the Works spreadsheet, you can control not only how entries align with regard to the left and right sides of the cells (called the horizontal alignment), but also how they align with regard to the top and bottom cell boundaries (the vertical alignment).

Follow these steps to change how entries align within cells:

To Do: Changing Cell Alignment

1. Select the cell(s) with the entries to align.
2. Choose Format | Alignment. The Format Cells dialog box appears, with its Alignment tab selected (see Figure 6.2).
3. In the Horizontal area, select a horizontal alignment.

Use the General choice in the Horizontal area if your selection includes both labels and values or formulas and you want to return all the cells to the default alignment(s). If you apply the Fill choice in the Horizontal area to a cell, Works repeats the cell entry to fill the entire width of the cell. For example, if the cell contained 0, Works would repeat it to display 00000000. To make an entry from one cell actually span over several cells, select the cell with the entry and one or more cells to the right of it. Display the Alignment tab of the Format Cells dialog box; then choose the Center Across Selection choice in the Horizontal area.

4. In the Vertical area, select a vertical alignment choice.

FIGURE 6.2

All the Works spreadsheet alignment options appear on the Alignment tab in the Format Cells dialog box.

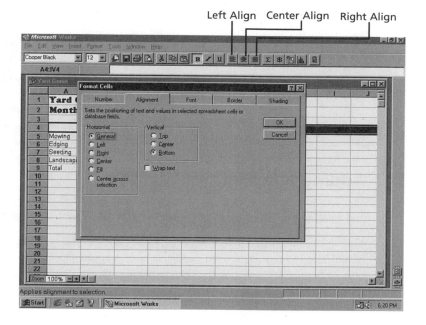

5. If entries in the selected cell(s) are too long but you don't want to increase the column widths, you can check the Wrap Text check box. Wrap Text formats the text in multiple lines within the cell.

6. Click OK to apply your alignment selections.

7. Click outside the selection to see the result of your changes.

You can click the Left Align, Right Align, or Center Align button on the toolbar to make a quick horizontal alignment change for selected cell(s).

> When it comes to a large block of cells that contain dollars and cents values or numbers using decimals, centered alignment makes the numbers more difficult to read. Your eye has to work harder to pick out the decimal point in each cell when it's centered. So, use centered or left alignment sparingly when it comes to dollar values and numbers with decimal places.

6

Formatting Cells and Ranges

The formatting changes you've seen so far apply to what's within your spreadsheet cells. Other formatting changes apply to the actual cells: the borders, shading, and cell size.

After you format your cell contents, you can apply complementary formatting to the cells, too. This section covers those formatting options.

> For examples of good spreadsheet design, use different spreadsheet TaskWizards to create a number of example spreadsheets. Look at where the TaskWizard designers applied particular fonts or effects such as borders and shading, and follow that lead in formatting your own spreadsheets.

Adding a Border or Shading

You can add a border to outline a range or background shading to highlight it. Borders and shading provide the most dramatic way to call attention to spreadsheet information.

You can add a border or shading to a single cell, but you're more likely to work with a range. Keep in mind that your border selection applies to the entire range. If you add an outline border, it surrounds the selected range; Works doesn't outline each cell within the range.

Follow these steps to apply a border and shading to a range:

To Do: Bordering or Shading a Range

1. Select the range to which you want to apply a border or shading.
2. Choose Format | Border. The Format Cells dialog box appears with the Border tab selected.
3. Under Border, click Outline to place a border around the entire range, or one or more of the other four choices (Top, Bottom, Left, or Right). Click any Border choice again to remove a previously applied choice.
4. Click the type of line you want to use in the Line Style area.
5. Click the color you want to use for the border in the Color list.
6. Click the Shading tab to display its options.
7. Click the shading style you want to use in the Pattern list (or None to remove a previously applied pattern).
8. Choose pattern colors to use from the Foreground and Background lists.
9. Click OK to close the Format Cells dialog box and apply your Border and Shading choices.
10. Click outside the selection to see the results. Figure 6.3 shows an example range with a border and shading applied.

FIGURE 6.3

Adding a border and shading highlights a range, as in cells B5:G9 here.

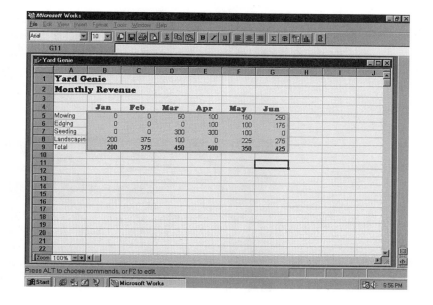

If you want to apply shading only to the selected range, choose Format | Shading to display the Format Cells dialog box with the Shading dialog box selected.

Many printers don't print shading and patterns very well. Shading and patterns can even make cells difficult to read onscreen, particularly if there's not enough contrast between the color of the cell contents and the fill color. You may need to experiment a bit to hit on shading that works for your spreadsheet.

Changing Column Width and Row Height

Earlier in this hour you learned that a row expands or contracts in height to mirror a font size you specify. However, Works can't take care of other column width and row height matters automatically. For example, refer to Figure 6.3 and look at cell A8. That cell appears cut off at the right because its entry is too long for the column and the cell to the right already contains an entry. A8's entry can't spill over to the right.

You can resize any row or column in a spreadsheet as needed to fit the size of the entries or to strategically add extra spacing. To resize a row or column, use one of these techniques:

6

• Point to the left border of the column header or the bottom border of the row header until you see the Adjust pointer (see Figure 6.4). Then, drag the border to the desired width or height, or double-click the border to have Works automatically choose the size that accommodates the widest entry in the column or tallest entry in the row.

FIGURE 6.4

You can drag a border for a column or row header to resize the column or row.

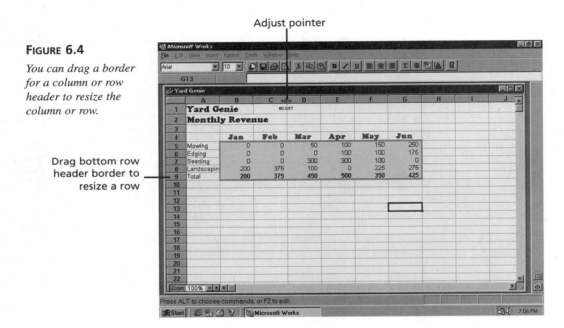

• Click a cell in the row or column to resize. Choose Format | Row Height or Format | Column Width. In the Format Row Height or Format Column Width dialog box that appears, enter a precise measurement in the Row Height (measured in characters) or Column Height (measured in points) text box; then click OK. Alternatively, you can click the Standard button in either dialog box to apply the default height or width, or the Best Fit button to apply the size that accommodates the widest or tallest entry.

Adding and Deleting Columns and Rows

Spreadsheets evolve over time, and Works gives you the flexibility to make needed improvements. For example, you might create a spreadsheet that totals sales for different products or services. If you later add a new product or service in your business, you need to add a row into the spreadsheet to include sales for the new item in the total. Conversely, you can delete a row or column of information that becomes obsolete.

When you add or remove rows and columns, keep formula referencing in mind. Normally, Works adjusts formulas to account for added and deleted cells. For example, if the formula in cell D9 reads =sum(D5:D8) and you add a new row below row 5, the formula moves to cell D10 and adjusts to read =sum(D5:D9). You have to be careful if you use absolute referencing or if you add a row or column at the edge of a range that is referenced in a formula. (See "Using Absolute Referencing," in Hour 5, "Calculating with a Spreadsheet.") The moral: Check your formulas after you add or delete a row or column.

Follow these steps to add or delete a row or column:

To Do: Inserting or Removing Rows or Columns

1. Click any cell in the row or column that you want to delete, or any cell in the location where you want to add a row or column.

2. Right-click the cell, and then choose the applicable command: Insert Row, Delete Row, Insert Column, or Delete Column. (Those four commands also appear on the Insert menu, and you can choose them there.) Works immediately adds or deletes a row or column.

When you delete a row or column, you remove all its contents from the spreadsheet. If you mistakenly delete a row or column, immediately choose Edit I Undo Delete Row or Edit I Undo Delete Column to reinstate it.

Working with Number Formats

Number formats control how numerical entries in a cell display. For example, formulas that perform division often produce results with many decimal places. You can apply a number format to a cell with such a formula to have it display only two or three decimal places. The number format doesn't change the calculated result; it only changes how Works displays that result.

To change the number format used for cells holding numeric entries, follow these steps:

To Do: Choosing a Number Format

1. Select the cell(s) to which you want to apply a new number format.

2. Choose Format I Number. The Format Cells dialog box appears, with the Number tab selected.

3. Click a choice in the Format list. A description for the format and any options for the format appear to the right. (Clicking the General choice returns the selection to the default format.)

6

Works offers 12 number formats, each of which offers different options. To learn how each format works, experiment with applying it to a cell and changing its options.

4. Specify options for the format as needed, until the Sample displayed at the bottom of the dialog box has the desired appearance. Figure 6.5 shows some formatting choices in progress, as well as some formats already applied to cells with numeric entries.

True/False format   Currency button

FIGURE 6.5

Use the Number tab in the Format Cells dialog box to control how the spreadsheet displays values in selected cells.

Fixed format, with four decimal places

Currency format, with two decimal places

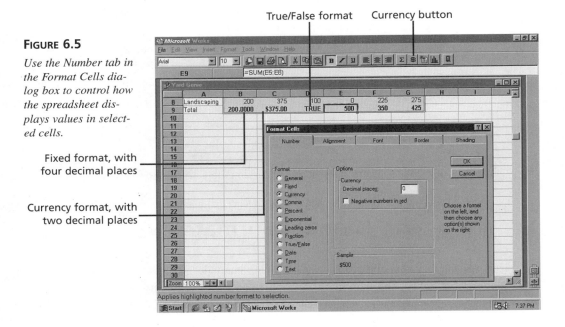

5. Click OK to close the dialog box and apply your choices.

 6. Click outside the selection to see the formatting results.

You also can click the Currency format to apply a dollar sign and two-decimal format to the contents of selected cells.

Using an AutoFormat

An AutoFormat in the Works Spreadsheet tool simultaneously applies a collection of formats to a range: fonts, font sizes, attributes, and color; alignment; borders and shading; and number formats. You can see the value here—apply an AutoFormat once, or spend your time making multiple formatting choices.

Follow these steps to apply an AutoFormat:

To Do: Applying an AutoFormat

1. Select the range to format.

2. Choose Format I AutoFormat. The AutoFormat dialog box appears.

3. Click the format you want in the Select a Format list. The Example area shows you how the formatting looks, as illustrated in Figure 6.6.

FIGURE 6.6

Select an AutoFormat from this dialog box to apply predefined formatting to the selected range.

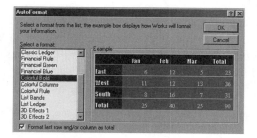

4. If the bottom row or far-right of your selection includes totals or other special entries to highlight, leave the Format Last Row And/Or Column as Total check box checked. Otherwise, clear the check box.

5. Click OK to close the dialog box and apply the AutoFormat.

 6. Click outside the selection to see the AutoFormat formatting.

Working with Page Formatting

The Works Spreadsheet tool provides a few notable page-formatting choices, geared primarily to improve the usability of spreadsheet printouts.

You might want to add a header or footer to print at the top or bottom of the spreadsheet. To do so, choose View I Headers and Footers. The View Headers and Footers dialog box appears. Enter the header text in the Header text box and the footer text in the Footer text box. To prevent the header or footer from appearing on the first page of the printout, click to check No Header on First Page or No Footer on First Page. Click OK to close the dialog box and finish creating the header or footer.

6

You also can change overall page settings in the Page Setup dialog box. Choose File |
Page Setup to display that dialog box. Make your choices on its three tabs; then click OK
to apply them:

- Margins   Specify top, bottom, left, and right margins, as well as margins for the
  header and footer.
- Source, Size & Orientation   Choose whether to print the spreadsheet in Portrait
  (tall) or Landscape (wide) orientation, and whether to use a paper size other than
  the standard 8.5" × 11".
- Other Options   Control whether gridlines between cells or the row and column
  header numbers and letters appear on the printout, as well as whether Works uses 1
  as the page number for the first page of the printout.

Charting a Selection

Although creating a chart might not seem like a formatting chore on its surface, charting
data provides perhaps the most dramatic illustration of what your data means. When you
present numbers graphically, the viewer can judge how the values compare and in particular, whether one of the values has more significance or whether any type of trend
emerges.

You can make a chart with a few simple choices, as these steps illustrate:

To Do: Creating a Chart to Illustrate Your Data

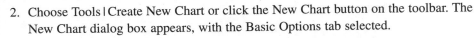

1. Select the range to chart, including cells holding any row or column labels that
   identify the range contents.
2. Choose Tools | Create New Chart or click the New Chart button on the toolbar. The
   New Chart dialog box appears, with the Basic Options tab selected.
3. Click a Chart Type choice in the What Type of Chart Do You Want area of the dialog box.
4. Enter a chart title in the Title text box.
5. To display a border around the chart, click to check the Border check box. To
   include gridlines that better clarify values, click to check the Gridlines check box.
6. Click OK to finish the chart. The chart appears in its own window onscreen, as
   shown in Figure 6.7.

FIGURE 6.7

When you chart your data, it appears in a separate window onscreen.

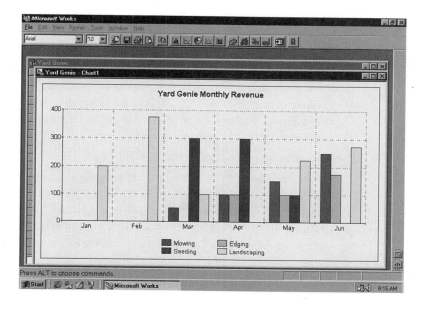

Although the chart appears in its own window, saving the spreadsheet file saves each chart you create based on the data in that spreadsheet file. To reopen a chart, choose View | Chart. Click the chart you want to display in the Select a Chart list of the View | Chart dialog box; then click OK. When the chart window is active, use the File | Print command to print the chart.

Summary

This Hour concludes your experimentation with the Works Spreadsheet tool. The last hour showed you how to create accurate spreadsheet information; this hour showed you how to create attractive spreadsheet information. You now know how to format cell contents, the cells themselves, and the spreadsheet page, as well as how to create a chart of spreadsheet data. When you want to work with lists of information rather than calculations, use the Works Database tool, the subject of Hour 7, "Capturing Lists in a Database."

6

Q&A

Q. **What quick and dirty formatting options do I have in the Spreadsheet tool?**

A. The toolbar offers several tools you can use to select another font and font size: apply bold, italics, or underlining; or choose left, right, or center alignment to the contents of selected cells. Or, if you want to apply a number of formats simultaneously, choose Format | AutoFormat, and choose an attractive AutoFormat for the selected range.

Q. **A number doesn't display the way I'd expect. How do I fix it?**

A. The number format you apply to a cell holding a numeric entry controls how that entry displays, without affecting the actual entry or calculated result. For example, if a cell holds a formula that calculates to a result with four decimal places, you can apply a number format that displays the result with only two decimal places and adds a dollar sign. To access the number format choices, choose Format | Number.

HOUR 7

Capturing Lists in a Database

If you have to capture and work with long lists of information, such as contact information for all the players on a soccer team or a list of product information, you can use the Works Suite Database tool to build and keep the list. The Works Suite Database tool makes it easy to find any item in the list, or sort the list as needed.

Your 60 minute introduction to the Works Suite Database tool shows how to

- Understand key database concepts.
- Create a database and enter list information.
- Find a particular database entry.
- Sort the database.
- Hide and display database information.
- Add and remove database information.

Understanding Database Terms

You use the Works Suite Database tool to keep and organize lists of information. A database *file* stores information in records and fields. For example, if you create an address book database, all the information about each person is a *record*, and each individual piece of information within a record (like the last name) is a *field*.

When you create the database file, you define which fields it holds. Then, you enter each record to build the database list.

Although you might use the Works Suite Database tool less often than you use the other Works Suite tools, don't write it off. Here are just a few situations in which you might want to create a database:

- Keep your address book.
- Keep an address list for greeting cards, and party invitations.
- Keep team, employee, and student contact information.
- Keep a list of emergency contacts.
- Document items you collect, such as audio CDs, movies, or antiques.

Creating a Database with a TaskWizard

You can use a Works TaskWizard to create a new database. The Works Suite Task Launcher includes a number of database TaskWizards. Each database TaskWizard suggests fields to include in the database, helping the database creation process proceed quickly.

Follow these steps to create a new database using a TaskWizard:

To Do: Using a Database TaskWizard

1. Click the Task Launcher button on the Works Suite toolbar to redisplay the Task Launcher.
2. On the TaskWizards tab, click the button for the category you want to open; then double-click the icon for the TaskWizard to use. The Task Launcher identifies database TaskWizards with address-card file icons.

Check the Names and Addresses category on the TaskWizards tab of the Task Launcher dialog box. It lists several of the available database TaskWizards.

▼

3. In the dialog box that appears, click the Yes, Run the TaskWizard button.

4. If you selected one of the TaskWizards that keeps an address book, such as the Sales Contacts database, verify that the correct database type is selected in the next TaskWizard dialog box. Click Next.

5. Review the information about the database fields in the next TaskWizard dialog box, and then click Next.

6. In the next TaskWizard dialog box, click either the Additional Fields, Your Own Fields, or Reports choice; then follow the onscreen directions for making modifications to the database. When you finish, click Create It.

7. Review the summary information in the next TaskWizard dialog box, and then click Create Document to finish. Works Suite displays the new database in its Form view, as shown in Figure 7.1. (See the section "Moving Between Form View and List View" later in this hour to learn more about the database views.)

FIGURE 7.1

This new database was created with the Sales Contacts TaskWizard.

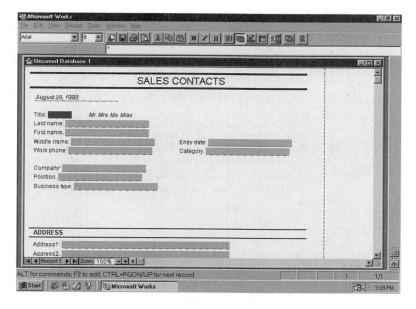

▲

Creating a Blank Database

The database TaskWizards cover many different purposes, but may include more fields than you need. For example, if you just need to create a team list with the player name, position, parent's name, and phone number, you can create a simple database that includes only those fields.

7

When you approach your first database design try to follow these eight steps, each with specific goals and end products. (Try to remember that designing the database is the hardest part; extracting and manipulating the data is far easier.)

1. Determine what the users want out of the database and what data is needed to provide the output.

2. Plan the data distribution.

3. Identify the fields for each table.

4. Assign a unique field for each table.

5. Determine the relationships between tables.

6. Review design and step through procedures with users.

7. Create tables and enter data.

8. Analyze database performance and optimize.

Here's the process for designing your own database:

To Do: Building a Unique Database

1. Click the Task Launcher button to redisplay the Task Launcher if needed.

2. Click the Works Tools tab.

3. Click the Database button. The Create Database dialog box appears.

> If the First-Time Help window appears after Step 3, click OK to bypass it. In fact, any time you see a First-Time Help window, you can click one of its choices to get Help about the operation you're attempting, or click OK to bypass the dialog box.

4. Type a field name in the Field Name text box. Figure 7.2 shows an example.

5. If needed, click the field type for the new field under Format. For entries that contain only letters (like names), use the General format. If an entry contains both numbers and special characters, such as a phone number or zip code, choose the Text format.

6. Click Add to add the new field.

7. Repeat Steps 4 through 6 to add as many fields as you need in your database.

8. Click Done to close the Create Database dialog box. Works Suite displays the new database in List view, as shown in Figure 7.3. (See the section "Moving Between Form View and List View" later in this hour to learn more about the database views.)

▼ FIGURE 7.2

Enter a unique name for each database field; then specify the field Format.

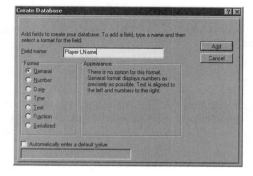

FIGURE 7.3

Create a database from scratch when you need unique fields or only a limited number of fields.

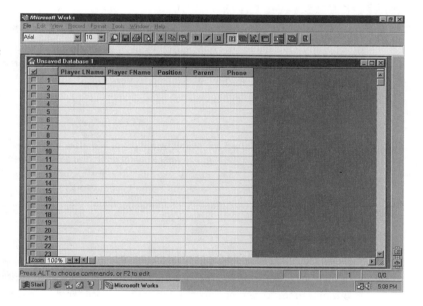

Moving Between Form View and List View

The Works Suite Database tool can display your database in either the Form view or the List view. The Form view resembles a paper form; you fill in each field in the underlined area beside the field name. The List view looks more like a spreadsheet grid; it holds each record in a row and the different fields in columns, with each field name at the top of the column. You can work in whichever view you prefer. You can easily switch to the view you need.

To change between views, you use a single command. Choose View | Form (F9) to change from the List view to the Form view. Choose View | List (Shift+F9) to change from the Form view to the List view.

7

The Form view displays the data form, and the List view displays the data list.

You print a database file by choosing the File | Print command. Works prints the current view—the data form or the data list—so, choose the view you want before you print.

Entering Records

Like any other file, your database file contains nothing until you enter its contents. Although making database entries might not be a fun or creative activity, it's worth the effort because of the work you'll save in the long run. You can enter database records in either Form view or List view, according to your preference. This section describes how to use either view to enter records.

Don't forget to save your database file after you enter a few records, periodically while you're entering records, and before you close the database file. (See "Saving a Works File" in Hour 1, "Introducing Works 4.5a," to review how to save and name files in Works.)

In Form View

The Form view displays the fields in a spacious form with one record (all the fields for one entry) in a single page. You use the Form view when you want to enter or view one record at a time. Note that Form view is not available in all the object areas.

The field that's ready to accept an entry (the selected field) appears in a darker gray than the other fields. For a new database, the selected field is the first field of the first record.

Use these steps to enter records and edit fields in the Form view:

To Do: Entering Records and Editing Fields in Form View

1. Type the information for the first field; then press Tab to select the next field.
2. Continue typing entries and pressing Tab to move to the next field. Figure 7.4 shows fields being entered in Form view.

▲ To Do

▼ **FIGURE 7.4**

Form view shows one record per page; type an entry in each field, and press Tab to move to the next field (or next record if you've finished the current one).

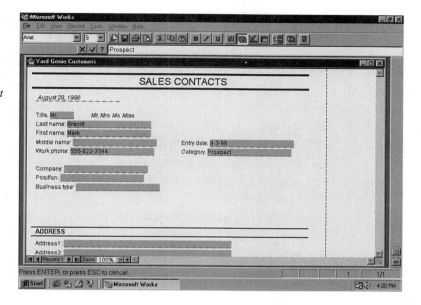

3. Press Tab after you fill in the last field to complete the current record and start a new one.

4. After you make entries in a few fields in a record, you can go back to a previous field. To do so, click the field you want, or press the left arrow key or Shift+Tab. You can then simply type a new entry for the field.

▲   5. Repeat steps 1-4 to enter additional records.

Depending on how many fields your database contains, you may not be able to see all of a record onscreen in Form view, or all the fields in the database in List view. Rather than pressing Tab multiple times to select the field you want in the current record, you can use Go To. Choose Edit I Go To. Click the field to go to in the Select a Field list; then click OK. You can then view or edit the entry in the selected field.

In List View

Each row in List view contains a single record. The compact list format enables you to display multiple records on a single page. The field that's ready to accept an entry (the selected field) has a heavy cell selector border around it, just as in a Works Suite spreadsheet.

7

Entering a record in the List view resembles entering a record in the Form view or even a Works Suite spreadsheet, as you'll see from the following steps:

To Do: Entering Records and Editing Fields in List View

1. Type the information for the first field; then press Tab to select the next field.

2. Continue typing entries and pressing Tab to move to the next field.

3. Press Tab after you fill in the last field to complete the current record, moving the cell selector to the first field in the next record.

4. You can go back to a previous field in any record. To do so, click the field you want, or press the left arrow key or Shift+Tab. You can then simply type a new entry for the field.

5. Repeat steps 1-4 to enter additional records.

Moving Between Records

To select a record to edit in List view, just scroll to display the record you want and click it. In the Form view, you have to use buttons to the left of the horizontal scrollbar to move between records and display a record to view or edit. Figure 7.5 illustrates the buttons to use, which include the following:

- Next Record button   Click to display the next record.
- Last Record button   Click to move to the end of the database, displaying a new, blank record.
- Previous Record button   Click to display the previous record.
- First Record button   Click to display the very first record in the database.

FIGURE 7.5

Click a button to display another record in the Form view.

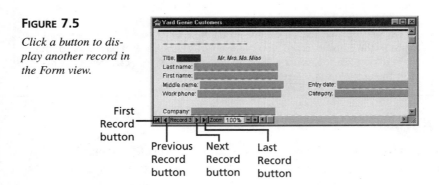

Finding a Record

When a database contains dozens or hundreds of records, it becomes too cumbersome to review records one by one until you find a record you want. You can instead perform a Find to go directly to the record you need. You enter the information to match (from any field in the database), and then tell Works Suite to display the next matching record or all matching records.

Follow these steps to perform a Find in either the List view or the Form view:

To Do: Displaying a Particular Record

1. The Find operation starts from the currently displayed record. To be sure that Works Suite examines all the records (if you find the next record instead of all matching records), press Ctrl+Home to display the first record before you perform the Find.
2. Choose Edit | Find (Ctrl+F).
3. Type a field entry from the record(s) you want to find in the Find What text box (see Figure 7.6).

FIGURE 7.6

Enter the field entry to match in this text box.

4. If you want to find all the matching records rather than only the next match, click All Records.
5. Click OK. Works Suite finds the matching record(s).
6. Review the matching record(s) in the view you want. (Use the navigation buttons to the left of the horizontal scrollbar in Form view.)
7. If you found all matching records, the database shows only the matching records. To redisplay all the records, choose Record | Show | All Records. (You also can manually choose to display only certain records. See "Limiting the List Display" later in this hour to learn how.)

7

Sorting Records

The database lists your records in the order in which you originally entered them. This means the records probably don't appear alphabetically. However, you can sort the data according to the entries in one or more fields. For example, if you want to reorder the records in a team database alphabetically according to the players' last names, you can sort by the Player LName field. If you sort by more than one field, such as the Player LName field and then the Player FName field, which holds the players' first names, the Database tool first sorts all records by Player LName. Then, if any records have the same entry in the Player LName field, the Database tool sorts those records again according to the first name.

Sort your database before you print if you want the records to be sorted in the printout.

Use these steps to sort your database:

To Do: Changing the Order of Database Records

1. Display the database you want to sort in either Form view or List view.
2. Choose Record | Sort Records. The Sort Records dialog box appears.
3. Choose the field you want to sort by first from the Sort By drop-down list.
4. Click Ascending or Descending to choose the sort order. The ascending sort order sorts records in A-Z or 1,2,3 order. The descending sort order sorts records in Z-A or 3,2,1 order.
5. Use the two Then By drop-down lists and accompanying Ascending and Descending buttons to specify a second (and third) sort field and sort order, if needed (see Figure 7.7).

FIGURE 7.7

Specify the sort settings in the Sort Records dialog box.

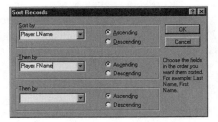

▼ 6. Click OK to finish the sort, and view and work with the sorted records. Figure 7.8 compares a database before and after sorting.

FIGURE 7.8

Here, you can compare records in List view before (above) and after a sort.

		Player LName	Player FName	Position	Parent Name	Phone
	1	Parks	Steve	Pitcher	John	555-1717
	2	Cambridge	Mark	Catcher	Anna	555-1234
	3	Stevens	Frank	1st base	Chris	555-0011
	4	Alley	Tom	2nd base	Steve	555-9343
	5	Presley	Hank	Shortstop	Scott	555-3443
	6	Fisher	Alex	3rd base	Frank	555-2222
	7	Castle	Curt	Left field	Elaine	555-6767
	8	Burden	Phil	Center field	Alan	555-9291
	9	Rogers	Cam	Right field	Haley	555-5858
	10	Terence	Hal	Pitcher	Bill	555-7777
	11	Pulaski	Ed	Catcher	Joe	555-8221
	12	Brown	Eli	All	Joel	555-0112
	13	Cambridge	Bill	All	Anna	555-1234

		Player LName	Player FName	Position	Parent Name	Phone
	1	Alley	Tom	2nd base	Steve	555-9343
	2	Brown	Eli	All	Joel	555-0112
	3	Burden	Phil	Center field	Alan	555-9291
	4	Cambridge	Bill	All	Anna	555-1234
	5	Cambridge	Mark	Catcher	Anna	555-1234
	6	Castle	Curt	Left field	Elaine	555-6767
	7	Fisher	Alex	3rd base	Frank	555-2222
	8	Parks	Steve	Pitcher	John	555-1717
	9	Presley	Hank	Shortstop	Scott	555-3443
	10	Pulaski	Ed	Catcher	Joe	555-8221
	11	Rogers	Cam	Right field	Haley	555-5858
	12	Stevens	Frank	1st base	Chris	555-0011
	13	Terence	Hal	Pitcher	Bill	555-7777

▲

To undo a sort, choose Edit I Undo Sort before you save the file or perform another action. Otherwise, you won't be able to undo the sort. If you want to be able to return database records to their original order after any sort, create a Record Number or ID field when you create the database; then enter the number for each record as you create it.

7

Limiting the List Display

When you perform a Find and find all matching records, all the found records have to have a common entry in one of the fields. If you want to display a list of records that don't necessarily match field for field, you need to tell the Works Suite Database tool which records to display and which not to. For example, if you have a database listing ball team members and you want to narrow your search scope, you might mark the records for the team captains, to make phone calls to only those players.

If you want to display only certain records in your database list, first you mark records in the database. Then you specify whether to show only the marked records or only the unmarked records in the database.

> Showing marked or unmarked records is different from hiding a record. Hiding a record means that it doesn't display at all (when you show marked, unmarked, or all records). To hide a record, display it in Form view or click a cell in it in List view. Choose Record | Hide Record. To redisplay the hidden records in the database, choose Record | Show | Hidden Records.

Marking and Unmarking Records

When you mark a record, you can subsequently choose whether or not to display it onscreen. You can mark or unmark a record in either the List view or the Form view.

Marking and unmarking records works easiest in the List view. Click to place a check in the check box to the left of the record number for each record to mark. Click to clear the check in the check box to the left of the record number for each record to unmark. Figure 7.9 illustrates marked and unmarked records.

FIGURE 7.9

The marked records have a check mark in the box beside the record (row) number.

Marked record —

		Player LName	Player FName	Position	Parent Name	Phone
☑	1	Parks	Steve	Pitcher	John	555-1717
☐	2	Cambridge	Mark	Catcher	Anna	555-1234
☐	3	Stevens	Frank	1st base	Chris	555-0011
☐	4	Alley	Tom	2nd base	Steve	555-9343
☐	5	Presley	Hank	Shortstop	Scott	555-3443
☑	6	Fisher	Alex	3rd base	Frank	555-2222
☐	7	Castle	Curt	Left field	Elaine	555-6767
☐	8	Burden	Phil	Center field	Alan	555-9291
☐	9	Rogers	Cam	Right field	Haley	555-5858
☐	10	Terence	Hal	Pitcher	Bill	555-7777
☐	11	Pulaski	Ed	Catcher	Joe	555-8221
☑	12	Brown	Eli	All	Joel	555-0112
☐	13	Cambridge	Bill	All	Anna	555-1234
☐	14					
☐	15					
☐	16					
☐	17					
☐	18					
☐	19					
☐	20					
☐	21					

Marking records in the Form view requires more time and effort, as these steps show:

To Do: Marking and Unmarking Records in Form View

1. Display a record to mark.
2. Choose Record | Mark Record.
3. Repeat steps 1 and 2 to mark additional records.
4. Display a record to unmark.
5. Choose Record | Mark Record to clear the check beside that command.

> The only way to tell if a record is marked in Form view is to open the Record menu and see whether Mark Record is checked.

6. Repeat steps 4 and 5 to unmark additional records.

> You can mark or unmark all the records in the database by clicking the small check mark button in the upper-left corner of the database window in List view. In Form view, choose Record | Mark All Records or Record | Unmark All Records to mark or unmark all the records.

Showing Only Marked or Unmarked Records

After you mark the records you want, you can control which records appear in either the Form view or the List view. Use one of these techniques to change the list display:

- Choose Record | Show | Marked Records to show only the marked records.
- Choose Record | Show | Unmarked Records to show only the unmarked records.

Redisplaying All Records

When you want to see all the records in your database rather than just marked or unmarked records, you need to redisplay all the records in the database. Choose Record | Show | All Records to return the list display to normal.

Inserting and Deleting Records

7

One of the drawbacks of using a paper address book is that it's difficult to update. You have to scribble out, erase, or paste paper over old entries that no longer apply. And, you might run out of space for more entries on the page for a particular letter. A Works Suite database eliminates both of those problems. You can add as many new records as needed, or delete any record that no longer applies.

To add a new record at the end of the database in the Form view, press Ctrl+End, type the new record information (press Tab between fields), and press Tab to finish the record. Or, you can click the first blank row in the List view and enter new record information.

You also can add a new field into all the records. You might want to do this if you forgot to include a piece of information that you realize you now need. For example, you might want to include a follow-up field in a customer database where you can enter what step you next need to take for that customer's account.

It's easiest to add a new field in the List view. Right-click the field name beside which you want to add a new field, point to Insert Field, and click Before or After. In the Insert Field dialog box that appears, enter the name in the Field Name text box; click to choose a field Format; click Add, and then click Done. You can then make an entry in the new field for each record in the database.

You can delete old records in either the Form view or the List view. Always save your database before deleting any records, because Works Suite doesn't warn you to confirm a record deletion. If you mistakenly delete a record, immediately choose Edit | Undo Delete Record to reinstate it. Or, if you later realize you've deleted records and can't undo the deletion, close the database without saving changes, and then reopen it to revert to the saved file version that still contains those records.

To delete a record, select the record you want to delete in either Form view or List view. Choose Record | Delete Record. Works Suite immediately removes the record from the database.

> You can choose multiple contiguous records in List view, and then choose the Record | Delete Record command to delete all of them. To select multiple records, click the row (record) number for the first record you want to delete. Press and hold the Shift key, and then click the row number for the last record you want to delete.

Summary

You've used the last hour to build your skills with the Works Suite Database tool. You learned how to create a database using a TaskWizard or from scratch and how to build the database by entering records in the database fields. You also learned how to find records, sort the database contents, or display only records that you select. To keep your database current, you also examined how to add and delete database records. The next hour shows you how to put your database information to good use in a mail merge with the Works Suite Word Processor tool.

Q&A

Q. I need a simple database. How do I create it?

A. That depends. Works Suite offers several database TaskWizards on the TaskWizards tab of the Works Suite Task Launcher. You can double-click one of those if it will meet your needs, to have the TaskWizard build your new database. If your database needs only a few fields, click the Database button on the Works Suite Tools tab of the Task Launcher. In the Create Database dialog box, enter a Field Name for each field; click a field Format, and click Add. Click Done after you create all the fields.

Q. How do I switch between views?

A. To change between views, you use a single command. Choose View | Form to change from the List view (which shows multiple records, with each record in its own row) to the Form view (which shows one record at a time). Choose View | List to change from the Form view to the List view.

Q. How do I enter or edit a record?

A. Type an entry in each field, and press Tab to move to the next field. When you make your entry in the last field of a record and then press Tab, you move to the first field of the next blank record. To edit an existing field, click to select the field, type your new entry, and then press Enter or Tab.

7

Hour 8

Merging Letters, Envelopes, and Labels

When you receive a letter addressed "Dear Occupant," you probably toss it right into the trash. When a letter comes addressed to you by name, though, you're likely to open it up and give it a look. Personalization increases the attention correspondence receives. By using the Works Suite Word Processor and Database tools together, you can create a personalized letter—even when you need to send a copy of the letter to 20 different people.

This hour shows you how to create customized copies of a document. You learn to

- Identify merging opportunities.
- Merge and print a document.
- Create merged envelopes and labels if you need to mail your merged letter.

When to Use Merging

To perform a merge, you first create a database using the Works Suite Database tool. Next, you create document text in the Works Suite Word Processor tool. Then, you specify where in the document the Word Processor should insert each database field. When you subsequently complete the merge, Works Suite creates one copy of the document for every record in the database, inserting the fields from that record where specified in the document.

You've most often seen merging used to create the form letter junk mail that hits your mailbox every day. Although the letters contain your name and address, inserted from some massive database, the text of the letters also appeared in copies sent to hundreds or thousands of other recipients.

Although the Works Suite Word Processor actually calls its merging command Form Letters, you can use merging for purposes other than form letters, such as the following:

- Addressing customer invoices, which you then edit to include the correct billing amounts before printing and mailing.
- Creating place cards (or personalized paper place mats) to organize seating at a party.
- Merging product information into a flyer, sales sheet, or brochure that includes attractive graphics and formatting.
- Generating nametags for a special event.
- Creating any other type of document where you want to combine database information with a document page layout, even if you only merge one record from the database.

Merging and Printing a Document

After you lay the groundwork, the Works Suite Word Processor leads you through the merge process. Follow these steps to perform a merge:

To Do: Performing a Merge in Works Suite

1. Use the Works Suite Database tool to create and save the database that holds the information to merge. It's easiest to save the database to the default \Program Files\MSWorks\Documents folder on your hard disk. You also can mark records and hide records if you only want to merge specific records in the list. Leave the database file open in Works Suite. Or, open an existing database to use it for the merge.

▼   2. Use the Works Suite Word Processor tool to create and save the document into which you want to merge the database information. Leave the document open in the Works Suite Word Processor tool.

> You can use a TaskWizard to create the document to merge, insert ClipArt and WordArt, and apply any fancy formatting you prefer.

3. Click to position the insertion point in the document where you want the first field of merged information to appear.

4. Choose Tools | Form Letters. The Form Letters dialog box appears.

5. If needed, review the information on the Instructions tab; then click the Database tab.

6. Click the database that holds the information to merge in the Choose a Database list (see Figure 8.1). (If the database you need doesn't appear in the list, you can click the Open a Database Not Listed Here button to find it.) Click the Recipients tab.

FIGURE 8.1

Click the database that holds the merge information on the Database tab.

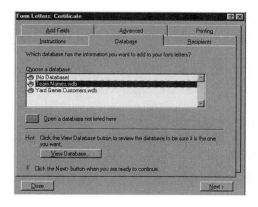

7. If you want to merge all the records, leave All Records in the Database selected. If you marked or hid records in the database, you can instead click Current Records Visible in the Database or Currently Marked Records in the Database. Click the Add Fields tab.

8. Click the field you want to insert in the Add a Field list; then click Insert Field. A field placeholder appears at the insertion point in the document (see Figure 8.2).
▼

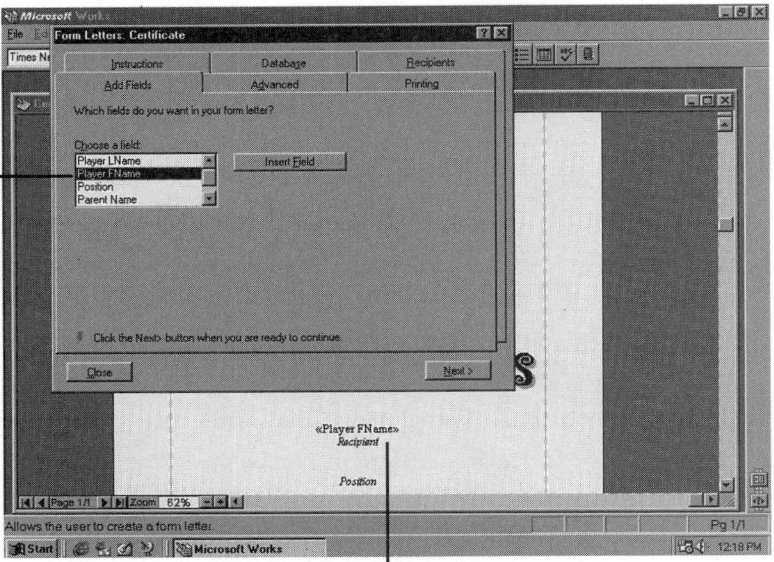

FIGURE 8.2

Use the Add Fields tab to specify a field to insert in the document.

Selected field

Field placeholder

9. Click the Close button to close the Form Letters dialog box.

10. Click in the document to position the insertion point where you want to insert the next field placeholder. If needed, enter any spaces or leading text before the field, or press Enter (if you're addressing a letter), to place the insertion point on the next line, so you can insert the field there.

11. Choose Tools | Form Letters and make sure the Add Fields tab is selected.

> You can close and redisplay the Form Letters dialog box as many times as needed before finishing the merge.

12. Repeat Steps 8-11 to insert additional field placeholders in the document. After you insert the last field needed, leave the Form Letters dialog box open.

13. (Optional) If you think you want to make further changes to the content or formatting of the document, click the Advanced tab; then click its Edit button. Make the needed changes in the document, and click the Go Back button.

14. Click the Printing tab; then click its Print button to merge and print the document copy or copies.

▼ 15. If Works Suite displays a message asking you to verify that you want to print all the records, click OK to confirm that you want to do so.

16. After Works Suite finishes sending the documents to the printer, click Close to
▲ close the Form Letters dialog box.

Figure 8.3 shows how a merge document looks onscreen in Works Suite, with its field placeholders in place.

FIGURE 8.3

This example shows merge field place-holders in a certificate document.

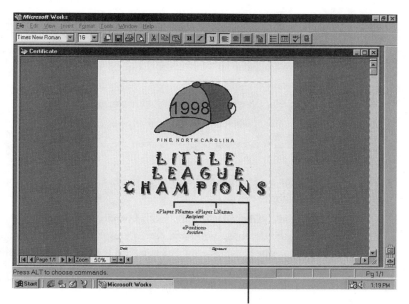

Field placeholders

Be sure to save the document before closing it and closing Works Suite, to ensure the field placeholders stay in place. You can reopen the document at any time and choose Tools | Form Letters to merge and print the letter again. You don't need to reselect the database; just click the Printing tab and click the Print button.

You can select any field placeholder to delete it. Or you can apply another font, font size, or other formatting to determine how the merged information looks when printed.

Merging Envelopes for Your Mailing

Works Suite also automates the process for creating personalized envelopes that you can use to mail your personalized form letters or other documents. Here's the process to follow to create envelopes:

To Do: Creating Personalized Envelopes

1. Use the Works Suite Database tool to create and save the database that holds the information to merge. It's easiest to save the database to the default \Program Files\MSWorks\Documents folder on your hard disk. You also can mark records and hide records if you want to merge only specific records in the list. Leave the database file open in Works Suite. Or, open an existing database to use it for the merge.

2. Open a blank Word Processor document.

3. Choose Tools I Envelopes. The Envelopes dialog box appears.

4. If needed, review the information on the Instructions tab; then click the Envelope tab.

5. Click the type of envelope to print in the Choose an Envelope Size list; then click the Database tab.

6. Click the database that holds the information to merge in the Choose a Database list. (If the database you need doesn't appear in the list, you can click the Open a Database not Listed Here button to find it.) Click the Recipients tab.

> If you left a merged letter open onscreen before displaying the Envelopes dialog box, the Envelopes dialog box automatically assumes you want to use the same database for the envelope merge, and selects that database for you. Works Suite also inserts the merge envelope as a separate page within the merged letter document, so you can save them both together. If you want to save the envelope in a separate document, be sure to create a blank document in Step 2.

7. If you want to merge all the records, leave All Records in the Database selected. If you marked or hid records in the database, you can instead click Current Records Visible in the Database or Currently Marked Records in the Database. Click the Return Address tab.

8. Type your return address in the Return Address text box. Click the Main Address tab. (This is where you insert the fields to merge the recipient address on each envelope.)

8

9. Click the first merge field to insert in the Choose a Field list; then click Add Field. The field appears in the Main Address text box.

10. Insert a space or type characters as needed to provide spacing or punctuation before you insert the next field. Or, click the New Line button to move the insertion point to the next line in the Main Address text box, so the next field appears there.

11. Repeat Steps 9 and 10 to add other fields. Figure 8.4 shows address fields entered into the Main Address text box.

FIGURE 8.4

For envelope printing, specify the merge fields on the Main Address tab of the Envelopes dialog box.

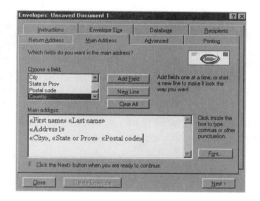

12. (Optional) If you think you want to make changes to the content or formatting of the envelope, click the Advanced tab; then click its Edit button. Make the needed changes in the envelope document, which Works Suite created automatically for you, and then click the Go Back button.

13. Click the Printing tab; then click its Print button to merge and print the document copy or copies.

14. If Works Suite displays a message asking you to verify that you want to print all the records, click OK to confirm that you want to do so.

15. After Works Suite finishes sending the envelopes to the printer, click Close to close the Form Letters dialog box.

16. Save and close the envelope document.

Using Merge to Create Mailing Labels

The process for merging labels is virtually identical to merging and printing letters (or documents) and envelopes, so this brief section highlights the key differences for labels.

1. After you create and save (or open) the database for the merge and a blank Word Processor file, choose Tools | Labels.

2. In the Labels dialog box that appears, click the Labels button. (You use the Multiple Copies of One Label button only if you want to create duplicates of the same label, not unique, merged labels.) Another Labels dialog box appears.

3. Click the Label Size tab and click the label size you want to use in the Choose a Label Size List. Make your choices on the Database and Recipients tabs as described for merging a document or envelope.

> When working with labels, make sure you write down the label manufacturer, size, and label number off your supply box. These pieces of information will prove to be invaluable when you are asked to define the label size.
>
> If you have chosen an Avery or Avery equivalent label, Works Suite has incorporated these predefined label sizes so you do not have to go through the painful task of custom designing the label width and length.
>
> With the Avery number at hand you can quickly choose the predefined label and be on your way to happy merging.

4. Click the Label Layout tab. Click the first merge field you want to insert in the Choose a Field list; then click Add Field. Add all the fields, punctuation, and new lines you need.

5. Use the Advanced tab to edit the label design, as needed; then click Print on the Printing tab to print the labels.

6. Click Close to close the Labels dialog box, and save and close the label document.

Summary

This last hour with Works Suite demonstrated how to merge information you've already captured in a Works Suite database into a Word document to create personalized letters, labels, envelopes, and other documents. The next hour shows you how you can use the Works Calendar to organize your appointments.

Q&A

Q. What do I use to merge?

A. Every merge involves a Works Suite database and a Works Suite document. If you're merging a letter or other document, you can create and design the document and then perform the merge. If you're merging envelopes or labels, Works Suite inserts them into the open document, so open a blank document first if you want to save the envelope or label merge in its own file.

Q. How do I start the merge?

A. Open or create and save the database. Then open or create the document file you want to merge. Choose Tools | Form Letters to begin the process for merging a letter or other document. Choose Tools | Envelopes or Tools | Labels to start the process for merging envelopes or labels.

8

HOUR 9

Preparing for Tomorrow with Works Suite Calendar

National and local media alike have repeatedly reported about how the average American puts in a longer work week than ever before and how busy we are during our free time as well. Microsoft Works Suite now includes the Works Calendar, a tool you can use to ensure you make it to the meeting, the soccer match, or the dentist's appointment on time.

If you can squeeze in an hour now to work with Calendar, you can learn to

- Start and exit the Calendar program.
- Specify how many days Calendar displays.
- Add an appointment.
- Delete an appointment.
- Print a copy of the Calendar for each family member.

Opening and Touring the Calendar

You can't access the Works Suite Calendar via the Works Task Launcher, like the other tools you've learned about so far. Instead, you have to launch Works Suite Calendar separately, using one of these methods:

- Double-click the Works Calendar shortcut icon on the Windows desktop.
- Click Start, point to Programs, and click Microsoft Works Calendar.

Calendar opens in its own window, as shown in Figure 9.1. It presents the schedule for the current day in the same type of list format you see in a schedule or appointment book. To display a different day, you click the Previous Day and Next Day buttons, which appear to the far left and right (respectively), on the Banner under the Calendar window toolbar. You can use the vertical scrollbar at the right side of the window to scroll the display to show an earlier or later time.

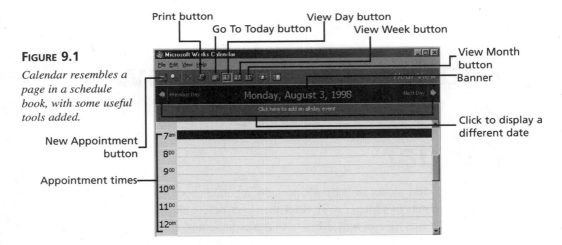

FIGURE 9.1

Calendar resembles a page in a schedule book, with some useful tools added.

Changing the Calendar View

Although you might want to view only the current day's appointments, you can view a full week or month in the calendar while you're planning upcoming activities. For example, you might want to get in the habit of spending some time Sunday evening entering and reviewing your personal and family activities for the upcoming week. Alternatively, you might want to look at a full-month calendar if you're trying to select a vacation week or need to block out some days when you're expecting visitors.

To display the Week view, which shows seven days, choose View | Week or click the View Week button on the toolbar. To display the Month view, which shows a full month, choose View | Month or click the View Month button on the toolbar. (Figures 9.2 and 9.3 compare the Week view and the Month view.) To return to the Day view from one of the other views, choose View | Day or click the View Day button on the toolbar.

FIGURE 9.2

Use the Week view in Calendar to see and plan a particular week's appointments.

Selected date —

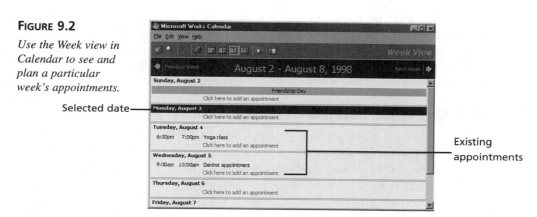

Existing appointments

FIGURE 9.3

To plan even further into the future, use the Month view.

Selected date —

Existing appointments

 When you're switching from the Week view or Month view to the Day view, click the date you want to display in the Day view. This saves you the trouble of clicking the Previous Day or Next Day button repeatedly to display the date you want.

When you're working in Week view or Month view, you can select a particular date by clicking it or by using the arrow keys. You can choose a different date in any view by clicking the Go To Today button on the toolbar. (In the Day view, of course, this action displays the calendar for the current date only.)

You also can use the Banner to display different dates in the current view. In Day view and Week view, click the Banner to display a smaller pop-up calendar; then click the day you want to display in the Day view or the first day of the week to display in the Week view. Clicking the Banner in Month view displays a drop-down list of months. Click the month you want to display in the list.

Working with Appointments

Now that you can move around in the various Calendar views, you're ready to set up appointments. Each appointment corresponds to a particular obligation you have at a particular time. Rather than writing your appointments in a paper schedule book, you can enter them in Calendar.

Although Calendar deals with appointments, you also can use it to track key to-dos for your family. For example, let's say that your son or daughter has a science project due at the end of the week. You can create a Friday morning appointment to remind you and your child to take the science project materials to school. In addition, you can enter an appointment or two for evenings earlier in the week to block out time when the two of you can work together on the project.

Scheduling an Appointment

You can use the same process for setting up an appointment, no matter what Calendar view you're working with. When you enter the appointment, you give it a name and specify when it starts and ends. You have the option of providing additional information, too, such as the appointment location.

When you're ready to enter an appointment, follow these steps:

To Do: Entering an Appointment in Calendar

1. Select or display the date on which you want to enter the appointment. (In the Day view, you also can click a particular time to later save you the trouble of specifying the appointment's starting time in Step 7.)

▼   2. Click the New Appointment button, or choose File | New Appointment. The New Appointment dialog box appears.

3. If the All Day Appointment check box is checked, click to clear the check box.

> An all day appointment denotes an event that occurs during an entire day, in addition to individual appointments during that day. For example, you could enter a child's birthday as an all day appointment, and then enter a specific appointment for the duration of the child's birthday party on the same day. All day appointments appear in a gray bar on the specified date, no matter what view you're working in. To create an all day appointment, leave the All Day Appointment check box checked, and specify any other available appointment options.

9

4. Enter the name of the appointment in the Title text box.

5. If needed, enter the place for the appointment in the Location text box.

6. Click the Category button, click to check one or more categories in the Select Categories list; then click OK. (See the following section, "Viewing Appointments by Category," to learn more about categorized appointments.)

7. If needed, use the drop-down lists beside Appointment Starts to specify the starting date and time for the appointment.

8. Use the drop-down lists beside Appointment Ends to specify the ending date and time for the appointment.

9. Open the Reminder drop-down list; then select how far in advance of the appointment you want the reminder to appear. For example, if it'll take you 30 minutes to travel to a meeting location, select 30 Minutes from the Reminder drop-down list. Then, the Reminders window opens 30 minutes before the appointment starting time to remind you of the appointment (assuming you have the Works Suite Calendar program running).

10. Click in the text box below the Reminder drop-down list and type any notes that apply to the appointment. Figure 9.4 shows the New Appointment dialog box with appointment information and notes specified.

▼   11. Click OK to add the appointment to your schedule in Calendar.

▼ **FIGURE 9.4**

This example illustrates all the details you can capture when you create an appointment.

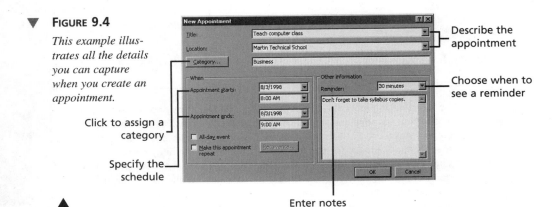

Describe the appointment

Choose when to see a reminder

Click to assign a category

Specify the schedule

Enter notes

▲

Works Suite Calendar *does* let you schedule overlapping or conflicting appointments, unlike some other scheduling programs. So, be on the lookout for instances where you've double-booked yourself. Or, if appointments have to overlap, such as when both your children have sports practice at the same time at different ball fields, make sure you note what transportation arrangements you've made.

If you later need to make changes to an appointment, you can edit the appointment. Double-click the appointment in any view to display the Edit Appointment dialog box, which offers the same options as the New Appointment dialog box shown in Figure 9.4. Make the needed changes; then click OK to close the dialog box.

Viewing Appointments by Category

Step 6 in the previous set of steps indicated that you can specify a category for each appointment. If you take the time to assign categories, you can then display the Category Filter and use it to display only appointments that fall within a particular category. For example, you can display only appointments to which you've assigned the Business category, to see your professional schedule for the week.

Follow these steps to use the Category Filter:

To Do: Filtering Your Schedule

1. Select the view you want to use.

2. Choose View | Show Category Filter or click the Show Category Filter button on the toolbar. The Category Filter appears at the left side of the Calendar window.

▼ 3. Click to clear the check beside any category that you no longer want to display. In Figure 9.5, every category is cleared except Business, so the Calendar lists only appointments in that category. Alternately, click to check any category of appointments to redisplay.

FIGURE 9.5

Check and uncheck categories in the Category Filter to control whether those appointments appear in your calendar.

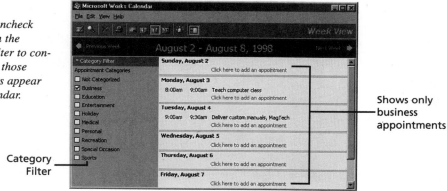

9

Category Filter

Shows only business appointments

▲ 4. When you finish working with the Category Filter, choose View |
Show Category Filter or click the Show Category Filter button on the toolbar again to hide the Category Filter.

The choices you make in the Category Filter remain active until you change them. To redisplay appointments in all categories, choose View | Category Filter | Show Appointments in All Categories.

Works Suite Calendar includes 10 default categories that you can assign to appointments. These general categories cover many bases but may not meet all your needs or enable you to filter your schedule as you'd like. You can create your own categories to supplement those that Calendar offers. For example, if you want to be able to display and print a separate schedule for each family member, create a category for each family member (each person's name or nickname). You can then apply each family member's category to appointments for that family member and use the Category Filter as just described to show his appointments.

Follow these steps to add a category in Calendar:

To Do: Creating a New Category

1. Choose Edit | Categories. The Edit Categories dialog box appears.
2. Type the name for the new category in the text box at the bottom of the dialog box (see Figure 9.6).

FIGURE 9.6

Enter a new category name at the bottom of the Edit Categories dialog box.

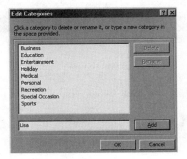

3. Click the Add button.
4. Click OK to close the Edit Categories dialog box.

Setting Up a Repeating Appointment

Many events and commitments repeat over time, such as a weekly ball game or monthly investment club meeting. Rather than enter similar appointment information over and over, you can set up a *recurring appointment*—an appointment that repeats at an interval you specify.

Use these steps to create a recurring appointment:

Repeating an Appointment

1. Enter the information for the first instance of the appointment in the New Appointment dialog box, or double-click the appointment you want to repeat to display the Edit Appointment dialog box.
2. Click to check the Make This Appointment Repeat check box. You have to specify the appointment scheduling information before enabling this check box, however.
3. Click the Recurrence button. The Recurrence Options dialog box opens.
4. In the Recurring area, specify how often the appointment should repeat. For example, to have an appointment repeat on Tuesday and Thursday of each week, choose the Weekly option button; then check the Tuesday and Thursday check boxes.

▼ 5. In the Range of Recurrence area, specify an End By date or an End After (X) Occurrences value to tell Calendar how many times to repeat the appointment. For example, Figure 9.7 shows an appointment set up to recur on Tuesdays and Thursdays for 20 occurrences.

FIGURE 9.7

Use the Recurrence Options dialog box to specify how often and how long to repeat an appointment.

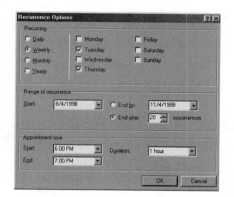

9

6. (Optional) Enter any schedule information in the Appointment Time area as needed.

▲ 7. Click OK twice to finish creating all the instances of the repeating appointment. Calendar automatically adds all the appointment occurrences to the schedule.

Deleting an Appointment

When someone cancels an event or you decide to shed a commitment, delete the corresponding appointment from your calendar. To start the process, you can click the appointment in any view and click the Delete button on the toolbar or choose Edit | Delete Appointment (Ctrl+D). Alternatively, you can right-click the appointment and click Delete Item. If the appointment is one of a set of repeating appointments, click Delete This Occurrence or Delete the Series; then click OK. Click Yes when Calendar prompts you to confirm the deletion.

> If you mistakenly delete an appointment, choose Edit | Undo immediately to return to the schedule.

Printing Your Calendar

Works Suite Calendar enables you to print a daily, weekly, or monthly calendar. You also choose a format that determines the layout for the printed pages. When you need to create a schedule printout for yourself or another family member, follow these steps:

To Do: Creating a Schedule Printout

1. Display the day, week, or month you want to print in Day view, Week view, or Month view.

2. If you want to print only appointments that fall in certain categories, use the Category Filter as described earlier in the section, "Viewing Appointments by Category," to display the desired categories.

3. Choose File | Print or click the Print button on the toolbar. The Print dialog box appears.

4. Under Style, click the page design you want to use.

5. If you didn't display the applicable day, week, or month in Step 1, use the settings in the Range area to specify which date(s) or time(s) to print.

> You can print a week's worth of schedule information using a style that prints a day per page, or a month using a style that prints a week per page. First, display the dates you want to print in the Week view (or Month view). Then choose a Day Page style (or Week style). Verify that the Range area lists the dates to print, and continue as directed here. Calendar prints multiple pages of schedule information for you.

6. In the Include area, specify whether to print All Appointments or Appointments Currently Selected in the Category Filter. (Make sure to choose the latter option if you filtered the schedule in Step 2.)

7. If you chose a page style that enables you to print appointment details such as the location and notes, you can check Appointment Details. Leaving that check box blank excludes detail information from the printout. Figure 9.8 shows settings for printing a calendar page, including Appointment Details.

FIGURE 9.8

Choose how the printout will look using the Print dialog box options.

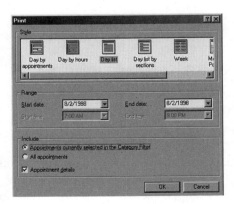

▼   8. Click OK. A second Print dialog box appears.

    9. Specify your options in this dialog box, such as the Number of Copies to print.

▲   10. Click OK to print.

Exiting Calendar

When you finish entering and printing appointment information, you can shut down the Works Suite Calendar program. To do so, choose File | Exit.

> Generally speaking, Calendar keeps all your schedule information together rather than making you save and manage files. When you exit Works Suite Calendar, it automatically saves your updated calendar information for you.

Summary

In an hour, you tackled the challenge of getting your family's schedule in order using Works Suite Calendar. You learned to start Calendar, choose a view, and enter appointments. You created categories and used them to control which appointments Calendar lists. Finally, you learned to print schedule copies and shut down the Calendar program. This concludes your work with Microsoft Works. Continue to Part II, "Learning Word 97 at Lunchtime," Hour 10 to begin working with Microsoft Word, a powerful word processor that offers more features than the Works Suite Word Processing tool.

Q&A

Q. How do I start and exit Works Suite Calendar?

A. Double-click the Works Calendar shortcut icon on the Windows desktop to start the program, and choose File | Exit to shut it down.

Q. Does it matter which view I use?

A. That's purely a matter of preference—in most cases. You can accomplish any task in any view, such as clicking a date and then clicking the New Appointment button to create a new appointment. You can save a little time when you print, however, by choosing a view before you choose the File | Print command.

Q. I don't see all my appointments. What's wrong?

A. You could have some categories filtered out with the Category Filter. To redisplay all your appointments, choose View | Category Filter | Show Appointments in All Categories.

PART II
Learning Word 97 at Lunchtime

Hour

HOUR 10

Building Documents with Word 97

Microsoft Word has been the top-selling word processing program for a number of years now. The word processor tool in Microsoft Works really is a smaller, streamlined version of the powerful favorite, Word. If you find that the Works word processor doesn't offer all the features you want, you can make a nearly painless transition to Word.

In both the Works Word Processor tool and Word, you use the same basic techniques to create and save documents. This hour helps you get started with Word, enabling you to

- Start and close Word 97.
- Create the text for your Word document.
- Save and insert AutoText entries.
- Make changes to improve your text.
- Save and open Word documents.

Getting Started

When you start the Word 97 program, its application window and tools display onscreen. There is no desktop shortcut for starting Word, so you need to use the Windows Start menu, as described in the following steps:

To Do: Starting Word

1. Click the Start button on the taskbar.

2. Point to Programs, and then click the Microsoft Word choice. The Word program opens.

3. If this is the first time you've started Word, the User Name dialog box appears (see Figure 10.1). If the Name and Initials text boxes are empty or contain the wrong information, enter the correct information, and then click OK to finish starting Word.

FIGURE 10.1

The first time you start Word, it prompts you to enter or verify your user information.

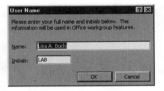

4. Word 97 also displays the Office Assistant, an automated online help character, the first time you start the program. To begin working, click the blue button beside Start Using Microsoft Word.

▲

> Even if you don't leave the Office Assistant open, it will pop up from time-to-time to ask if you need help with an activity in Word. You can choose one of the Help options the Office Assistant presents, or close the Office Assistant. To close it, click the Close (X) button at the right end of its title bar.

Entering Text

Unlike when you start Works, starting Word also opens a new, blank document onscreen. The blinking vertical insertion point appears in the upper-left corner of the new document window, so you can start tapping away at your keyboard to enter your document's text.

The techniques for entering text in Word are the same as those you learned for the Works Word Processor (see Hour 2, "Building Documents with the Word Processor"). To save

you the trouble of skipping back to that information, here's a brief review of how to
enter text:

- Each character you type appears at the insertion point and moves the insertion
  point to the right.

- When you're nearing the end of the line, just keep typing. Word automatically
  wraps text to the next line.

- Press Enter to start a new paragraph; this is called inserting a *paragraph break*. You
  have to press Enter for every paragraph, even short, one-line paragraphs as in an
  address (see Figure 10.2).

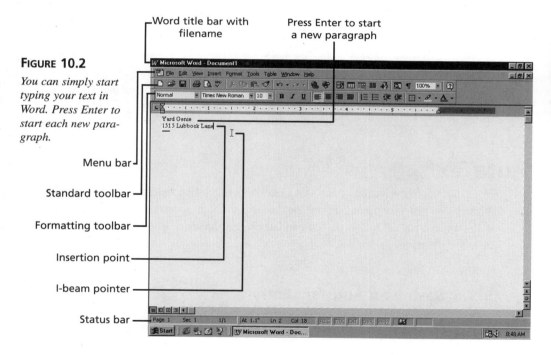

FIGURE 10.2

*You can simply start
typing your text in
Word. Press Enter to
start each new para-
graph.*

Word title bar with
filename

Press Enter to start
a new paragraph

Menu bar

Standard toolbar

Formatting toolbar

Insertion point

I-beam pointer

Status bar

10

- After you type a page's worth of information, Word inserts a *soft page break* (an
  automatic page break) to start a new page for you. You keep typing, and Word
  starts filling the new page. In Normal view (the default view for Word), a hard
  page break appears as a dotted line across a page.

- After you type text, you can use the arrow keys to move the insertion point, or
  click with the mouse to position it where needed. You also can press PgDn and
  PgUp to move the insertion point by one screenful of information at a time.

- If you need to control where a new page starts, you can insert a *manual* or *hard* page break. To start a new page at a particular location, choose Insert | Page Break or press Ctrl+Enter. In Normal view, a hard page break appears as a dotted line across a page, with the words Page Break in the center.

> By default, Works doesn't display each file window at its maximized size. Instead, you can see the document window title bar in the work area below the Works toolbar. Word, on the other hand, maximizes the document (file) window by default, so that the Word title bar also includes the filename, and the right end of the Word menu bar shows the buttons for controlling the file window, such as the Close (X) button.

> Word offers numerous toolbars with numerous buttons. To identify a toolbar button—to find the one you need—point to it with the mouse. A yellow pop-up ScreenTip appears with the name (and function) of the button.

AutoText

Word offers a feature called AutoText that works much like the Easy Text feature in the Works word processor. You can use the AutoText feature to save a block of text and assign a name to that block, so you can later insert the block into the document just by choosing its name.

Follow these steps to create an AutoText entry:

To Do: Saving an AutoText Entry

1. Type the text that you want to save as an AutoText entry, and then drag over it to select or highlight it.
2. Choose Insert | AutoText|New (Alt+F3). The Create AutoText dialog box appears.
3. The Create AutoText dialog box suggests a name for your new AutoText entry, usually the first few words or line of the text you selected in step 1. The name appears highlighted in the Please Name Your AutoText Entry text box, so you can simply begin typing to replace the suggested name with another of your choice.
4. Click OK to finish creating the AutoText entry.

After you create an AutoText entry, position the insertion point where you want to insert the entry's contents in the document. Then use one of these two methods to insert the AutoText entry:

- Choose Insert | AutoText | AutoText. The AutoCorrect dialog box appears, with the AutoText tab selected. Scroll down the list under the Enter AutoText Entries Here text box, and then click the name of the AutoText entry you want to insert, as shown in Figure 10.3. Check the preview to ensure you've chosen the right entry, and then click Insert to insert it into the document.

FIGURE 10.3

When you click an AutoText entry to insert it, the Preview area shows the selected AutoText entry's contents.

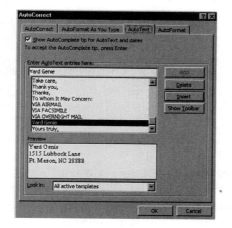

10

- Begin typing the name of the AutoText entry where you want it to appear in the document. If at any time a yellow pop-up box appears and shows the beginning of the AutoText entry, that means that Word has recognized the AutoText entry; you can then press F3 to insert its contents into the document. Otherwise, type the full name of the AutoText entry. (Do not press Spacebar after the name.) Then press F3.

Word offers a number of built-in AutoText entries that it might prompt you to insert if you're typing what looks like the name for one of those entries at the beginning of a new paragraph. For example, if you type Your, a yellow pop-up box might present the *Yours truly,* AutoText entry, so you can just press F3 to insert *Yours truly,* into the document. Keep an eye out for Word's helpful AutoText suggestions.

Editing Text

As with virtually everything discussed in this hour, the editing techniques you use in Word are the same as those you learned about in the Works word processor.

After you position the insertion point at a location where you want to make an edit, press the Backspace key to remove the character to the left of the insertion point. Press the Delete key to delete the characters to the right of the insertion point. You can press Backspace and Delete multiple times to delete multiple characters. To delete a hard page break, click to position the insertion point at the beginning of the paragraph that follows the page break, and then press Backspace.

> To undo an edit, choose Edit I Undo (Action), click the Undo (Action) button on the Standard toolbar, or press Ctrl+Z. (The names of the Undo command and button change based on the action you last performed.)

After you delete characters as needed, you can type new text to insert it into the document. However, be careful to check whether you're working in Insert mode or Overtype mode. In Insert mode, Word inserts characters you type at the insertion point, and existing text moves to the right to make room for the inserted information. When you switch to Overtype mode by pressing the Insert key or double-clicking the OVR indicator on the status bar, text you type replaces or types over existing text to the right of the insertion point. Press Insert or double-click the OVR indicator again to return to Insert mode.

Selecting Text

You must be comfortable with selecting text in a document because you must select text before you perform most operations on it. This includes making many types of edits or applying formatting.

For a detailed look at all the options for selecting text in the Works word processor and in Word, refer to Table 2.1 in Hour 2, "Building Documents with the Word Processor." Briefly, though, you can drag over any amount of text to select it, double-click a word to select it, or Ctrl+click a sentence to select the whole sentence.

> Be careful when you have some text selected. If you accidentally press a key, that new character replaces the entire selection. Click the Undo button on the Standard toolbar or press Ctrl+Z immediately to get your text back.

Copying, Moving, and Deleting Text

You'll save time if you become a recycling advocate—a *text* recycling advocate, that is. Copying or moving text to another location saves you the time of retyping it and reduces the likelihood that you'll introduce new typos.

When you need to copy or move text in Word, follow these steps:

To Do: Copying and Moving Word Text

1. Select the text to copy or move.

2. Choose Edit I Copy (Ctrl+C) or Edit I Cut (Ctrl+X). Or, click the Copy or Cut button on the Standard toolbar.

3. Move the insertion point to the location where you want to insert the copied or cut text. (To insert the text in another document, open the document as described later in this hour or display the other file by choosing its name from the bottom of the Window menu.)

4. Choose Edit I Paste (Ctrl+V) or click the Paste button on the Standard toolbar. The copied or cut material appears at the insertion point.

5. (Optional) Repeat Steps 3 and 4 to paste the text into additional locations.

Alternatively, you can use the shortcut menu to copy, cut, or paste text. Right-click a selection, and then click Cut or Copy in the shortcut menu. Position the insertion point to the location where you want to insert the cut or copied information, and then right-click to display the shortcut menu again (see Figure 10.4). Click the Paste command to paste the information at the insertion point location.

FIGURE 10.4

You can right-click to display a shortcut menu with commands for cutting, copying, and pasting text.

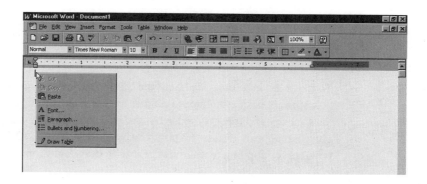

To remove text from your document, select it, and then press the Delete key or choose Edit I Clear. Clearing text does not place it on the Clipboard, so you have to type it or use Undo to retrieve it.

Word offers much more powerful undo capabilities than Works. In Word, you can undo multiple previous actions. To do so, click the drop-down list arrow beside the Undo button on the Standard toolbar. In the list that appears, click the action that you want to undo; Word undoes the selected actions, plus all the other actions listed above it. After you undo one or more actions, the Redo button becomes active. Click the drop-down list arrow beside that button, and click the action to redo in the list that appears. Word redoes that action plus any others listed above it.

Using Drag-and-Drop

For quick copy or move operations within the same paragraph or so of information, you can use drag-and-drop. Drag-and-drop certainly makes editing faster, especially if you're comfortable with the mouse. You can make a drag-and-drop edit in one, smooth sweep of the mouse.

If you have to move information between different pages in a document, I don't recommend using drag-and-drop because it's difficult to get the document to scroll to display the destination where you want to drop the text. Also, if you have a notebook computer with an integrated pointing device that you're not used to, you might have trouble dropping the text in the right position. In these situations, I suggest using the full-blown copy/cut and paste procedure described earlier.

Here's how to use drag-and-drop to move or copy text:

To Do: Dragging and Dropping Text in Word

▲ To Do

1. Select the text to move or copy.
2. To move the text, press and hold the left mouse button, and drag the text; a gray box appears beside the mouse pointer as you drag. To copy the text, press and hold the Ctrl key and the left mouse button, and then drag the text; a gray box with a plus sign appears beside the pointer as you drag. Figure 10.5 shows the mouse pointers for copying and moving text with drag-and-drop.
3. Drag until the gray insertion point appears where you want to insert the text. Release the mouse button (and the Ctrl key, if needed) to drop the moved or copied information into place.

▼

FIGURE 10.5

When you use drag-and-drop, the mouse pointer changes depending on whether you're moving (left) or copying the text.

Managing Document Files

Whether you're organizing information in a home or business setting, you'll be working with both paper documents and word processor document files stored on a computer disk. This section instructs you in essential document file-management skills in Word, including saving a file, closing and opening files, and creating a new file from scratch.

10

Saving and Closing a File

As you create new documents, Word names them *Document1*, *Document2*, and so on. (See "Opening a New, Blank Document," later in this hour and "Creating a New Document Using a Template" in Hour 13, "Using Templates and Styles to Save Time.") To provide a document (file) a unique name and store it on disk, you have to save the document.

By default, Word prompts you to store files in the \My Documents\ folder on your hard disk. However, you can save the document to another folder, when, for example, you create a separate folder to store the files related to each project you're working on.

Use these steps to save the current document file (the file that's displayed) in Word:

To Do: Saving Your Word Document File

1. Choose File | Save (Ctrl+S) or click the Save button on the Standard toolbar. The Save As dialog box appears.

2. To save to a folder other than the default one, click the Up One Level button on the dialog box's toolbar once or twice. This is called "moving up a level in the folder tree." (You also can click to open the Save In list, and click a folder higher on the tree to select it.) Then, double-click the folder to select in the list of folders that appears in the dialog box.

3. Double-click the entry in the File Name text box to select it, if needed, and then type the name you want for the file. (Figure 10.6 shows an example filename.)

Your filenames can be very descriptive because they can include more than 200 characters, spaces, and special capitalization. By default, Word suggests the first line of text in the file as the File Name text box entry, so you could skip this step if that name is acceptable.

Up One Level button

FIGURE 10.6

You can enter a lengthy name for the Word document you're saving.

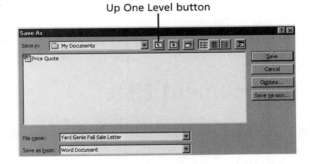

4. Click the Save button. After you save and name the file, its name appears in the file window title bar.

> After you name your file, you can choose File I Save As to redisplay the Save As dialog box. If you enter a new filename and then click Save, Word saves a copy of the file under the new name. Also note that any folder you selected previously appears in the Save In text box in the redisplayed Save As dialog box. To save to another folder, use the Up One Level button or Save In list to select it.

After you save your file the first time, resaving it adds your recent changes to the file without renaming the file. You should save it every 10 minutes or so to ensure that you won't lose your work if your system reboots due to power fluctuations. The Word application has a habit of freezing up from time to time, especially on systems that have less than 32MB of RAM, which can also cause you to lose work you haven't saved. To resave a Word document after you've saved it the first time, choose the File I Save command (Ctrl+S) again or click the Save button on the Standard toolbar.

When you've finished working with a file, you can choose File I Close to close it. If it contains work that you haven't saved, Word displays a dialog box reminding you to save your changes. Click Yes to do so and close the file.

Opening an Existing File

You can open as many files as your computer handles in Word. When you open a file, it becomes the current or active (top) file in the Word window. You can then make changes to the file or print it.

To open a file in Word, use these steps:

To Do: Opening a Word Document File

1. Choose File | Open (Ctrl+O) or click the Open button on the Standard toolbar. The Open dialog box appears, listing the files stored in the default folder (\My Documents\).

2. To open a file stored in a folder other than the default one, click the Up One Level button on the dialog box's toolbar once or twice. (You also can click to open the Look In list, and click a folder higher on the tree to select it.) Then, double-click the folder you want to select in the list of folders that appears in the dialog box.

3. In the list of files shown in the dialog box, click the file you want to open.

4. Click the Open button to open the file in Word.

If you've recently worked with a file you want to open, you can probably open it directly from the bottom of the File menu, which by default lists recently used files. Open the File menu. If the file you want to open appears there, click its filename to open it (see Figure 10.7).

FIGURE 10.7

Open the File menu and click the name of a file shown there to open that file.

To open Word and an existing document, click the Start button, and then choose Open Office Document from the top of the Start menu. In the Open Office Document dialog box that appears, navigate to and click the Word file you want to open, and then click the Open button.

Files you open remain open until you close them. It's possible to have several files open at one time. If you happen to have several files open and need to work in a different one, open the Window menu and click the name of the file you want to use. It becomes the current or active file.

Opening a New, Blank Document

Any time you're ready to create a new document, you can open a new, blank document and start your work. Use one of the following techniques to open a new document:

- Click the New button on the far-left end of the Standard toolbar.
- If you've already chosen File | New to display the new dialog box, click the Blank Document icon on the General tab (see Figure 10.8), and then click OK.

FIGURE 10.8

Choose the Blank Document icon in the New dialog box to open a new document.

New button

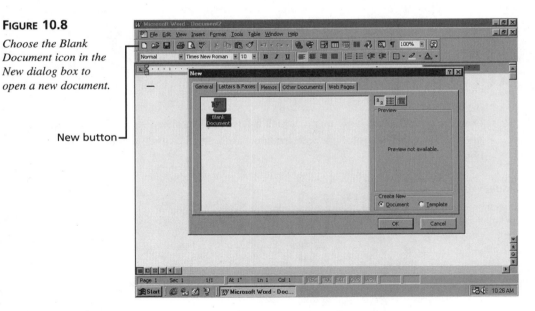

The new, blank document appears onscreen, with the insertion point in its upper-left corner, so you can begin your work.

Exiting Word

When you're finished working in Word, you can exit the program. You should always exit Word (and other applications) before you shut down your computer for the day, to ensure that you don't lose any work and that the system shuts down properly.

To exit Word, either click the Close (X) button at the far-right end of the Word title bar, or choose File | Exit. If one or more open files contain changes you haven't saved, Word displays a message box like the one shown in Figure 10.9. Click Yes to save your work for each open file. Word saves and closes each file, and the Word application window closes.

FIGURE 10.9

Word prompts you to save your work before it shuts down.

 If you shut down Windows but forget to exit Word first, you should still see a message like the one in Figure 10.9 prompting you to save any open Word files that have unsaved work. To exit Windows, choose Start | Shut Down from the Windows taskbar; choose the Shut Down option button, and then click OK.

10

Summary

Creating documents in Word requires skills like those you learned for the Works Word Processor tool. You now can feel confident starting Word, entering and editing text, and saving and opening files. From here, you can move on to learn how to format your Word documents with new text and page settings, some of which are again similar to those you saw in the Works word processor.

Q&A

Q. How do I start or exit Word?

A. From the Windows desktop, choose Start | Programs | Microsoft Word to start the Word program. Choose File | Exit in Word to shut down Word; click Yes to save your unsaved work in any file.

Q. What do I need to know about entering and editing text?

A. Literally, the same things you needed to know in Works. Type text and let Word wrap it to the next line. Press Enter only to create a new paragraph. You can click or press an arrow key to reposition the insertion point, and then press Backspace or Delete to delete a character to the left or right. You need to select a larger block of text before you can delete or format it. Drag to select or highlight any block of text. Double-click a single word to select it, or press Ctrl and click a sentence to select the entire sentence.

Q. How do I save the file I've created?

A. Choose File | Save or click the Save button on the Standard toolbar. Use the Save In list to select the disk and folder in which you want to save the file. Type a name in the File Name text box; then click Save.

Q. What's the fastest way to create a document?

A. Click the New button at the far-left end of the Standard toolbar to open a new, blank document in Word.

Hour 11

Formatting Word Documents

New Word documents look rather plain by default—they use 10-pt. Times New Roman text with no fancy spacing or other embellishments. To make your document stand out from others in the pack (or the pile), you can change its formatting.

This hour presents basic text, paragraph, and page formatting techniques in Word. Word's formatting features resemble those in the Works Suite Word Processor, as described in Hours 3 and 4, so this hour highlights key skills only. You learn to

- Select another document view.
- Change fonts, font sizes, and attributes.
- Work with paragraph alignment, spacing, and borders.
- Control the page formatting.
- Add graphics to illustrate the document.

Choosing a View

Like the Works Suite Word Processor, Word offers a *Normal view,* which hides bells and whistles so you can focus on the text. Like Works Suite, it also offers the *Page Layout* view, showing your document just as it will print, with graphics, margins, and other formatting fully in place. Word offers some additional views, too:

- Online Layout　Shows how the document would look if you saved it as an HMTL (Web) page.
- Outline　Enables you to organize your document in traditional outline style by promoting and demoting information to different outline levels.
- Master Document　Enables you to combine documents into a cohesive whole. The individual documents remain intact, as well.

You use one of the views listed previously when you're creating sophisticated or lengthy documents. This book won't explain or cover those views because they are so specific and the discussion here is more general.

Instead, you'll work primarily in Normal view while you're entering text or Page Layout view when you're working with graphics, text, and page formatting. As in the Works Suite word processor, Word automatically displays the Page Layout view for you when you perform certain actions such as inserting a graphic.

To display the current document in a different view, open the View menu and click the view you want to use.

Formatting with the Formatting Toolbar

By default, Word displays two toolbars. The Standard toolbar just below the menu bar offers tools for managing your file. The Formatting toolbar below the Standard toolbar offers tools strictly for formatting a text selection. Figure 11.1 identifies the Formatting toolbar buttons you learn about in this hour.

Most often, you'll use these tools on the Formatting toolbar:

- Font and Font Size　You can select another font (lettering style) and size for selected text using these drop-down lists.
- Bold, Italic, and Underline (*font style or attributes*)　Click one of these buttons to add or remove the attribute of your choice. You also can use the keyboard shortcuts Ctrl+B, Ctrl+I, or Ctrl+U to add and remove boldface, italic, and underlining for a selection.

- Font Color   Click this button to apply the font color it currently shows. To select another color, click the drop-down list arrow beside the Font Color button; then click the new color you want to use.

FIGURE 11.1

Word's Formatting toolbar offers a variety of formatting buttons.

Different font and font size

Different attributes

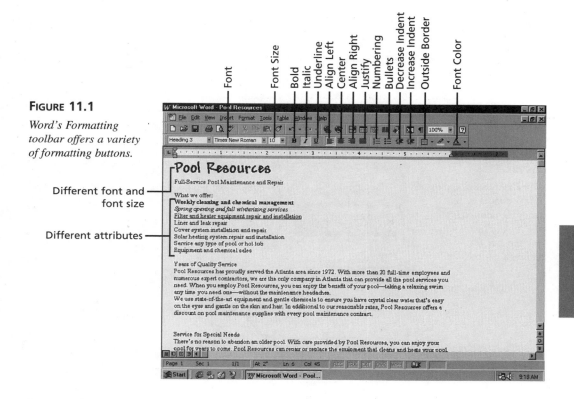

 As in Works Suite, press Ctrl+Spacebar to remove all formatting changes you make from a selection.

Using the Font Dialog Box

Word offers many more text formatting choices than the Works Suite word processor, such as making text superscript, changing the spacing between characters, or even animating the text. It would take volumes of written text to explain every formatting setting; the scope of this hour is narrower and reviews how to access the settings in Word's Font dialog box.

Follow these steps to use the Font dialog box:

To Do: Formatting Text with the Font Dialog Box

1. Select the text to which you want to apply the new formatting.

2. Choose Format | Font. The Format Font dialog box appears.

3. On the Font tab, which is selected by default, specify the Font, Font Style, Size, Underline choice, Color, and Effects that you want.

4. Click the Character Spacing tab, and use its settings to adjust the spacing between the characters in a selection. Figure 11.2 shows this tab and an example of changing the spacing between letters.

These setting changes...

FIGURE 11.2

Word's Font dialog box offers dozens of settings for controlling the look of text, including the spacing between characters.

Original spacing

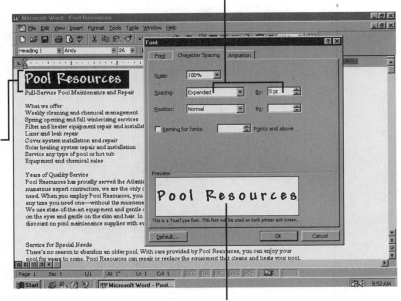

...have this effect

5. Click the Animation tab; then click an effect you want to use from the Animations list.

6. Click OK to close the Font dialog box and apply your settings.

An animation you apply to text appears only when the document is open onscreen. Animated text prints normally.

> The fact that Word offers more formatting options than Works Suite doesn't mean you should use all those options at the same time. Remember to keep your document designs simple, and consider your reader's needs and tastes at all times. Too much fancy stuff will make your documents hard to read.

Formatting Paragraphs

After you update the text formatting in your Word document, you can move on to paragraph formatting. Controlling how paragraphs align and how they're spaced can really affect the mood and readability of your document. For example, centering everything in a document makes it tough to read. Adding an indent to the first line of each paragraph makes it easier to read. This section provides an overview of the different paragraph formatting adjustments you can make in Word. Refer to Hours 3 and 4 if you encounter any term that doesn't seem familiar to you.

Changing Alignment and Paragraph Spacing

The Formatting toolbar offers several buttons for controlling how the selected paragraphs align in relation to the document margins. (You can simply click in a paragraph before applying paragraph formatting or select multiple paragraphs, first.) Click one of these buttons to apply the described effect:

- Align Left, Center, or Align Right   Aligns the left side of the paragraph to the left margin, centers every line of the paragraph, or aligns the right side of the paragraph to the right margin, respectively.
- Justify   Inserts spacing between words in the paragraph so that both sides of the paragraph align to the margins.
- Increase Indent   Applies .5" of indention to the left side of all lines in the paragraph each time you click the button.
- Decrease Indent   Removes .5" of indention from the left side of the paragraph each time you click it.

The Formatting toolbar buttons offer only general control over paragraph alignment, and they don't enable you to adjust the spacing between lines or between paragraphs. You can instead change text alignment and gain control over line and paragraph spacing as follows:

11

To Do: Controlling Alignment and Spacing with the Paragraph Dialog Box

1. Select the paragraph(s) for which you want to change alignment.

2. Choose Format | Paragraph. The Paragraph dialog box appears with the Indents and Spacing tab selected.

3. Choose an alignment from the Alignment drop-down list.

4. To indent all lines in the selected paragraph(s), enter a measurement in the Left or Right text box. Or, open the Special drop-down list and choose First Line or Hanging; then enter a measurement for the first line or hanging indention in the By text box.

A *hanging indent* occurs when all lines *but* the first line in the paragraph indent from the left by the measurement you specify.

You can indent the whole paragraph from the left and apply a first line or hanging indent. Just make sure to enter a By text box measurement that's larger than the one you enter in the Left text box.

5. To add spacing before or after the paragraph, increase the Before or After text box settings.

6. To adjust the line spacing within the paragraph, make a choice from the Line Spacing drop-down list. If you chose Exactly, you can enter a corresponding measurement in the At text box. After you make all your alignment and spacing choices, the Preview area shows a sample of how they'll look, as shown in Figure 11.3.

7. Click OK to close the dialog box and apply the alignment and indention.

FIGURE 11.3

The Preview area at the bottom of the Paragraph dialog box illustrates the settings you've chosen.

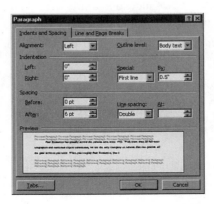

Adding Bullets, Numbering, and Tabs

Word enables you to apply bullets or numbering to paragraphs with just a click of the mouse. Select the paragraphs to which you want to apply bullets or numbering; then click the Numbering or Bullets button on the Formatting toolbar. Word numbers each paragraph in sequence or applies the default bullet style (see Figure 11.4). By default, Word also applies a hanging indent to the numbered or bulleted paragraphs, so that any text wrapping below the first line aligns neatly with the first line text—not the margin or the number or bullet. Click the applicable button again to remove the number or bullet from a selected paragraph.

FIGURE 11.4

Numbering is applied to the first four paragraphs in the list, and bullets are applied to the next four paragraphs.

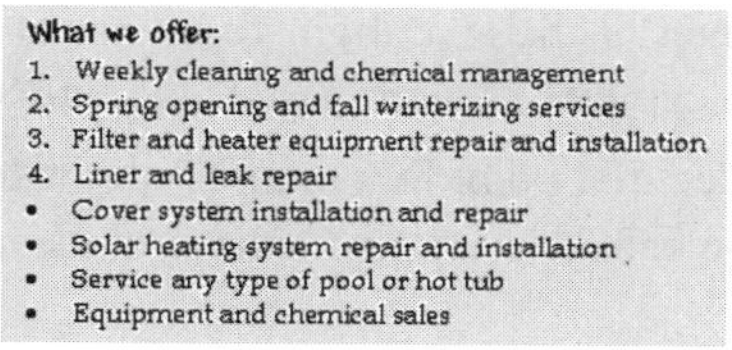

What we offer:

1. Weekly cleaning and chemical management
2. Spring opening and fall winterizing services
3. Filter and heater equipment repair and installation
4. Liner and leak repair
- Cover system installation and repair
- Solar heating system repair and installation
- Service any type of pool or hot tub
- Equipment and chemical sales

You can't apply both a bullet and a number to a paragraph. If you want to apply another bullet or numbering style to a selection, choose Format | Bullets and Numbering. Click a bullet style you want to use on the Bulleted tab or a numbering style to use on the Numbered tab; then click OK.

> If a numbered or bulleted item needs to consist of more than one para-graph, use Shift+Enter to insert the paragraph break. If you simply press Enter, Word adds a number or bullet to the new paragraph.

11

Although bullets and numbering enable you set off individual items in a list, tabs enable you to align lists between the margins of the document. You set up *tab stops* where you want items to align between the margins and then press the Tab key to push the text over to the next tab stop. The fastest way to create a tab stop is to use the ruler, as described next:

To Do: Aligning Text with Tabs

▼ To Do

1. If you don't see the ruler at the top of the document, choose View | Ruler.

2. Select the paragraphs to which you want to apply the tab stops.

3. Click the button at the far-left end of the ruler until it displays the marker for the type of tab you want:

   • Left tab   The left side of the text aligns to the tab stop. Its marker looks like a capital "L" with part of the top cut off.

   • Right tab   The right side of the text aligns to the tab stop. Its marker looks like a backward capital "L" with part of the top cut off.

   • Center tab   The center of the text aligns to the tab stop. Its marker looks like an upside-down capital "T" with part of the tail cut off.

   • Decimal tab   The decimal point in a number aligns to the tab stop. Its marker looks like the center tab marker, with a decimal point added to the right side of the tail.

4. Click the ruler at the measurement where you want to set the tab stop.

5. Repeat steps 3 and 4 to set additional tab stops.

6. Click to position the insertion point within the paragraph(s) to which you applied the tab stops, and press the Tab key to align text to the next tab stop. (Of course, if the text already included tabs, it automatically aligns when you create the tab stops.) Figure 11.5 shows tab stops on the ruler and some text aligned to the tabs.

FIGURE 11.5

The ruler provides the fastest way to set tabs in a document.

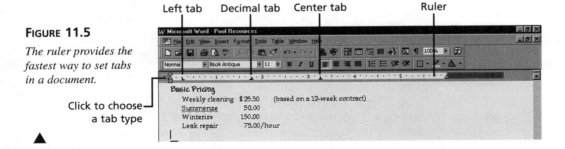

To move a tab stop, drag it to a new position on the ruler. To delete a tab stop, drag it off the ruler.

Using Borders and Shading

You can apply a border and shading to any selected paragraph. The Formatting toolbar includes the Outside Border button. You can click that button to apply the border style it displays to the selected paragraph(s). To apply another border style using that button, click the drop-down list arrow beside the Outside Border button, and then click the type of border you want to use. Click the Outside Border button to apply the new border style.

To apply a fancier border to a selection or to also include shading or a pattern, use these steps:

To Do: Adding a Border and Shading to a Selection

1. Select the paragraph(s) to which you want to apply a border or shading.

2. Choose Format | Borders and Shading. The Borders and Shading dialog box appears.

3. With the Borders tab selected, click one of the Setting choices. Click the type of border you want to use in the Style list; then use the Color and Width drop-down lists to adjust the selected style. Then, in the Preview area, click any side of the paragraph for which you'd like to remove the border. Figure 11.6 shows some border choices on the Borders tab of the Borders and Shading dialog box.

FIGURE 11.6

Apply a paragraph border using this Word dialog box. Word offers more border styles than its cousin, the Works' Suite Word Processor.

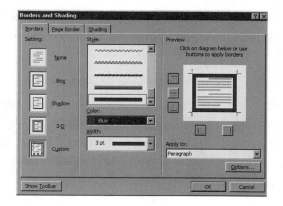

4. To apply shading only to the selection, click the shading color in the Fill area. Alternatively, under Patterns, select a pattern to apply from the Style drop-down list; then choose the pattern foreground color from the Color drop-down list.

5. Click OK to close the dialog box and apply your border and shading choices.

Formatting Pages

Word offers roughly the same page formatting choices that you saw in the Works Suite Word Processor, with a few extras along the way. For example, with Word you can change the page margins and add page headers and footers. In addition, you can add a page border or background. You're more than halfway through this hour, so there's no room remaining to cover each page formatting choice. However, the following set of steps introduces you to the key commands that lead you to the available page formatting settings.

Follow these steps to explore your page setup choices in Word:

To Do: Discovering Word Page Design Choices

1. Choose File | Page Setup. The Page Setup dialog box appears.

2. On the Margins tab, adjust any measurements as needed. On the Paper Size tab, choose the appropriate paper size and choose whether to use a Portrait or Landscape orientation. (You can explore the other two tabs on your own, if needed.) Click OK to apply the page settings.

3. Display the page on which you'd like to start including a header or footer; then choose View | Header and Footer. A Header area and Header and Footer toolbar appears. Click the Switch Between Header and Footer button to move to the footer area if needed. Type the text for the header or footer. Use the Insert Date, Insert Page Number, and other toolbar buttons to insert special elements. Figure 11.7 illustrates a header in progress.

FIGURE 11.7

Use the Header and Footer toolbar to add elements to your header text.

Insert Page Number   Insert Date

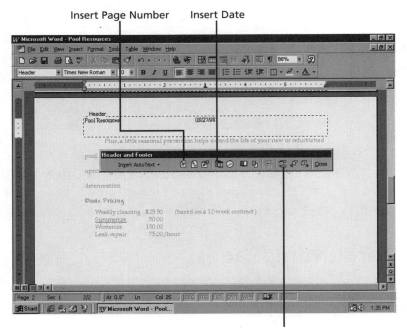

Switch between Header and Footer

To see your header and footer, switch to the Page Layout view.

4. You can select the header and apply any formatting you want; then click the Close button on the Header and Footer toolbar to finish creating the header or footer.

5. To add a border to every page in the document, choose Format I Borders and Shading; then click the Page Border tab. Click one of the Setting choices. Click the type of border you want to use in the Style list; then use the Color and Width drop-down lists to adjust the selected style. You also can select a graphical border style from the Art drop-down list. Then, in the Preview area, click any side of the page for which you'd like to remove the border. Click OK to close the Borders and Shading dialog box. Figure 11.8 shows a page with a graphical border applied.

FIGURE 11.8

When you add a page border, you can see it in Page Layout view.

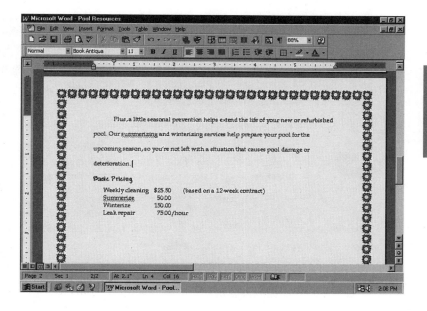

11

A page border you add might cover your header or footer. Redisplay the Page Setup dialog box and adjust margin settings to resolve this problem.

6. If you plan to save the document as an HTML (Web page file) sometime in the future, you can add a background for all the pages in the document. To do so, choose Format I Background. Click a color to apply it as the background (or No Fill

to remove the background). You also can click Fill Effects; choose a Gradient, Texture, Pattern, or Picture using the tabs of those names in the dialog box that appears; then click OK.

7. Because applying a page background switches the document to the Online Layout view, choose View | Page Layout to see the results of your page formatting changes and to resume your work.

▲

Inserting Pictures

You can incorporate Clip Art and WordArt images, as well as other types of electronic images you create or somehow gain access to, into your document. As you learned in Hour 4, " Formatting Pages," graphics enhance and illustrate your document, but should be used sparingly so they don't overwhelm your text or bog down your printer.

For Clip Art, Word uses the same Microsoft Clip Gallery you can access in Works Suite. (As a *shared component*, Clip Gallery can be used by other applications.) The process for inserting Clip Art in a Word document is identical for adding ClipArt in Works, with the exception of the command you use to get started. After you insert the CD-ROM into your CD-ROM drive, choose Insert | Picture | Clip Art. Then continue with the steps described in "Adding ClipArt" in Hour 4.

After you insert a graphic, you can click it to select it. Selection handles appear around the graphic. Drag the selected graphic to move it to a new location. Press Delete to remove the selected graphic from the document.

The process for creating WordArt in Word differs a bit from the process in Works. Use these steps to create and insert WordArt into your Word document:

To Do: Adding WordArt to a Word Document

1. Click to position the insertion point at the approximate location where you want the WordArt graphic to appear.

2. Choose Insert | Picture | WordArt. The WordArt Gallery dialog box appears, as shown in Figure 11.9.

3. Click the design that you want to use in your document; then click OK. The Edit WordArt Text dialog box appears.

4. Type the text you want to format as a WordArt graphic. Use the Font and Size drop-down lists and Bold and Italic buttons to change the WordArt text formatting, if needed; then click OK. Word inserts the WordArt graphic into the document.

▼

FIGURE 11.9

Click the WordArt design you want to use in this dialog box.

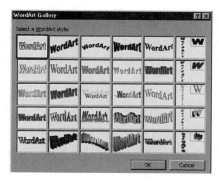

5. If needed, use the buttons on the WordArt toolbar that appears to enhance the WordArt graphic.

6. Click outside the WordArt graphic to finish it.

When you want to edit the WordArt graphic, click it. Doing so places selection handles around the graphic and redisplays the WordArt toolbar. Drag a selection handle to resize the WordArt, use the toolbar buttons to make other changes, and click outside the graphic to finish.

To insert a graphics file in another format (such as .GIF, .JPG, .PCX, or .BMP), choose the Insert | Picture | From File command. The Insert Picture dialog box appears. Use the Look In list to navigate to the disk and folder that holds the graphics file you want to insert. When you see the file in the list in the dialog box, click it and then click Insert.

Summary

This hour reviewed all the formatting changes you can make in a Word document—text, paragraph, and page formatting—as well as how to insert different types of graphics in a document. The next hour delves into creating columns in documents and using a Word feature that's not available in Works Suite: the Table feature.

Q&A

Q. What types of formatting does Word offer?

A. Word offers virtually all the same text, paragraph, and page formatting options as the Works Suite Word Processor tool. Word offers extra settings not found in Works Suite, such as the capability to insert graphical borders around a page.

11

Q. How can I apply quick and dirty formatting?

A. Use the Formatting toolbar, the second toolbar that appears by default in Word. It offers more than 15 tools for adjusting text formatting, paragraph alignment, and indention.

HOUR 12

Working with Tables and Columns

Just think how difficult it would be to read a newspaper or magazine that used one huge column per page. You wouldn't be able to find key statistics, and your eye would tend to wander off the page rather than travel all the way to the end of each line.

In contrast, when you properly break up and align information in a document, you not only lend a more professional appearance to the document, but you also make the information more readable and accessible. Word enables you to create tables and columns to give your document information the special treatment it warrants.

You can use this hour to learn to

- Create a table to align information.
- Make entries in table cells.
- Select and delete table cells.

- Improve your table's appearance.
- Divide a block of text into columns.
- Adjust the columns.

Inserting a Table

Documents often include lists of information. Formatting a list becomes a challenge, though, if each line in the list contains multiple items that need to align vertically. You learned about one solution for lining up lists in the last hour—setting tab stops on the ruler. However, Word 97 offers an even better option—inserting a *table* into the document.

A Word table consists of a spreadsheet-like grid of cells aligned in rows and columns. The grid automatically aligns cell entries both horizontally and vertically; you just create the table and make your entries.

Follow these steps to insert a table into your document:

To Do: Adding the Table Grid

1. Click to position the insertion point on the blank line where you want to insert the table.

> Inserting a table within a paragraph splits the paragraph information, interrupting your reader. So, it's preferable to stick with inserting a table after the paragraph that describes it or that it illustrates.

2. Click the Insert Table button on the Standard toolbar. A grid appears below the button.

3. Move the mouse down and to the right (you don't have to press the mouse button) until you highlight cells representing the number of rows and columns you want in your table (see Figure 12.1). The bottom of the grid tells you how many rows and columns the table will have. For example, *4 x 2 Table* denotes a table with 4 rows and 2 columns.

4. Click the lower-right highlighted cell. Word inserts the table grid into the document.

FIGURE 12.1

Use the grid for the Insert Table button to specify how many rows and columns your table contains.

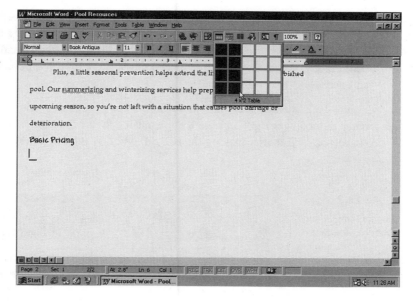

To add a table, you also can choose Table I Insert Table. In the Insert Table dialog box, enter the Number of Columns and Number of Rows for the table; then click OK.

If you have text that you aligned using the Tab key and tab stops, you can convert that text to a table. Select all the text; then choose Table I Convert Text to Table. Make sure the Convert Text to Table dialog box displays the correct Number of Columns entry and that Tabs is selected under Separate Text At. Click OK.

12

Entering and Editing Table Information

The table grid appears in your document with the insertion point in the upper-left table cell. To enter text in any cell, just type the text.

If your cell entry exceeds the current cell width, Word automatically wraps the cell text within the cell. This capability alone makes a table easier to use than tab stops. You don't have to worry about entries that are too long to work with the tab stops. In fact, you can even press Enter within a table cell to force text to wrap to the next line.

After you finish each cell entry, you can press Tab to move to the next cell to the right, or to the first cell in the next row if you're finishing the entry for the rightmost cell in the row. Alternately, you can press an arrow key to finish your entry and move to another cell. Finally, you can click any table cell to place the insertion point in it and type the cell entry.

Figure 12.2 illustrates the initial entries in a new table. After you finish making the last entry in the lower-right table cell, click outside the table or press an arrow key to finish. (If you press Tab after making the last cell entry, Word adds another row to the table.)

FIGURE 12.2

Type an entry in each table cell, and then press Tab or an arrow key to move on.

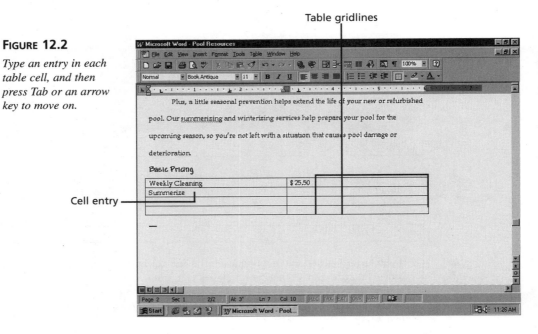

To make a change to an entry in a table cell, click in the cell. You can then use the Backspace, Delete, and other keyboard keys to make changes to the text. You can double-click a word in the table cell to select it, and then press Delete to delete the word. In short, most of the editing techniques you use elsewhere in a Word document also work within a table cell.

Selecting Table Cells

Unlike clicking to place the insertion point within a table cell for editing, selecting the table cell highlights the entire cell. After you highlight one or more table cells, you can press Delete to delete the contents of all those cells, add or remove cells in the table, or format those cells. Use one of these techniques to select table cells:

- Drag over a contiguous group of cells to highlight them.

- To select a row, point to the far-left side of the row until the mouse pointer arrow tilts to the right. Click the mouse to select a single row, or drag down to select multiple rows.

- To select a column, point to the top of the column until the mouse pointer changes to a down-pointing arrow, and then click. Drag to the right to select multiple columns.

- To select the entire table, click any table cell and then choose Table | Select Table.

Deleting and Adding Table Cells

If you're creating a large table, you might not have estimated the number of rows or columns you needed correctly. Or, you might find that you need to insert or delete a cell somewhere within the table. Depending on whether you're working with a few cells or entire rows and columns, the technique for adding and deleting cells differs slightly.

Use these steps to add or delete selected cells in a table:

To Do: Removing or Adding a Few Table Cells

1. Drag to select the cells you want to remove or the cells currently in the location where you want to insert new cells.

2. Right-click the selection; then click Delete Cells or Insert Cells. Either the Delete Cells or Insert Cells dialog box appears.

3. If you're deleting cells, choose either Shift Cells Left or Shift Cells Up to tell Word how to move remaining table cells to fill in the area formerly occupied by the deleted cells. If you're inserting cells, choose Shift Cells Right or Shift Cells Down to tell Word how to move existing table cells to make room for the new cells.

4. Click OK to finish the deletion or insertion.

In contrast, follow these steps to delete or add a new row or column in the table:

To Do: Deleting or Adding a Table Row or Column

1. Select the row or column you want to remove or the row or column that occupies the location where you want to insert a new row or column.

2. Right-click the selection to display a shortcut menu, as shown in Figure 12.3.

3. Click Delete Rows (or Delete Columns, if you selected a column) to remove the selection from the table. Click Insert Rows (or Insert Columns, if you selected a column) to add a new row or column at the selection location.

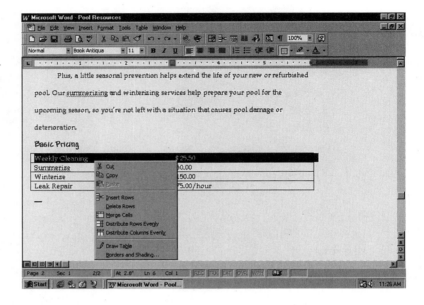

FIGURE 12.3

Right-click a selected row or column; then choose Insert Rows (or Columns) to add a row or column or Delete Rows (or Columns) to remove the selection from the table.

Formatting Tables

Most of the formatting techniques you learned about in the last hour work for tables, as well. Select the table cells with the contents you want to format; then use the buttons on the Formatting toolbar to choose another font, apply attributes, change how the information aligns in the table cells, and so on. You also can use the Format | Font and Format | Paragraph commands to apply formatting for the table text.

Similarly, you can format the border used for the table gridlines or apply shading to table cells. Just select the cells you want to format, and choose the Format | Borders and Shading command. The settings you make on the Borders and Shading tabs apply to the selected cell(s).

By default, each table you insert spans from margin to margin in your document. Based on the table entries you make, you might find that you need to make a column wider or narrower, or adjust the height of a particular row. To change column width or row height, select the row(s) or column(s) you want to adjust. Choose Table | Cell Height and Width to display the Cell Height and Width dialog box. On the Row tab, open the Height Of drop-down list, and choose Exactly; then enter a measurement in the At text box. On the Column tab, adjust the measurements in the Width Of and Space Between Columns text boxes; then click OK to apply your settings.

If you don't need a precise column width, you can drag to resize table columns. Point to the gridline between columns until the mouse pointer changes to a double-headed arrow with a double vertical bar; then drag the column border until it's the width you want (see Figure 12.4) and release the mouse button.

FIGURE 12.4

Resize table columns by dragging the column border until the vertical guideline reaches the desired width.

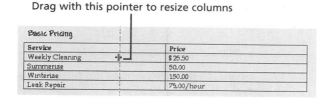
Drag with this pointer to resize columns

To save you all this work, though, Word provides the Table AutoFormat feature. Table AutoFormat provides a collection of predefined formatting settings to a table, so you can dress up the table without having to make multiple selections or later remember what settings you chose. Follow these steps to apply an AutoFormat to a table:

To Do: AutoFormatting a Table

1. Click any cell in the table.
2. Choose Table | Table AutoFormat. The Table AutoFormat dialog box appears.
3. Scroll down the Formats list; then click the format you want to use. The Preview area at the right shows how the selected AutoFormat looks, as shown in Figure 12.5.

FIGURE 12.5

Choosing an AutoFormat enables you to apply a variety of formatting settings at the same time.

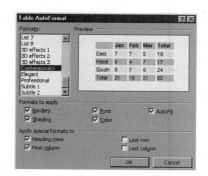

4. In the Formats to Apply area, click to remove any checks beside settings from the Auto Formatting that you do not want to apply.

5. In the Apply Special Formats To area, be sure to click to check any part of the table to which you want to apply specialized formatting. For example, in most tables, you want to call attention to the first row or Headings Row, which typically contains labels that identify the column contents. If your table totals information, you might also want to check Last Row to apply special AutoFormatting to the last row in the table.

6. Click OK to apply the selected AutoFormat to the table.

An AutoFormat you apply overrides any formatting you previously applied to the table. Therefore, if you want to improve on any of the formatting from an AutoFormat, make your changes after you apply the AutoFormat.

Because a table can call such attention to the information in a document and because AutoFormatting applied to a table can look so dramatic, think about using tables in cases when you otherwise wouldn't. For example, rather than simply entering a bulleted list of brief items, enter the list in a table. Instead of burying statistics in paragraph text, pull them out into a table.

Formatting a Document in Columns

When you want to use a smaller font to cram more information on a page, you should break the text into multiple columns; the shorter column width makes each line easier to read in the small font.

In Hour 4 you learned that you can display the text in a Works Word Processor document in multiple columns. You can do the same in Word, but you have more control. You can format all of a document with multiple columns. You can format part of a document in one column, part of it in two columns, and so on. Position the insertion point where you want new column settings to take effect; then specify how many columns Word should use.

Follow these steps to divide text into multiple columns within a Word document:

To Do: Creating Columns in Word

1. Choose View | Page Layout. You need to be working in Page Layout view to see the results of your column choices.

▼ 2. Click to position the insertion point where you want to begin dividing text into columns.

3. Choose Format | Columns. The Columns dialog box appears.

4. In the Presets area, click one of the multiple column designs. Alternatively, change the Number of Columns text box entry to specify the number of columns you want to use.

5. If you want the columns to be uneven in width, click to clear the Equal Column Width check box; then edit the settings for each column in the Width and Spacing area.

6. Open the Apply To drop-down list and choose whether the new column settings should apply to the Whole Document or apply from This Point Forward.

7. Click to check Line Between if you want Word to display and print a line between each column.

8. If you want Word to move the text after the insertion point to the top of a new column (rather than the top of the first column), click to check Start New Column.

9. When the Preview area shows the column look you want, click OK to apply the settings. Figure 12.6 illustrates column settings in the Columns dialog box and how they look in the preview and when applied in the document.

FIGURE 12.6

In this case, the top of the document uses one column and the body uses three columns with lines between them.

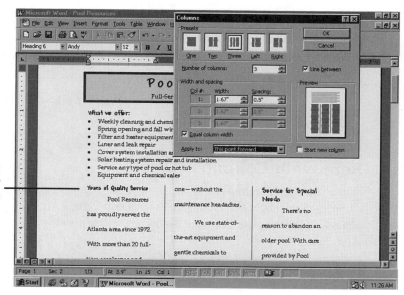

This was clicked before the new column settings were specified

12

Manually Inserting a New Column Break

Often, you need to control when text from one column wraps to the next column. For example, let's say you have text that's divided into three columns. A heading appears near the bottom of the second column, and you'd prefer that the heading instead move to the top of the third column for a neater appearance.

To insert a *column break*, which bumps all text following the column break to the top of the next column, follow these steps:

To Do: Using a Column Break to Balance Columns

1. Click to position the insertion point where you want the new column to start.
2. Choose Insert | Break. The Break dialog box appears.
3. Click Column Break, as shown in Figure 12.7.
4. Click OK.

FIGURE 12.7

Use this dialog box to insert a column break.

To remove a manual column break, click to position the insertion point at the beginning of the new column where the break takes effect; then press Backspace.

> As in the Works Word Processor, you can press Ctrl+Enter to insert a page break wherever you need one, even within columns.

Removing Columns

When you want to remove columns from your document, it's easiest to remove all the columns in the document. To do so, choose Edit | Select All. Then choose Format | Columns to display the Columns dialog box. Click the One design in the Presets area; then click OK.

Summary

This Hour showed you how to organize and highlight document information using tables and columns. You learned to insert a table with as many rows and columns as needed, how to enter and edit table text, and how to add and remove table cells. You also learned to format the table contents and table grid, and to add and remove columns within a Word document. The next hour shows you how to improve your document formatting using templates and styles.

Q&A

Q. How do I create a table?

A. Click where you want the table to appear; then click the Insert Table button on the Standard toolbar. In the grid that appears below the button, click the cell that identifies the number of rows and columns for the table. The table appears with the insertion point inside each cell. Type each cell entry, pressing Tab or an arrow key to complete the entry.

Q. What's the fastest way to format a table?

A. Apply a Table AutoFormat. Click any cell in the table; then choose Table | Table AutoFormat. Click the style you want to use in the Formats list, specify any other options as needed, and then click OK.

Q. How do I create columns in Word?

A. Click where you want the new column settings to start; then choose Format | Columns. Click a Preset; then choose This Point Forward from the Apply To drop-down list. Choose any other column options you want, and then click OK.

12

HOUR 13

Using Templates and Styles to Save Time

Each of us tends to develop certain preferences for dealing with our documents. You might like to use a specific font for document headings or body text, or use certain paragraph alignment settings. Word offers techniques you can use to save and reuse your favorite formatting—styles and templates.

You'll save many hours in the future after you teach yourself to

- Understand when to use a style and when to use a template.
- Select and fill in a template to create a new document.
- Modify a template style or develop and save your own style.
- Make a new template from an existing one.
- Create your own template.
- Design a Web page.

Understanding Templates and Styles

Every Word document—even a blank one—has a template that controls the document's formatting and other aspects of the document. A template can contain the following:

- Styles   A *style* is a named formatting setting that you can apply to any paragraph. The style specifies such formatting as the font and font size, alignment, and line spacing. The "Formatting with the Formatting Toolbar" section in Hour 11, "Formating Word Documents," explains how to choose a font from the Style drop-down list on the Formatting toolbar.

- Page Formatting   The template might use particular margins or include a header or footer, for example.

- Content   Templates can offer standard text and graphics. They also can contain stored AutoText entries.

- Automation   Templates can include custom menus, toolbars, and other special features. Although this book won't teach you how to create and work with automated features, you might encounter them when you use templates in the future.

You can create a new document by choosing a template to serve as the basis for that document. That new document then contains the styles, page formatting settings, content, and automation stored in the template. For example, if you create a document based on one of Word's memo templates, the new document contains special styles such as the DOCUMENT LABEL and COMPANY NAME styles. It includes text specified by the template, such as the TO and FROM lines. It also includes prompts that you can click and then type in your new text, which automatically appears in the right position with the right style.

So, in essence, to format an entire document, you use a template. To format a specific paragraph, you use a style.

A blank document you create by clicking the New button on the Standard toolbar uses the Normal.dot template. (Even though you won't typically see filename extensions, Word templates use the .dot extension, whereas documents use the .doc extension, which Word adds automatically when you save a document.) The Normal template offers a number of predefined styles, including the Normal style for default text and three heading styles.

Creating a New Document Using a Template

The best time to choose a template is when you create a new document. The templates that come with Word save you some work by entering the starter content from the template. Choosing the template from the start also ensures that you'll be using relatively harmonious formatting for the text in the new document. You can use the template's styles as you go, rather than go back and create the styles and formatting for your document after you enter its content.

Follow these steps to create a new document from a template:

To Do: Making a New Document with a Template

1. Choose File | New (Ctrl+N). You *cannot* click the New button to choose a template other than the default one. The New dialog box appears.

2. Click a tab in the dialog box to select a template category.

3. Click the template you think you might want to apply. If it includes a preview image, it appears in the Preview area at the right side of the dialog box, as shown in Figure 13.1.

Preview of selected template

FIGURE 13.1

Choose a tab in the dialog box, and then select the icon for the template you want to use.

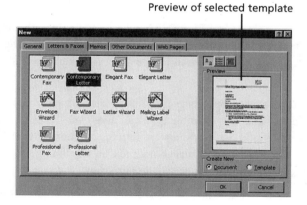

4. After you select the template you want, click OK to open a new document that uses the design, content, and so on for the template.

You also can simultaneously start Word and select a template to create a new document. Click the Start button on the Windows taskbar, and then click the New Office Document choice near the top of the Start menu. The New Office document dialog box that appears looks nearly identical to the New dialog box shown in Figure 13.1. Select the template to use as just described in Steps 2 through 4. Word opens and creates a new document based on the template.

13

You can apply a different template to a document after you've created it. To do so, choose Tools | Templates and Add-Ins. Click to check the Automatically Update Document Styles check box, and then click the Attach button. Select the new template in the Attach Template dialog box, and then click Open. Click OK back at the Templates and Add-Ins dialog box to apply the new template.

Just be aware that choosing a new template doesn't always translate smoothly, especially if you try to switch from, say, a fax template to a résumé template. In such a case, the document usually retains the content from the original template (including any text you changed or added), but uses the styles from the newly applied template.

Filling in Template Placeholders

Most users jump right into entering text after creating a new document based on a template. Most of the templates that come with Word offer not only starter text such as labels, but also prompts and placeholder text that show you where to enter your unique information and how the template will format the text based on the template's styles.

The template prompts appear in square brackets and begin with the phrase Click Here. The rest of the prompt describes what to enter in that location. Click one of those prompts to highlight it, as shown in Figure 13.2, and then type the text specified by the prompt.

You have to edit other placeholder text, such as the Company Name Here title that appears in Figure 13.2. For example, you can drag over the placeholder document title, and type your own title. Unless you start getting into more advanced Word skills, you'll probably just enter this kind of placeholder text in any templates you create, rather than set up a Click Here prompt, a more challenging task.

Review the placeholder text near the body area of the template-based document to learn more about how to use the template and to check whether the template you've selected offers any special features.

At some point after you start entering content into your template-based document, make sure you save and name the new file as described in "Saving and Closing a File" in Hour 10, "Building Documents with Word 97."

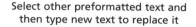

Select other preformatted text and
then type new text to replace it

FIGURE 13.2

*A document created
from a template pre-
sents placeholders to
prompt you to fill in
your own text.*

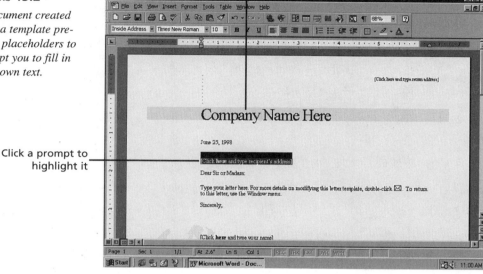

Click a prompt to
highlight it

Editing a Style

You're not stuck with all the styles offered in a particular template. If you like most of a
template's styles but would prefer to change the font, size, or other formatting used by a
particular style, Word enables you to do so. For example, you might want to make text
formatted with the Normal style slightly larger, so it's easier to read. You also can choose
whether to change the style for the current document only or to add the style change to
the template.

Follow these steps to edit a style:

To Do: Changing a Style

1. Choose Format | Style. The Style dialog box appears.
2. Click the style that you want to modify in the Styles list at the left side of the dialog box. Information about the style's formatting settings and a preview of the style
   appears at the right side of the dialog box.
3. Click the Modify button to display the Modify Style dialog box.
4. Click the Format button (see Figure 13.3), and then click the command for the
   type of formatting you want to alter. For example, you can click the Font choice

13

to display the Font dialog box. Make your changes in the applicable dialog box, and then click OK to apply them. Use as many other choices from the Format button menu as needed to update the style. It's OK to experiment until you're satisfied. Just check the Preview area of the Modify Style dialog box to see the impact of a formatting change, and then change it back if needed.

FIGURE 13.3

Use the Format button in the Modify Style dialog box to specify which aspect of the style you want to modify.

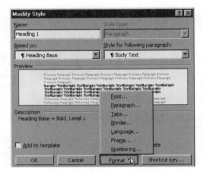

5. After you modify the style formatting as needed, decide whether you want to check the Add to Template check box. Doing so tells Word to apply your style change to both the current document and the template you used to create the document. Leaving the check box empty applies the style change in the current document only.

6. If you want to be able to change the style (in the current document only) without displaying the Modify Style dialog box, you can click to check the Automatically Update check box. Then, when you apply new formatting to any paragraph in the document that uses the selected style, Word updates the style to use the new formatting.

I tend not to check the Automatically Update check box, especially if I'm going to share my file with someone else. If that person accidentally formats a paragraph using a style that automatically updates, he could be stuck with an ugly document and might not know how to fix it. It's also very easy to change a style inadvertently with Automatically Update on. Then you might have to go back and re-create the style from scratch, requiring you to recall the settings you used to create the style.

7. Click OK to close the Modify Style dialog box.

8. Click Apply to close the Style dialog box and apply the newly changed style to the paragraph that holds the insertion point.

▼

9. You can continue working with the document, and then save and close it. If you checked the Add to Template check box as described in Step 5, Word displays a message box asking whether you want to save your changes to the document tem-

▲   plate. Click Yes to do so and finish closing the document.

Creating Your Own Style

At some point, you'll be fiddling with the formatting in a document and realize that you really like the look of a particular heading or paragraph. You can use the example you've already created as a model for a new style, without in any way having to go back through all the settings you've applied.

To save a new style from an example in your document, follow these steps:

To Do: Using Example Formatting to Create a New Style

1. Select the paragraph that has the formatting you want to save as a style.
2. Choose Format|Style. The Style dialog box appears.
3. Click the New button. The New Style dialog box appears, as shown in Figure 13.4.

Example text on which new style is based

FIGURE 13.4

Use the Name text box of the New Style dialog box to name the style you're creating.

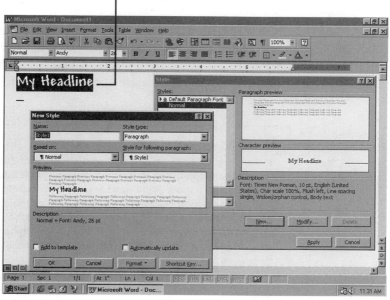

13

▼

4. Enter a name for your new style in the Name dialog box.

5. Check the Add to Template check box to add the new style to both the current document and the template you used to create the document. Leaving the check box empty creates the new style in the current document only.

6. If you want to be able to change the style (in the current document only) without displaying the Modify Style dialog box, you can click to check the Automatically Update check box. Then, when you apply new formatting to any paragraph in the document that uses the new style, Word updates the style to use the new formatting.

7. Click OK to close the New Style dialog box.

8. Click Apply to close the Style dialog box and apply the newly changed style to the paragraph that holds the insertion point.

9. You can continue working with the document, and then save and close it. If you checked the Add to Template check box as described in Step 5, Word displays a message box asking whether you want to save your changes to the document template. Click Yes to do so and finish closing the document.

▲

Creating a New Template from an Existing Template

Say that you like the design for one of Word's templates, or a template that you or a colleague has created, but you would prefer that the template contain some different starter text. In such a case, you can basically copy an existing template, make changes to it, and then save it under a new name.

Although you can open any template and change it, it's not a good idea to modify any of the templates that come with Word. If you modify one of Word's templates but then for some reason decide you need the original template formatting, you'd have to rerun Word's Setup program and reinstall the templates. Ouch! For this reason, I only show you how to create a copy of that template and modify and save the copy. (You also could copy an original template file from another user's machine to your own. Look for template files in the subfolders of the \Program Files\Microsoft Office\ Templates folder.)

When you're ready to create a modified version of an existing template, try these steps:

To Do: Basing Your New Template on an Existing One

To Do

1. Choose File | New. The New dialog box appears.

2. Click a tab to select a template category, and then click the icon for a template on the tab. Check the Preview area to verify that you've selected the correct template.

3. In the Create New area below the Preview, click the Template option button.

4. Click OK to close the New dialog box and open a new template file based on the original. Word displays *Template1*, *Template2*, or so on in the title bar to tell you that you're currently working with a template file rather than a document file. Word uses the temporary name with the number until you save the template under a new name as described later in these steps.

5. Make any changes you want to the template's styles and page formatting, contents, or automation features.

6. Choose File | Save (Ctrl+S) or click the Save button on the Standard toolbar. The Save As dialog box appears. In this case, the Save As Type choice has been set to Document Template and then disabled. This is because Word only enables you to save the template file as a template.

7. (Optional) You can store the new template in a particular template category so that it appears on the tab for that category in the New dialog box. In the Save As dialog box, double-click the folder that corresponds to the desired tab or category where you want to include the new template.

> If you save your template to a folder other than the one Word suggests by default (\Program Files\Microsoft Office\Templates) or one of the category folders within that folder, you won't be able to use the New dialog box to apply your new template. For easy access to your new template, save it in the default folder (which is selected in Figure 13.5) or one of the category folders in Figure 13.5.

13

8. Click in the File Name text box, and type a name for the new template.

9. Click the Save button to save the template.

10. Choose File | Close to close the template. The next time you choose File | New, you'll be able to choose the template and use it for a new document.

Folders correspond to
New dialog box tabs

FIGURE 13.5

When you save a file opened as a template, you can only save it as a template.

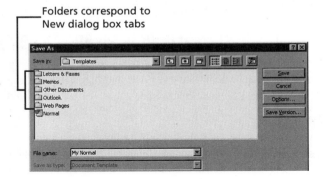

Saving Your Own Work as a Template

For some of us, creating a new template and then using it to build a document might be putting the cart before the horse. Instead, you might enter a document's text, alter its styles and other formatting, and only then realize that the document would make a perfect template. Shoot!

Don't worry. You can save a document that you've created as a template so that you can reuse the information and styles. Follow these steps to save a document file (.doc file) as a template file (.dot file):

To Do: Creating a Template from a Document

1. Choose File | Save As. The Save As dialog box appears.
2. Open the Save As Type drop-down list, and then click Document Template, as shown in Figure 13.6. The Save In list automatically changes, selecting the default templates folder (\Program Files\Microsoft Office\Templates) for you.

FIGURE 13.6

Use the Save As Type drop-down list to save an existing file as a template.

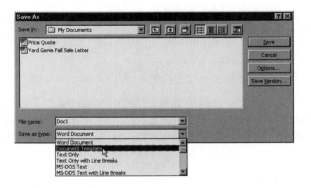

▼ 3. (Optional) To store the new template in a particular template category so that it appears on the tab for that category in the New dialog box, double-click the folder that corresponds to the desired tab.

4. Click Save.

5. Choose File | Close to close the template. The next time you choose File | New,
▲ you'll be able to choose the template and use it for a new document.

Using the Web Page Wizard to Create a Web Page

Word 97 provides tools to help you create your own pages to display on the World Wide Web. Although the specifics of adding a Web page to a Web site are beyond the scope of this book, you can experiment with Word's Web tools and consult other resources to learn how to post your work.

| Web page files use the HTML file format. |

Word by default offers a couple of unexciting Web page templates that you can use to get started. But it also offers the Web Page Wizard, which you access just like a template. The Web Page Wizard enables you to choose a layout and a design for your new Web page.

Follow these steps to use the Web Page Wizard and create an HTML document:

To Do: Creating a Web Page in Word

1. Choose File | New. The New dialog box appears.

2. Click the Web Pages tab to display Word's Web template offerings.

3. Click the Web Page Wizard icon, and then click OK to start the Wizard.

4. If Word displays the Connect to the Internet dialog box, you can click Yes to launch your Web browser, connect to the Internet, and display a Web page from which you can download additional Web templates and graphics. (If you do so, you might have to restart the Wizard). To proceed with the Wizard, click No.

5. You can use the first Web Page Wizard dialog box that appears to select the layout for the Web page. The layout provides placeholder text for different elements such as the title, body text, tables, hyperlinks, and so on. It also specifies the relative position of each element. Click a layout in the list, and Word displays the layout

▼

To Do (sidebar)

13

▼   design, as shown in Figure 13.7. After you view different layouts and select the one
           you want, click Next to continue.

FIGURE 13.7

*First choose the page
layout to use for your
Web page.*

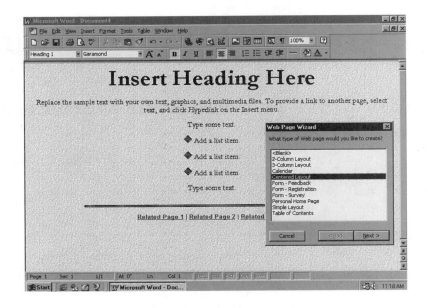

> Check out the right half of the toolbars in Figures 13.7 and 13.8. When
> you're working with a Web page, Word displays its new Web tools. Again, I
> can't cover the full scope of Word's Web tools in this book, but you won't
> do any harm by experimenting on your own with the new tools that appear
> as you work. But, for example, the Standard toolbar offers a Picture button
> (seventh from the right) for inserting a graphic onto the page. The
> Formatting toolbar offers the Background button (second from right) for
> choosing an attractive page background.

6. The next Web Page Wizard dialog box lists different styles or designs for your
   page. The design controls the fonts, background colors, graphics, and other
   aspects of the page appearance. Click a design to see how it looks, as shown in
   Figure 13.8. When you've selected the design you want to use, click Finish.

7. Choose File | Save or click the Save button on the Standard toolbar. (Although you
   could wait to save the file, some operations require you to save and name the Web
   page first, so you might as well do so right off the bat.) By default, the Save As
▼   dialog box displays HTML Document as the Save As Type choice, so you don't

have to change that setting. Instead, type a new document name in the File Name text box, and click Save.

FIGURE 13.8

Then choose a pleasing design.

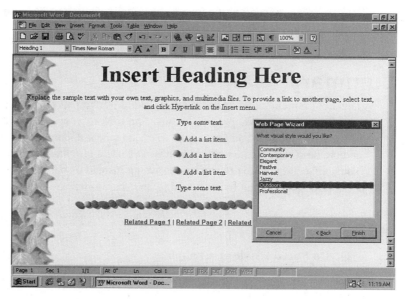

8. Edit and format the page text as needed. You also can insert Clip Art images or other types of graphics.

9. Most of the Web page layouts include hyperlink placeholders formatted in blue, with underlining. See the Related Page 1 link near the bottom of Figure 13.8 for an example. If you want to replace a placeholder with a link to another page on your Web site, first drag over the link text, and then type a new name for the link. For example, if you're creating a link to Microsoft's home page, type `Microsoft Home Page`. Right-click the link placeholder, and then click Hyperlink. In the Insert Hyperlink dialog box, type the link address (such as `http://home.microsoft.com`) in the Link to File or URL text box, and then click OK to close the dialog box.

See Part III in this book, "Late Afternoon Online—Internet Explorer and Outlook Express," for more information about the Internet, Web browsing, hyperlinks, and other facets of the online world.

10. Click the Save button on the Standard toolbar to save your finished page.

11. Choose File | Close to close the file. You can then copy (post) the file to the appropriate folder on your Web site.

13

You can save any Word file as a Web document (HTML file). To do so, choose File | Save As HTML. In the Save As HTML dialog box, HTML Document appears as the Save As Type choice. Enter a name in the File Name text box, and then click Save to save the file.

Summary

This hour concluded your self-study of Word 97. You've taught yourself how styles and templates can help you provide a consistent look to your documents and to create documents more rapidly. You know how to create a new document based on a template, edit and create styles, create new templates, and use a template wizard to create a Web page. You can spend the next two hours browsing instead of building—in the next sections you learn how to go on the Internet to find and share information.

Q&A

Q. Do I need a style or a template?

A. A style contains formatting for a paragraph, including such things as font size and line spacing. To format a paragraph, choose a style from the Style drop-down list at the left end of Word's Formatting toolbar. A template provides even more document creation help. Each template offers styles and page formatting, and can include starter text and automation tools. Every document uses a template—blank documents use the Normal.dot template. However, you can select another template to create a new document with more styles and content.

Q. OK then, how do I use a template to create a new document?

A. Choose File | New (Ctrl+N). Click a tab in the dialog box to select a template category. Click the template you think you might want to apply. If it includes a preview image, it appears in the Preview area at the right side of the dialog box. When you've selected the template you want, click OK to open a new document that uses the template. Click a prompt in the document to select it, and then type new text. Alternatively, drag over plain placeholder text, and then type your replacement text. From there, you can edit, format, and save the new document as needed.

Q. What's the fastest way to create my own style?

A. Do it by example. Format some text with the style settings you want, and then select the text. Choose Format | Style. The Style dialog box appears. Click the New button. In the New Style dialog box, enter a name for your new style in the Name dialog box. Select the Add to Template check box or the Automatically Update check box. Click OK to close the New Style dialog box. Click Apply to close the Style dialog box. If you chose the Add to Template check box, when you close the document, Word displays a message box asking whether you want to save your changes to the document template. Click Yes to do so and finish closing the document.

13

PART III

Late Afternoon Online— Internet Explorer and Outlook Express

Hour

HOUR 14

Preparing to Go Online

The first time I set up a computer to connect to the Internet, I struggled for two hours or so to get the connection to work and then it was an unreliable beast. Microsoft had a choice: either make it easier to go online, or start doling out sedatives with every copy of Windows. Microsoft chose the former path, including more help and automation with the second release of Windows (called OSR2) and now, Windows 98. Windows 98 makes it much easier to set up your connection to the Internet.

In this hour, you use Windows 98's features to get your system ready to connect to the Internet. You'll accomplish the following:

- Get motivated to log on to the Internet to see what it offers.
- Use Windows 98 to create a connection to the Internet and find a service provider, if needed.
- Dial and hang up your Internet connection.
- Clear up problems with your connection.

Looking at What You Can Do Online

The *Internet*, that worldwide network of computers that you can dial into with your computer's modem, serves as a repository and exchange medium for an astounding amount of information. In many professional and educational settings, you can't compete without Internet skills. Likewise, more and more folks connect to the Internet at home. Some estimates say that at least 20 percent of us go online at least once a week—based on my personal experiences, I'd say that number is even higher.

Most of us use the Internet in three ways (although the Internet offers other functions, too):

- Finding information on the Web   The *World Wide Web* (or just the *Web*) organizes information in graphical *Web pages*. You can search for and find a Web page providing information about virtually any topic, from personal finance help to online job listings to recipes for meals. The Web offers games you can play, files you can download, and news and informational magazines you can read. Because it fills a variety of business, computing, entertainment, and other needs, the Web continues to emerge as the most important resource on the planet.

- Exchanging *electronic mail (email)*   Even though it's not instantaneous, email messages transmitted over the Internet arrive much more quickly than letters sent via U.S. mail (snail mail). Email enables you to ask questions and receive responses with more immediacy. It also enables you to attach and send files of various types, such as a photo of your kids or a spreadsheet with important calculations.

- Reading and posting news   The Internet also offers Usenet *newsgroups*, areas where users with common interests can read and post public messages. Each newsgroup holds postings about a particular topic, such as a software program or a popular music group. Newsgroups enable you to interact with and meet other people around the world.

You view Web pages using *Web browser software*, also called simply a *browser*. Similarly, you use *email software* to send, receive, and store email messages. A year or two ago, you had to obtain separate *news reader software* to work with newsgroups, but now some browsers and email programs include newsgroup capabilities. The next two hours in this book cover how to use a browser and read email and news.

With Windows 98 and Works Suite 99, you have almost everything you need to begin using the Web. Windows 98 features Internet Explorer 4.0 (Microsoft's latest Web browser software) and Outlook Express (an email program that also enables you to read newsgroups and more) already installed for you. If you don't have Windows 98, Works Suite 99 includes Explorer 4.01 and Outlook Express, and you can run these programs with Windows 95. See Appendix C, "Installing Works Suite 99," to learn how to install those applications with an older version of Windows.

Hours 15 and 16 introduce you to the basics of using Explorer and Outlook Express. The rest of this hour helps you lay the groundwork for connecting to the Internet.

Creating Your Internet Connection

The browser and email software you use doesn't connect directly with the Internet. Instead, it relies on the Windows Dial-Up Networking software, which dials your computer's modem and connects your computer with an *Internet service provider (ISP)* computer. Dial-Up Networking uses a communication method (protocol) called TCP/IP to exchange information with the ISP.

ISPs generally charge a flat monthly fee for Internet access, which includes a main Internet account (used for Web browsing), as well as an email account and access to newsgroups. The ISP provides you with the information that Dial-Up Networking needs to connect to the Internet. Windows 98 provides the *Internet Connection Wizard (ICW)*, which leads you through the process of setting up a Dial-Up Networking connection to use to connect with your Internet account from your ISP.

If you've already installed software for using Internet email and newsgroups—Outlook Express, in this case—you've already completed a lot of the work. Then, Windows 98's ICW can automatically set up Outlook Express to connect with your ISP's *mail servers* (systems that traffic and store email) and your ISP's *news server,* which provides access to newsgroups.

If your ISP provides setup software, chances are that software will set up an Internet connection for you. The Microsoft Network (MSN), for example, provides setup software. Use Windows 98 ICW if your ISP doesn't provide setup software. If Explorer 4.0 and Outlook Express have already been installed on your computer, you can simply skip installing the ISP's setup software.

14

Before you can dial into the Internet, you need to use the ICW to set up your Internet connection (that is, a Dial-Up Networking connection for dialing your Internet account) whether or not you already have an account with an ISP. If you don't have an account, the ICW can help you find one. The rest of this section describes each scenario.

This book shows you how to use the Windows 98 Internet Connection Wizard. Likewise, Windows 95 offers an ICW, which works much like the one described here. After you start the Windows 95 ICW, follow the wizard's instructions to set up your connection.

This book also assumes that your computer's modem is correctly set up under Windows 98. See Windows 98's online help if you need to learn how to set up a modem.

One last note: If you've set up multiple users under Windows 98 or use a program such as Compaq's Homebase to set up multiple users, so each can log on to his own unique desktop, you need to run the ICW for each desktop. For example, say you have two users—Lisa and Steve—set up under Windows 98. First log on as Lisa and run the ICW to set up her Internet connection on her desktop. Then log on as Steve and run the ICW to set up his connection on his desktop.

If You Already Have an Internet Account

The ICW asks you a series of questions about your Internet connection. You supply the answers, and the ICW saves the connection for later use. If you already have an account, your ISP should have provided the following information, which you in turn need to supply to the ICW:

- Username and password   Your ISP provides these when you create your account. Your username might be some variation on your own name, or it might be a random alphanumeric combination.

- ISP phone number   This is the number you dial to connect and log on (not the number you called to set up your account). Make sure your ISP provides a local number. If you have a notebook computer and plan to connect to the Internet while you travel, also make sure you get a toll-free number. You can re-run the ICW and set up a separate connection for dialing the toll-free number.

- Internet email account information   You need to provide your email address. In addition, you need to identify the ISP's server for incoming mail, called a POP3 server, as in *pop.myisp.com*. You also need to identify the ISP's server for mail you're sending, called the SMTP server, as in *mail.myisp.com* or *smtp.myisp.com*. Your ISP also should tell you whether or not your email account name and password are the same as your overall Internet account's username and password.

- Internet news account information   Generally, you need to specify only the name of your ISP's news server, as in *news.myisp.com*.

After you have your account information, follow these steps to use the ICW:

To Do: Setting Up a Connection to Your Existing Internet Account

1. Double-click the Connect to the Internet shortcut on the desktop (see Figure 14.1). Or, choose Start|Programs|Internet Explorer|Connection Wizard.

FIGURE 14.1

Double-click this desktop shortcut to launch the Internet Connection Wizard.

If you haven't yet set up your Internet connection, the ICW also starts if you double-click the Internet Explorer icon (Windows 98) or Internet icon (Windows 95) on the desktop.

2. In the first Internet Connection Wizard dialog box that appears, click the second option button, I Have an Existing Internet Account Through My Phone Line or a Local Area Network (LAN). Then click Next.

3. In the next dialog box, leave the top option button selected. That option button tells the ICW that you want to connect to the Internet through your ISP. Click Next.

4. In the next dialog box, titled Set Up Your Internet Connection, leave the Connect Using My Phone Line option button selected, and then click Next.

5. The Dial-Up Connection dialog box appears. Leave the Create a New Dial-Up Connection option button selected, and then click Next. The Phone Number dialog box appears (see Figure 14.2).

FIGURE 14.2

After you make a few preliminary selections, the ICW begins prompting you to enter information about your connection, such as your phone number.

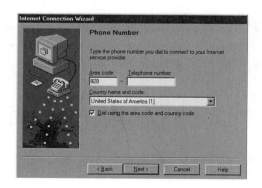

14

▼ 6. Enter the number to use to dial your ISP account in the Telephone text box. If your computer can always dial the call as a local call, you can click to clear the check beside Dial Using the Area Code and Country Code. Click Next.

7. The next dialog box prompts you to enter your username and password. Enter them in the User Name and Password text boxes, as shown in Figure 14.3; then click Next.

FIGURE 14.3

Tell the ICW what username and password your ISP has assigned to your account using this dialog box.

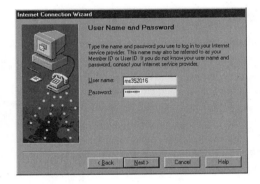

8. The next dialog box, titled Advanced Settings, asks whether you want to manually specify any advanced settings for your connection. Because doing so is unnecessary, leave the No option button selected, and then click Next.

9. The Dial-Up Connection Name dialog box asks what name you want to assign to your dial-up connection. Type the name you want in the Connection Name text box (see Figure 14.4), and then click Next.

FIGURE 14.4

Type a name for your Internet connection in this dialog box.

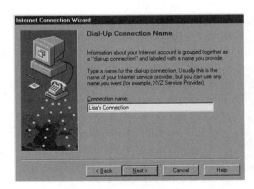

10. The next dialog box asks whether you want to set up your Internet mail program (Outlook Express) to send and retrieve your email. Leave the Yes option button selected, and click Next.

▼

If you previously ran the ICW and set up your mail and newsreader programs, the ICW might not ask you to do so again. In which case, you can
skip any of the following steps that don't apply.

11. The Your Name dialog box appears. It asks you to enter a *display name*, the name
    that identifies you when you send messages. (This is not your username or email
    address.) Type the name you want to use in the Display Name text box, and then
    click Next.

You don't have to enter your real name or full name. You can enter a nickname or "handle," instead, if that's how you prefer to be identified when
corresponding.

12. In the next dialog box, enter your actual email address in the E-Mail Address text
    box, and then click Next.

13. The next dialog box (see Figure 14.5) asks you to specify the names for your
    ISP's mail server. Enter the POP3 server's name (as in pop.myisp.com) in the
    Incoming Mail (POP3 or IMAP) Server text box. Enter the SMTP server (as in
    mail.myisp.com or smtp.myisp.com) in the Outgoing Mail (SMTP) Server text
    box. Click Next.

FIGURE 14.5

*Enter the names for
your ISP's Internet
mail servers here.*

14. The Internet Mail Logon dialog box appears. In most cases, leave the Log On
    Using option button selected. Then enter your email username (which is either the
    same as the username for your overall Internet account or is the portion of your

▼ email address that appears prior to the @ symbol) in the POP Account Name text box. Then enter your email password in the Password text box; this password might or might not be the same as the one used for your Internet account. Click Next.

15. If you want to give a friendly name or nickname for your Internet email account, enter it in the Internet Mail Account Name text box of the dialog box labeled Friendly Name. Click Next.

16. In the Set Up Your Internet News Account dialog box, leave the Yes option button selected, and then click Next.

17. Another dialog box titled Your Name appears. Enter a *display name*—the name that identifies you when you post news messages. (Most people use a nickname rather than a username or email address.) Type the name you want to use in the Display Name text box, and then click Next.

18. In the Internet News E-Mail Address dialog box, enter your actual email address in the E-Mail Address text box. This address enables other users to reply to you via email in response to messages that you post in a newsgroup. After you make your entry, click Next.

19. The Internet News Server Name dialog box appears. Type the name of your ISP's news server (as in news.myisp.com) in the News (NNTP) Server text box. If your ISP requires you to log onto its news server, also click to check the My News Server Requires Me to Log On check box. Click Next.

20. If you want to give a friendly name or nickname for your Internet news account, enter it in the Internet News Account Name text box of the dialog box labeled Friendly Name. Click Next.

21. Most users can leave the No option button selected in the Set Up Your Internet Directory Service dialog box. (You need to select Yes only if your ISP provides an LDAP account—for directory service—and you signed up for one.) Click Next.

22. In the Complete Configuration dialog box, click Finish to finish setting up your Internet connection. The ICW closes, and you should be ready to log on to the
▲ Internet.

If You Need an Internet Account

If you live in a larger city, you can find an ISP in your area simply by looking up Computers—Internet Access Providers (or a similar category) in the yellow pages. If your area doesn't have any local ISPs, or if you travel and want a regional or national ISP that provides access numbers in a number of cities, you need a different way to find an ISP.

The ICW can connect you to the Microsoft Referral Service, which lists ISPs. To use the ICW to find an ISP and set up your Internet connection, grab your credit card, and then follow these steps:

To Do: Using ICW to Sign Up for and Set Up an Internet Connection

1. Double-click the Connect to the Internet shortcut on the desktop. Or, choose Start|Programs|Internet Explorer|Connection Wizard.

2. In the first ICW dialog box that appears, leave the top option button, I Want to Sign Up and Configure My Computer for a New Internet Account, selected. Click Next.

3. In the next ICW dialog box, enter the correct code in the Area Code text box; then click Next.

4. After your computer dials the Referral Service, it displays a list of ISPs that offer service in your area, as shown in Figure 14.6.

Select an ISP here...

FIGURE 14.6

The Microsoft Referral Service connects you with a number of ISPs, so you can select one to use.

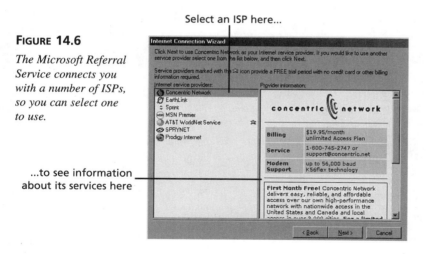

...to see information about its services here

5. Click an ISP from the Internet Service Providers list at the left. Information about the ISP appears in the Provider Information list at the right.

6. When you find the ISP you want to work with, make sure you click its name in the Internet Service Providers list. Then, click Next to continue.

7. Follow the onscreen instructions for establishing your account. After your account is established, the ICW leads you through the process of setting up the connection, as described previously in the section, "If You Already Have an Internet Account."

14

Dialing Your ISP, If Needed

Generally, when you start Internet Explorer or Outlook Express, those programs find your Internet connection and either dial it automatically or prompt you to confirm that you want to connect.

There might be instances where you need to dial your connection manually, however. For example, you might want to test your connection, or you might be disconnected without being prompted to reconnect.

If you need to dial your Internet connection, follow these steps:

To Do: Dialing Your Internet Account

1. Double-click the My Computer icon on the desktop, and then double-click the Dial-Up Networking icon. Or, choose Start|Programs|Accessories|Communications|Dial-Up Networking.

2. Double-click the icon for the connection you want to dial (see Figure 14.7).

FIGURE 14.7

You can double-click the icon for an Internet connection to dial that connection.

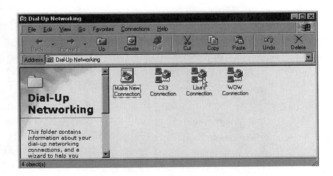

3. In the Connect To dialog box that appears, click the Connect button. Your modem dials your ISP and transmits your log-on information.

4. If the Connection Established dialog box appears, review the information it presents, and then click Close to close it.

Closing the Connection, If Needed

In Explorer 4.0 and Outlook Express, you can *work offline*. This means that after you download certain Web pages, newsgroups, or your email messages to your computer, you

▼   can disconnect from the Internet and read that information. In each of these programs, you choose the File|Work Offline command to go offline. In addition, however, you need to hang up your Internet connection manually. You also might need to hang up your connection manually, for example, if you simply dialed it to test your connection.

Follow these steps to hang up your modem and disconnect from the Internet:

To Do: Hanging Up Your Internet Connection

1. Double-click the small Internet Connection icon in the system tray area of the taskbar (see Figure 14.8).

FIGURE 14.8

Double-click the icon that looks like two small computers to display information about your connection or to disconnect from the Internet.

Internet Connection icon

2. In the Connected to (Connection Name) dialog box that appears, click the Disconnect button. Your modem hangs up, and the connection icon disappears from the tray.

▲

Troubleshooting Your Connection

You try to connect to the Internet, and get a message that Windows can't find your modem, can't make a Dial-Up Networking connection with your ISP, or something else. Or, your connection is slow or unreliable and disconnects just before you finish receiving that big email. Bummer.

Don't despair. Windows can give you some help. Click Start, then click Help. In the Windows Help window, click the Contents tab at the left; then click the Troubleshooting topic. Click Windows 98 Troubleshooters, and then click Modem in the list that appears. As shown in Figure 14.9, you can simply click the option button beside the description of the problem you're having and then click Next to continue. Follow Help's lead through a series of questions and actions to (I hope) fix the problem.

Another possibility is that you haven't provided quite enough information for your Internet connection to work correctly. Some ISPs require that your Dial-Up Networking

14

connection give an *IP (Internet Protocol) address* or *Domain Name Service (DNS) server address* to log on. These addresses identify your ISP's servers on the Internet. IP and DNS addresses always have four sets of 1–3 numbers each, separated by periods, as in 207.69.160.185. Most ISPs automatically (dynamically) assign an IP address to your system when you log in; however, if your ISP doesn't dynamically assign addresses, you do need to specify one for your connection. In contrast, many ISPs do require that you specify your ISP's Domain Name Service (DNS) server address to connect. If either of these addresses is missing but your ISP requires them, your computer won't be able to connect with the ISP.

FIGURE 14.9

Use the Window's Help system's troubleshooters to fix connection problems.

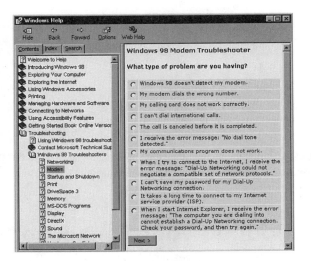

When you're using the ICW as described earlier in the section, "If You Already Have an Internet Account," you can choose Yes in step 8 and then click Next to tell the ICW that you want to specify advanced settings for your Internet connection. Then, the ICW prompts you to enter more specific settings for the connection, such as the type of connection (generally a PPP account), the IP address, and the DNS address. Follow the wizard's onscreen instructions to specify the appropriate information.

You can manually adjust your existing Internet connection to give the appropriate IP and DNS addresses. To do so, follow these steps:

To Do: Updating Your Dial-Up Internet Connection with IP and DNS Addresses

1. Double-click the My Computer icon on the desktop, and then double-click the Dial-Up Networking icon. Or, choose Start | Programs | Accessories | Communications | Dial-Up Networking.

2. Right-click the icon for the connection you want to adjust, and then click Properties in the shortcut menu.

3. Click the Server Types tab.

4. Near the bottom of the tab, click the TCP/IP Settings button. The TCP/IP Settings dialog box appears.

5. To designate a specific IP address to use, if required, click the Specify an IP Address option button. Then, enter the address to use in the IP Address text box.

> When you enter an IP or DNS address, you must type the periods, where needed, to separate the groups of numbers in the address.

6. To designate one or more DNS addresses to use, click the Specify Name Server Addresses option button. Then, enter an address in the Primary DNS text box. You also can enter an additional address in the Secondary DNS text box.

7. Click OK to close the TCP/IP Settings dialog box.

8. Click OK again to close the dialog box for the connection and apply the new settings. The connection should now work, and work reliably.

> If your connection still doesn't work after you specify the IP and DNS addresses, check to make sure your modem line is firmly plugged in at the back of the computer and at the wall jack. Also make sure that others in the household are staying off the telephone.

14

Although it's not as common as it used to be, you might encounter situations where you just can't get your Internet connection to work reliably. If you've made attempts to fix it on your own and have worked with your ISP's tech support department, but still can't get it to work, the culprit may be your modem. You can check your modem's operation by choosing Start|Settings|Control Panel from the Windows taskbar. Double-click the Modems icon in the Control Panel window; then click the Diagnostics tab in the Modems Properties dialog box. In the list on the tab, click the port the modem uses, and then click the More Info button. After a few moments, the More Info dialog box will tell you how the modem responded to a number of commands. If you see a lot of error messages in the Response column, the modem might not be operating correctly. Some older modems or modems from lesser-known manufacturers might not connect reliably with your ISP, even if the modem checks out as OK. (I know, because it happened to me.) The only remedy for an unreliable connection might be to replace your modem with one from a more well-known manufacturer such as 3Com, Boca Research, Motorola, or U.S. Robotics.

Summary

You've just spent a valuable hour preparing your system to connect with the Internet. You've created a Dial-Up Networking connection (your Internet connection), to dial into and connect with your account at an Internet service provider.

The next two hours show you how to put that connection to good use, using Internet Explorer 4.0 to find information on the Web and Outlook Express to work with private email or public newsgroup messages.

Q&A

Q. How do I start the Internet Connection Wizard?

A. Double-click the Connect to the Internet shortcut on the desktop. Or, choose Start|Programs|Internet Explorer|Connection Wizard.

Q. How do I find an ISP?

A. Start the Internet Connection Wizard; then in the first ICW dialog box that appears, leave the top option button, I Want to Sign Up and Configure My Computer for a New Internet Account, selected. Click Next. Select the ISP you want from the Internet Service Providers list that appears, and then click Next and continue with the onscreen instructions to find and set up an ISP.

Q. If I already have an ISP, how do I set up my connection?

A. Start the Internet Connection Wizard, and then in the first ICW dialog box that appears, select the second option button, I Have an Existing Internet Account Through My Phone Line or a Local Area Network (LAN). Click Next, and supply the wizard with the information it prompts you for.

Q. What do I do to dial my connection, if I need to?

A. Double-click the My Computer icon on the desktop, and then double-click the Dial-Up Networking icon. Double-click the icon for the connection to dial.

Q. How do I hang up if I need to?

A. Double-click the Connection icon in the system tray at the right side of the taskbar, and then click the Disconnect button.

14

Hour 15

Exploring the Web with Internet Explorer 4.0

Explorer 4.0 hangs some new features on its time-tested framework. Designed to help you find information on the World Wide Web even more easily, Explorer works well on its own or in concert with the Windows 98 desktop.

Spend the next hour getting acquainted with Explorer and the World Wide Web and learn how to

- Start Explorer and begin viewing Web pages.
- Display Web pages using different techniques.
- Search for a Web page that has information you need.
- Save a file from the Web to your hard disk.
- Customize Explorer for a better browsing experience.
- Exit the Explorer program when you finish surfing.

Launching Internet Explorer

When you need to connect to the Internet and begin viewing Web pages, you can start Internet Explorer 4.0. Use one of these three techniques to start the program:

- Double-click the Internet Explorer icon on the desktop (see Figure 15.1).
- Choose Start | Programs | Internet Explorer | Internet Explorer.
- Click the Launch Internet Explorer Browser button on the Quick Launch toolbar on the taskbar (see Figure 15.1).

FIGURE 15.1

The desktop offers multiple ways to launch Internet Explorer.

Double-click this icon...

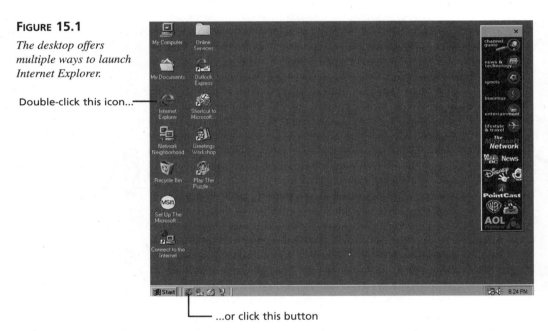

...or click this button

After you start Internet Explorer, it dials your Internet connection and logs on if it's set up to do so automatically. Otherwise, the Dial-Up Connection dialog box appears to ask you to verify that you want to dial your Internet Connection. Click the Connect button to dial your Internet account and log on. (If you have trouble connecting, see "Troubleshooting Your Connection," at the end of Hour 14, "Preparing to Go Online.")

If you click to check the Connect Automatically check box in the Dial-Up Connection dialog box, in the future Explorer will dial your Internet connection without displaying the Dial-Up Connection dialog box to prompt you.

After your system connects to the Internet, Explorer displays a *start page*—the first page from the Web that your browser is set up to display each time you log on to the Internet. By default, Explorer displays the page shown in Figure 15.2 as its start page.

FIGURE 15.2

Explorer displays this start page by default when you connect to the Internet; from here, you can display other pages on the Web.

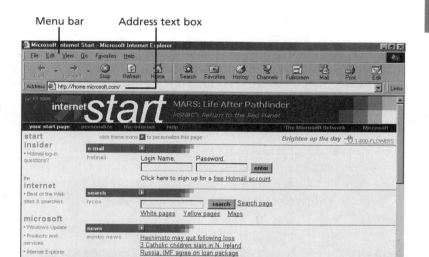

Menu bar   Address text box

Status bar

Browsing the Web

Web browsing—moving from page to page on the Web—provides an experience like reading through a newspaper. You can scan through the headlines, begin reading the story you want, and skip to a later page for more in-depth coverage. Along the way, you'll spot photos, graphs, and other graphics that illuminate the information or provide a bit of entertainment.

You can use a number of techniques to display a different Web page, described next.

Using Web Links

Web pages display information and graphics, and also offer *links* (or *hyperlinks*) to other Web pages. Click a link to display the page it represents (also called following the link). Both text and graphics on a Web page can serve as links, so Web page designers usually use special formatting for links on a page. For example, a text link usually appears with a color that differs from the rest of the text on the page, or is underlined. It might also have a special font. A button or graphic link might have a special border, or a label that cues you to click it.

> If you click a link to display a particular page and then go back to the page that holds that link, the used link appears in a different color or perhaps includes a border so that you can tell which links you've already selected.

You can tell whether highlighted text or a graphic represents a link by using the mouse. Point to the information that you think represents a link. The pointer changes to a hand when it's over a link. The status bar at the bottom of the Explorer window displays the Web address (or a shortcut for that address) that the link represents, as in Figure 15.3. For linked graphics, a pop-up description might also appear.

Enter URLs here

FIGURE 15.3

When you point to a link, the mouse pointer changes to a hand and the link address appears in the status bar.

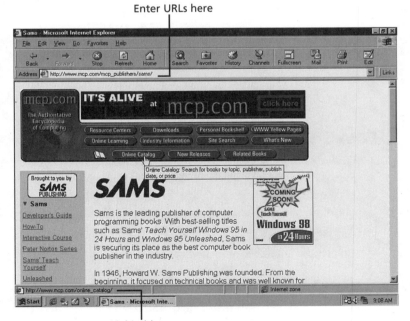

Link address

15

 If Explorer loads the start page first, then what's a *home page*? Home page can be used as another name for start page. In addition, a home page is the main page of an individual's or organization's Web site. The home page typically gives you information about the site and includes links to other pages in the site.

Using URLs

Web pages are special files stored on Web server computers connected to the Internet. Because the Web consists of so many computers, it uses a special method to identify each Web page file. Each Web page has a *Web address* called the *Uniform Resource Locator (URL)*. Each Web URL (typically pronounced "Earl") consists of a few parts:

- Content Identifier   The content identifier at the beginning of each URL, `http://` identifies the address as a Web address.

- Web site   The next part of the URL identifies the Web site—the location on a particular computer connected to the Web. Examples include `www.microsoft.com` or `espn.sportszone.com`. The Web site name can begin with `www`, `home`, or nothing at all. Likewise, the site name can end with `.com`, `.org`, `.net`, or other extensions, as in `www.mcp.com` or `www.circle.net`.

- Directory and Filename   As with files stored on your computer, Web computers organize files in directories (folder), by file (page) name. Use forward slashes to separate folders, as in /nba/. For some addresses, the filename, as index.htm, is optional. The filename can end with a number of different extensions: `HTM`, `HTML`, `ASP`, and so on.

A full Web address looks like this: `http://espn.sportszone.com/nba/index.html` or `http://home.microsoft.com/exploring/exploring.asp`.

To display a particular Web page by entering its URL, follow these steps:

To Do: Displaying a Page by Entering Its URL

▼To Do

▲

1. Click in the Address text box at the top of the Explorer window. This highlights (selects) the entire URL it holds.

2. Type the URL for the page you want to display, such as `http://home.microsoft.com/exploring/exploring.asp`. You must type the site name, directory, and page name exactly—including using forward slashes, no spaces, correct capitalization, any special characters like a hyphen or tilde (~).

3. Press Enter.

Explorer no longer requires you to type the content identifier (http://) portion of the URL in the Address text box. You can simply type an address, as in www.fortune.com. When it displays the page, however, Explorer does display the full URL in the Address text box.

After you display the page you want, click the Print button on the Explorer toolbar to print it.

Moving Back and Forward

Browsing definitely involves jumping around between pages. For example, you can follow a link or go to a particular URL and find out the page doesn't include the information you were looking for. At that point, you might want to redisplay the previous page and try another link it offered.

You can use the Back and Forward buttons on the Explorer toolbar to display pages you've already seen. Here's how to use these buttons:

- Point to the Back button to see a pop-up description of the previous page; then click the button to display that page.
- Click the Back button additional times, as needed, to display earlier pages.
- After you use the Back button one time, the Forward button becomes active (meaning it's no longer grayed out). Point to the Forward button to see a pop-up description of the next page, and then click the button to display that page.

By default, Explorer displays Microsoft's home page, http://home.microsoft.com, as the start page. To go back to the home page from any other page, click the Home button on the Explorer toolbar.

If you've been online for some time, however, it's too slow to click the Back or Forward button several times, because Explorer tries to reload each page. Explorer offers a couple of different methods you can use to return to a page you've previously visited, without

15

having to back up page by page or remember and enter an URL. To redisplay a Web page, use one of these techniques:

- Click the drop-down list arrow at the right end of the Address text box, and click the URL you want to display.

- Click the drop-down list arrow beside either the Back or Forward button (see Figure 15.4), and, in the list that appears, click the title of the page you want to redisplay.

- Click the History button on the Explorer toolbar to display the History list at the left side of the screen. Click an URL to display the pages on that site that you've visited; then click the name of the page you want to display. You can click the History button again to hide the History list.

FIGURE 15.4

You can use either the Back or Forward button drop-down lists or the History list to return to a Web page.

Click to display a list
of pages to revisit

Click to display or
hide the History list

Click to display
a page

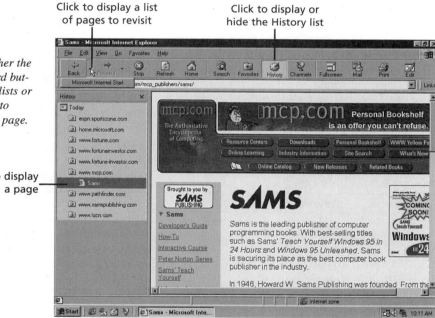

The Back and Forward buttons (and their drop-down lists) track only pages you've displayed during your current work session on the Web. In contrast, the History list tracks pages you've visited in the last 20 days, by default.

Stopping and Refreshing

Even though the Web isn't a living, breathing being, it is organic in the sense that it grows, changes, and evolves daily. People add and remove pages, move them to other locations, and so on. (If you try a link and get an error message that the page no longer exists, you can simply back up to an earlier page.)

The Web also teems with traffic. The Web becomes more crowded at certain times of the day, usually late afternoon and early evening. If too many people try to display the same page at the same time, the Web can't handle the traffic and displays a message that the server is too busy. In other cases, the destination page simply never appears, although Explorer continues to try to access it. If the page doesn't appear or you click the wrong link, click the Stop button (Esc) on the Explorer toolbar to stop loading the page, and then try another link. Or, you can click the Refresh button (F5) on the Explorer toolbar to try a link again, or update the current page.

Performing a Search

There's probably a Web page for any topic you can think of. Trying to find the page you need by clicking endless links or guessing at URLs would progress as quickly as trying to find a particular blade of grass on a golf course. You can identify pages that cover a topic of interest using your choice of several search tools offered on the Web. Table 15.1 lists popular search tools, each of which is operated by an independent company, on the Web.

TABLE 15.1   WEB ADDRESSES FOR SEARCH TOOLS (SEARCH ENGINES)

Name	Address
Excite	`http://www.excite.com`
InfoSeek	`http://infoseek.com`
Lycos	`http://lycos.com`
Yahoo!	`http://yahoo.com`

According to experts at the NEC Research Institute, the Web now consists of more than 320 million pages, and the number of Web pages out there will increase by 1,000% during the next few years. Don't rely on search engines alone. The experts also estimate that the current search engines only catalog about 40% of the pages out there. Follow links between pages to explore on your own. Also look for pages that list links to numerous other pages about a topic; many helpful people out there gather and post such reference pages so you don't have to repeat their legwork.

After you display a search tool, you enter one or more *search words* (topics) and then begin the search. The search tool searches its directory of catalogued or registered pages and then lists the pages that include your search words. Usually, the listing includes a brief description of or excerpt from each page. Each page's URL appears so you can click the linked URL to display the page. Some tools group the search results listings in categories or try to rank how likely each page is to provide the information you need.

> A search tool might enable you to perform a second, more targeted search within the listed pages only. Or, it might list links to other pages similar to one listed in the search results. Browse around as needed, but be aware that search tools can't keep up with the Web's changes, so you might encounter a lot of bad links or missing pages. You can always click the Back button to return to the search results list.

You can go directly to a search tool by entering its URL. Or, you can use the Search button on the Internet Explorer toolbar to display a search tool. The following steps illustrate how to display a search tool and perform an example search. (Keep in mind that each search tool looks and works a bit differently.)

To Do: Searching for Information on the Web

1. Click the Search button on the toolbar. The Search list appears at the left side of the screen, suggesting a search tool for you to use (see Figure 15.5). Each time you click the Search button, Explorer displays a different search tool, so you might not see the one shown in Figure 15.5. You always can click the Choose a Search Engine link to display a list of other search tools, and then click the tool you want to use.

2. To see the search tool better, right-click the title bar for the Search list, and then click Open in Window. Internet Explorer opens a separate window so you can see the search tool and its results more clearly.

3. Click in the text box displayed by the search tool, and type your search words. For example, type recipes. If you enter more than one search word, as in *vegetarian recipes*, most search tools list Web pages that contain any of the search words.

4. Click the button that starts the search, which will be named something like Search, Go Get It, or Search Now.

5. The search tool might prompt you to provide more information. For example, if you use Lycos to search for *recipes*, Lycos displays its Recipedia page. Enter another search word to help narrow the search in the text box provided, and click

▼

the button provided to search again. For example, you could enter vegetarian in the text box on Lycos' Recipedia page, and then click Go Get It.

FIGURE 15.5

The search tool initially appears in the pane at the left.

Enter search words here

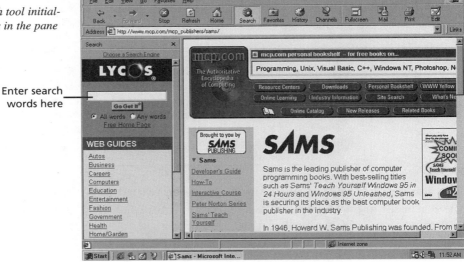

To display only pages that contain all the search words you enter, type quotation marks around the search words or use a plus sign or AND between them, as is *"vegetarian recipes"*, *vegetarian+recipes*, or *vegetarian AND recipes*. (Alternatively, the tool shown in Figure 15.5 enables you to click an option button to search for pages that include All Words—all the search words you entered—or Any Words.) Then, the search results will list pages that better match your needs.

6. As shown in Figure 15.6, the search tool lists matching entries. From there, you can browse around. Click a matching page's link to display that page. Click the Next Page link (or Next 10 or similarly named link) to display additional matching entries. The page also provides a link for returning to previously listed entries. In addition, you can click a link to matching or similar categories of entries, if the search page offers such links.

7. After you finish working with the search results, you can simply display other Web pages. You also can click the window Close (X) button to close the separate window you opened for the search tool in Step 2.

▼

FIGURE 15.6

Search tools list links to pages that include or cover the search words you specified.

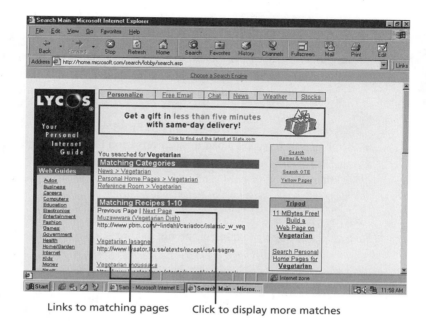

Links to matching pages   Click to display more matches

From time to time, Internet Explorer might display a Security Alert dialog box. When it appears, click Yes to continue working.

Transferring Files to Your Hard Disk

Many Web sites offer free files that you can *download* (transfer over your Internet connection) to your computer, save on your hard disk, and use at your leisure while you're working offline. For example, you might find articles, research documents, software, sound files, graphics, and other types of files available for download. Software publishers such as Microsoft also offer software patches that update a program or fix small bugs.

Before you begin downloading, though, be aware of these issues:

- A file you download might carry a computer *virus* program, which could damage your Windows software or other files. If you plan to download files often, you should purchase and install an antivirus program such as McAfee VirusScan, Thunderbyte Antivirus, or Norton Antivirus.

- Most software on the Web is *shareware*. If you plan to use the software after you test it out, you need to send a modest payment to the shareware author. Please pay your shareware fees to support the folks who write and distribute shareware.

- When you download a program, make sure you understand whether you're down-loading the final version or a beta (test) version of the software. Betas can work unreliably, cause your system to crash or even write over crucial files shared by your Windows applications. Use caution before you install any beta, and make sure you back up your Windows system files and other crucial files before you install a beta.

- You should assume anything you download is copyrighted and protected by law. You can save or download most information for your personal use, but you can't use it for commercial purposes without permission from (and often payment to) its author, creator, or publisher.

Web pages generally display a link or a button that you click to download the specified file. After you click a download link, Explorer uses a communication method called *FTP* (*file transfer protocol*) to transfer the file to your system from the Web site. Follow these steps to download a file:

To Do: Downloading a File

1. Display the Web page with files you want to download. For example, you can go to `http://www.greetingsworkshop.com/isapi/addonpks/clipart.gww` to download free clip art images to use with Greetings Workshop. (You might need to navigate through pages with categories of files to display the page with the actual link to the file to download.)

2. Click the link or download button for the file you want to download.

3. If a page prompts you to review a software license agreement, review the informa-tion and click I Agree to continue.

4. In the File Download dialog box that appears, leave the Save This Program to Disk or Save This File to Disk option button selected, and then click OK.

5. Open the Save In list in the Save As dialog box that appears and click the disk to which you want to save the file. In the list of folders that appears, double-click the folder in which you want to save the file (and repeat to save to a subfolder, if needed).

6. If needed, edit the entry in the File Name text box to use another name for the file.

7. Click Save. The File Download dialog box informs you of the download's progress and the download time remaining (see Figure 15.7).

8. After the entire file is transferred, a message box informs you that the download is complete. Click OK, and continue working on the Internet.

FIGURE 15.7

Downloading a file transfers it from a Web site to a folder on your computer's hard disk.

 You can save Web page graphics to your hard disk, and then use them in your Works or Word documents. To try to save a graphic or picture, right-click it, and then click Save Picture As. Use the Save In list to choose the disk to save to, and then click Save. Or, right-click the picture and click Set As Wallpaper to use it on your Windows desktop. As noted earlier, assume that images you save are copyrighted and use them for personal (fun) purposes only.

Streamlining Internet Explorer

You can customize many aspects of Internet Explorer 4.0's appearance and behavior. Although I don't have time in this hour to cover all the possibilities, I can take a few moments to identify the most useful changes you can make.

Changing the Start Page

You might not want to start every Web browsing session by going to Microsoft's home page. You might prefer to display the day's business news, check out last night's sports scores, or go to a page on your company's Web site to check for news.

You can change the start page (or home page) that Internet Explorer displays when you first log on any time you want, or as frequently as you want. Follow these steps to select a new start page:

To Do: Selecting a New Start (Home) Page

1. In Explorer, display the page that you want to use as your new start page.
2. Choose View | Internet Options. The Internet Options dialog box appears, with its General tab selected.
3. In the Home Page area at the type of the tab, click the Use Current button to place the URL for the new start page (the page you displayed in step 1) in the Address text box. (Or, you can type the URL for any other page into the Address text box, although it's easier to just display a page first.)

▼
▲
4. Click OK to close the Internet dialog box and finish specifying the new start page. The next time you launch Internet Explorer and connect to the Web, that page displays first.

Adding and Displaying a Favorite

Although the History list remembers sites you visited more effectively than you can, the list can become long and unwieldy. Additionally, because History deletes pages you haven't visited in the last 20 days, you can't always rely on it to go back to a page you want. If you identify a page that's an important resource that you know you'll need to visit in the future, you can add it to your list of *Favorites*.

A *favorite* represents a Web page's URL. You can select the favorite to display the page. Explorer stores the favorites you mark on the Favorites menu or in the Favorites list that appears when you click the Favorites toolbar button.

Follow these steps to mark a favorite page:

To Do: Adding a Page to Your List of Favorites

1. In Explorer, display the page that you want to mark as a favorite.
2. Choose Favorites | Add to Favorites to display the Add Favorite dialog box.
3. Leave the No, Just Add the Page To My Favorites List option button checked.
4. Edit the entry in the Name text box to give the name you want to your favorite.
5. (Optional) To place the favorite in a folder that appears on the favorites list (enabling you to group similar favorites, such as all favorites related to finances or sports), click the Create In button, and then click the name of the folder to use. If you need to create a new folder to hold the favorite, click the New Folder button, type a name in the Folder Name text box, and then click OK.
▲
6. Click OK. Explorer adds the folder to the Favorites list.

To go to a favorite page in Explorer you can use either the Favorites menu or the Favorites list:

- Open the Favorites menu. If the favorite is in a folder, point to that folder to open it. Then click the favorite to display that page.
- Click the Favorites button on the toolbar. In the Favorites list at the left side of the screen, click the folder that holds the favorite, if needed (see Figure 15.8). Click the favorite you want to display the page it represents. Click the Favorites button again to close the Favorites list.

15

A folder I added,
with two favorites

FIGURE 15.8

You can click a favorite in the Favorites list to display the page the favorite represents; create folders to organize your favorites.

Other favorites

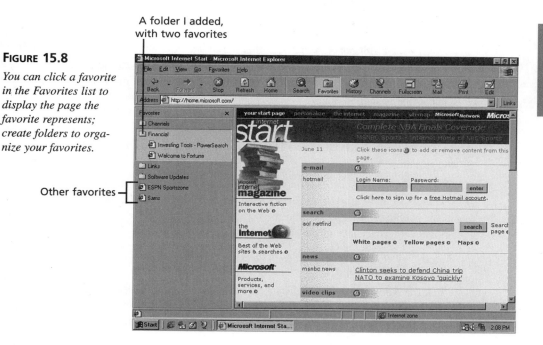

 You also can display a favorite from the Windows Start menu. Choose Start I Favorites. If the favorite is in a folder, point to that folder. Then click the favorite. Windows starts Explorer and connects to the Internet, if needed, and then displays the page.

Working with Channels

With Windows 98 and Internet Explorer 4.0, you can train your computer to retrieve Web content automatically—saving you the trouble of browsing and selecting pages—via *push technology*. Basically, this means that you select information that you want to receive regularly from a Web site (called *subscribing*). Then, each time you connect to the Internet and visit the channel, the Web site automatically downloads the content to your computer (so you can read it offline). Even better, most sites let you subscribe for free.

There's a lot you can do with subscribing to and using channels, so please consider the next few minutes an opportunity to get your feet wet with this exciting new technology.

Subscribing to and Viewing a Channel

Even though your Explorer bar appears to list a number of channels, the channels don't work until you subscribe to them. You have to manually subscribe to each channel you want to use, and specify what type of information to retrieve from that channel. Here's how to subscribe to a channel:

To Do: Setting Up and Using a Channel

1. In Explorer, click the Channels button. The Channels list appears at the left side of the screen.

2. Click one of the choices in the Channels list, such as Lifestyle and Travel. The channels in that category appear in the Channels list under the category name, and in the Web page that appears to the right. (If there's only one channel choice, it appears automatically to the right.)

3. Select a channel either by clicking it in the Channels list or by clicking the graphic for it in the Web page.

4. Click the Add Active Channel button (sometimes called the Subscribe button) in the Web page that appears for the channel. The Modify Channel Usage dialog box appears.

5. To fully subscribe to the channel so that it alerts you of updates and downloads its content to your computer, leave the bottom option button (Yes, Notify Me of Updates and Download the Channel for Offline Viewing) selected. (To learn what the other choices do, click the question mark button in the upper-right corner of the dialog box, and then click the option button.)

6. To control what should download when you log on, click the Customize button. The Subscription Wizard starts.

7. Make your choices in each Subscription Wizard dialog box, and then click Next to continue. The choices vary, depending on the kind of information the channel offers. Click Finish at the last wizard dialog box.

8. Click OK to Close the Modify Channel Usage dialog box and finish subscribing to the channel. The selected channel appears in Explorer, in Fullscreen view.

9. Click the Fullscreen button on the toolbar to return to the normal view of Explorer.

10. Work and browse as you'd like in Explorer.

15

A Web site needs to be specially programmed as an *active channel* to enable it to act as a channel. If you want to search for active channels to which you can subscribe, click the Microsoft Active Channel Guide at the top of the Channels list. Then, click the Search button on the page that appears at the right to begin your search.

After you subscribe to a channel, you can visit (display the Web page for the channel) to view it and download its content to your hard disk. Although viewing a channel might seem like viewing a Web page, the channel content you see is different from the home page for the Web site that offers the channel. Subscribing offers you more customized information than you'd get by browsing.

To display a channel (and download its information if you've subscribed fully), click the Channels button on the toolbar to display the channels list in the Explorer bar. Click the channel category that holds the channel to view, and then click the channel name. For example, Figure 15.9 shows the Microsoft Expedia Travel channel. You also can display a channel using the windows Start | Favorties | Channels submenu, or using Internet Explorer's Favorites | Channels submenu.

FIGURE 15.9

The channel that is clicked at the left appears in the pane at the right.

To manually update a subscribed channel and download its new information to your hard disk, choose Favorites | Update All Subscriptions in Explorer.

Working Offline

After you visit a channel and download its information to your computer, you can use Offline mode at any later time to review the information without being connected. This cuts down on the connect time you use (if you don't have unlimited access), or enables someone else in the household to log on to the account with another computer.

To work offline, click the Work Offline button in Dial-Up Connection dialog box that appears when you launch Internet Explorer. This starts Explorer without connecting to the Internet.

If your system is set up to dial your Internet connection automatically or if you know you'll want to work offline the next time you start Explorer, choose File | Work Offline to toggle that command on before you exit Internet Explorer for the day. Then, the next time you launch Explorer, it does not connect to the Internet. Instead, your start page (home.microsoft.com by default) appears and you can begin browsing your downloaded channel information or pages that have been stored in the History list (which means they've been downloaded to a History folder on your hard disk).

Then, you can click the Channels button and select a channel to which you've subscribed to view it. Alternatively, click the History button and select a page in History that you want to view. If you click a link that Explorer can't follow while it's offline (such as if the channel hasn't been updated recently, so that all its information isn't on your hard disk), the URL Not Found in Offline Mode dialog box appears. You can click the Connect button to connect and download the information, or click Stay Offline and view something else, instead.

To resume working online, choose File | Work Offline in Internet Explorer to toggle that command off. Explorer can connect to the Internet as it normally would the next time you start it or try to display another Web page.

Exiting Internet Explorer

Shutting down Internet Explorer 4.0 resembles shutting down other applications. To start the shut down process, choose File | Close or click the Close (X) button in the upper-right corner of the application window. The application window closes.

If you're working online, the Disconnect dialog box appears to ask you to verify that you want to hang up your connection to the Internet. Click Yes to hang up the modem and close the dialog box.

 Internet Explorer does have an idiosyncrasy. It tends to spawn or open multiple copies of itself when you display other pages. If this occurs, you'll need to use File | Close to close each instance of Explorer. When you close the final instance, it'll prompt you to hang up your Internet connection.

Summary

You've just spent the first of what will probably be many interesting hours exploring the Web and all its content. You learned both basic browsing steps and techniques that can save you legwork, such as creating a favorite—a shortcut to a favorite page. The next hour covers how to use email over the Web and how to work with Internet newsgroups using Outlook Express.

Q&A

Q. How do I start and exit Internet Explorer?

A. To open Explorer, double-click the Internet Explorer icon on the desktop or click the Launch Internet Explorer Browser button on the Quick Launch toolbar. If the Dial-Up Connection dialog box appears, click the Connect button to dial your Internet account and log on. To close Explorer, choose File | Close. If the Disconnect dialog box appears to ask you to verify that you want to hang up your connection to the Internet, click Yes.

Q. Who's this Earl guy everyone talks about, and what do I need to know about him?

A. "Earl" is actually the pronunciation for URL—Uniform Resource Locator. Each URL is the Web address for a Web page, as in `http://home.microsoft.com/exploring/exploring.asp`. To display a Web page using its URL, type the URL in Explorer's Address text box, and then press Enter.

Q. What's the most convenient way to display another page?

A. That depends on your preference. Casual users might just click underlined link text or linked graphics to browse from page to page. Or, if you know exactly what you want to view, type the URL in the Address text box, and press Enter. To revisit a page you've viewed recently, click the History button. In the History list at the left, click a Web site URL; then click the name of a page on that site to redisplay it.

HOUR 16

Using Email and More with Outlook Express

Email encourages communication. It eliminates the need to buy stationery and stamps, saves time for anyone who's a decent typist, and provides an easy way to share information with multiple people at the same time. Public newsgroups do the same—in addition to providing you a way to meet other people, explore varying opinions, and get referrals to resources you need.

Settle in for an hour or so to teach yourself about the online communication capabilities—email and newsgroup reading—of Outlook Express. You'll learn to

- Start and close Outlook Express.
- Make sure Outlook Express is set up to handle your email and newsgroups.
- Create and send your email messages.
- Respond to the messages you receive.
- Subscribe to newsgroups.
- Read a newsgroup posting, or post your own message.

Launching and Exiting Outlook Express

Before you can choose to send email or work with newsgroups, you need to open the Outlook Express program. To start Outlook Express, either double-click the Outlook Express shortcut on the desktop or click the Launch Outlook Express button on the Quick Launch toolbar on the taskbar. Note that you also can choose Start | Programs | Internet Explorer | Outlook Express.

> The first time you start Outlook Express, you have to specify a few settings. See the next section, "Setting Up for Email," to learn about these extra settings.

If the Outlook Express dialog box appears to prompt you to dial your Internet connection, select the connection you want to use from the Select the Connection You Would Like to Dial drop-down list; then click OK. Figure 16.1 illustrates the tools you can use to start Outlook Express and shows the initial Outlook Express window that appears.

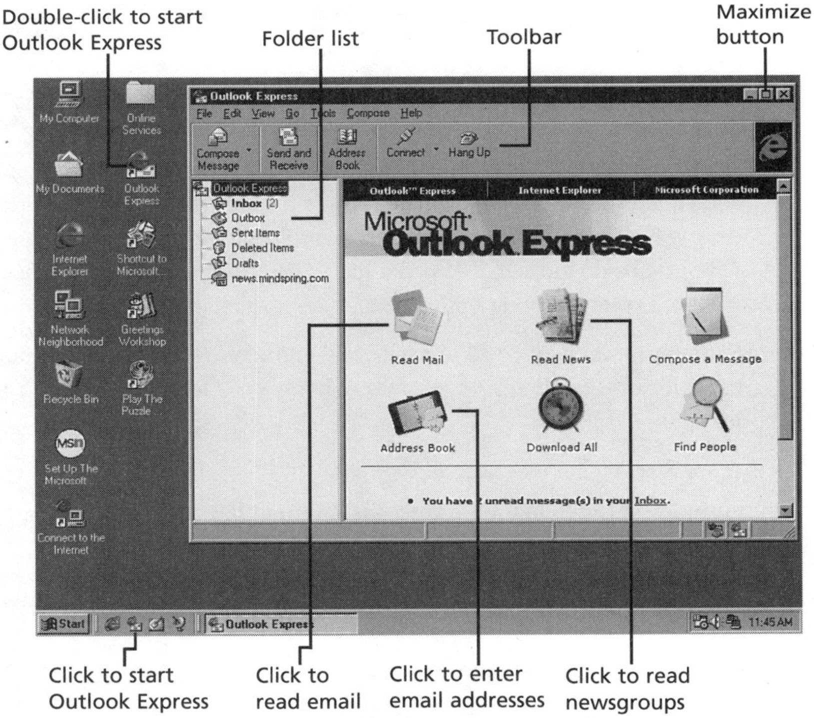

Double-click to start Outlook Express   Folder list   Toolbar   Maximize button

FIGURE 16.1

The desktop offers two ways to open the Outlook Express program, shown here in its window.

Click to start Outlook Express   Click to read email   Click to enter email addresses   Click to read newsgroups

You can click the Maximize button to expand the Outlook Express window to fill the desktop, if needed. Initially, the pane at the right side of the Outlook Express window displays large picture icons that you can click to choose what to do in Outlook. The folder list at the left shows a folder tree. You can click a folder to see what it contains; for example, you'll learn soon to go to the Inbox to review messages you've received.

To close the Outlook Express program when you finish working, choose File | Exit or click the Close (X) button in the upper-right corner of the Outlook Express window. If the Outlook Express dialog box appears to ask you whether to hang up your connection, click Yes to do so.

Setting Up for Email

The first time you start Outlook Express, the Browse for Folder dialog box might appear, as shown in Figure 16.2. (This dialog box always appears if you have more than one user set up under Windows 98.) Use the Browse for Folder dialog box to verify the folder in which Outlook Express should store your email messages. You can simply click OK to accept the suggested folder, or you can click another folder to select it before clicking OK. (Click the small plus beside a folder to display the subfolders it holds.)

FIGURE 16.2

If prompted, use this dialog box to select a folder to hold your email messages.

After you specify a folder to hold your messages, the Outlook Express dialog box appears. You use it to indicate which Internet connection Outlook Express should dial to connect to the Internet. Open the Select the Connection You Would Like to Dial drop-down list and click the name of the connection you want to use. If you want Outlook Express to always use that connection, click to check the Set as the Default Connection check box; if you don't check this check box, the Outlook Express dialog box appears every time you start Outlook to prompt you to choose a connection. Click OK to finish selecting the connection and continue. Your computer dials your Internet connection and logs on to the Internet.

If the Internet Connection Wizard didn't prompt you for mail account information, or if you later change Internet service providers, change your mail password, or want to change other mail information, you must change the corresponding settings in Outlook to ensure that it can retrieve your mail. To do so, choose Tools | Accounts. Click the Mail tab in the Internet Accounts dialog box; then click the name of your mail account, as in `pop.mindspring.com`, in the list. Click the Properties button to display a Properties dialog box for the connection. You can then change settings as needed. Most likely, you'll need to change entries on the General, Servers, and Connection tabs, changing such entries as the account name and log on password for your mail account. To review what specific entries mean, see "Creating Your Internet Connection" in Hour 14, "Preparing to Go Online." After you change the needed settings, click OK; then click Close to resume working in Outlook Express.

Working with Email

Some families find themselves moving every few years due to job changes, taking them hundreds of miles away from family, friends, and colleagues. While email isn't the same as being there, it sure provides a convenient, fast, and inexpensive avenue for sharing greetings, discussing plans, giving an update, or even passing along a photo snapped with a digital camera.

If you're like me, you might even find that email enables you to do a better job of staying in touch with others. This section shows you how to use Outlook Express to share your thoughts via Internet email and respond to news you hear.

Adding an Address Book Entry

So many millions of us are online now that it's often tough to get an Internet email address that sounds like plain English. Your cousin Dan's email address might be something like `z152man@myisp.com`, and your friend Sally's email address might be `slm7077@internet.net`.

Although it's certainly possible to type your recipient's Internet email address for each new message, it's more convenient to instead use the Outlook Express Address Book. The Address Book not only remembers cryptic email addresses for you, but also enables you to select each person's address by choosing their real name or a nickname rather than an address.

Before you jump into creating and sending email messages, you might want to take some time to add the addresses you'll be using to the Address Book, using this process:

To Do: Adding a Contact to the Address Book

▼ To Do

1. Choose Tools | Address Book (Ctrl+Shift+B); click the Address Book button on the Outlook Express toolbar, or click the Address Book icon in the right side of the Outlook Express window. The Address Book window opens.

2. Choose File | New Contact (Ctrl+N) or click the New Contact button on the Address Book window's toolbar. The Properties dialog box appears.

3. Type the parts of the recipient's real name in the First, Middle, and Last text boxes. You can then edit the contents that appear in the Display text box; the Display entry is the one that appears in your Address Book list. You also can enter a shorter nickname in the Nickname text box.

4. In the Email Addresses section of the dialog box, click the Add New text box, type the recipient's email address; then click Add. Figure 16.3 shows information entered for a new contact.

16

Addresses I've already added
to my Address Book

FIGURE 16.3

The Address Book captures a variety of information about a contact, including the contact's email address, so you can easily address messages.

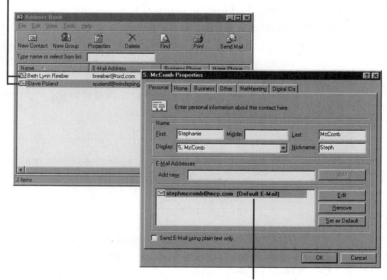

The new recipient's email address

5. (Optional) You enter additional information about the person on other tabs in the dialog box. For example, you can enter the person's home address, phone, and fax number on the Home tab.

▼ 6. Click OK to finish adding the new contact to the Address Book list.

▼ 7. Repeat Steps 2 through 5 to add the email addresses for more people to your
      Address Book.

   8. To close the Address Book window, choose File I Close or click the Close (X) but-
▲   ton at the upper-right corner of the Address Book window.

Creating and Transferring Messages

You've got news to share with a friend. You're working at home and need to send price
quotes to a colleague in another state. You read about a cool product in a magazine and
want to request more information.

When it's time to send an email message to handle such situations, follow these steps:

To Do: Sending an Email

   1. Choose Compose I New Message (Ctrl+N), click the Compose Message button on
      the Outlook Express toolbar, or click the Compose a Message icon on the right side
      of the Outlook Express window. The New Message window appears.

   2. The insertion point appears in the To text box by default. You can either type a
      recipient's email address in that text box, or click the small cardfile icon beside the
      text box to display the Select Recipients window, which lists your Address Book
      entries. To specify one or more recipients to whom you want to send the message,
      click each recipient's name in the list at the left; then click the To button. To send a
      carbon copy or blind carbon copy to one or more recipients, click the recipient
      name; then click the Cc or Bcc button to add it to the appropriate list. Click OK
      when you finish specifying recipients.

> When you use the Address Book entries to specify a recipient, the recipient's
> Display name appears in the To, Cc, or Bcc text box, not the recipient's email
> address.

   3. If you didn't use the Recipients window to Cc or Bcc other recipients, you can
      click the prompt that appears beside either the Cc or Bcc at the top of the New
      Message window, and type a recipient's email address.

   4. Click the prompt for the Subject line, and type the subject of your message.

   5. Click in the message area at the bottom of the window, and type the text of your
▼   message.

You also can drag over text in the message to select it; then use any of the buttons on the toolbar just above the message area to format the text. The Format menu offers even more options for jazzing up your message. However, your recipient must have an email program that supports message formatting, like Outlook Express, to see the special formatting.

6. If you want to attach a file to the message, choose Insert | File Attachment or click the Insert File button (it has a paper clip on it) on the window toolbar. In the Insert Attachment dialog box that appears, use the Look In list to select the disk and folder that holds the file you want to attach. When the file appears in the list in the dialog box, click the file; then click the Attach button. Repeat to attach additional files. A new pane opens in the message window, displaying an icon for each attached file.

7. When you finish creating your message, click the Send button at the left end of the toolbar at the top of the window. (Figure 16.4 shows a message that's ready to go.) Outlook Express dials your Internet connection, if needed, and transfers your messages.

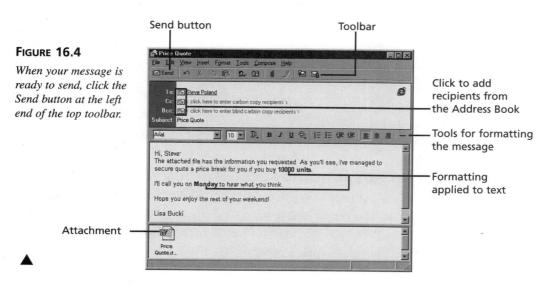

FIGURE 16.4

When your message is ready to send, click the Send button at the left end of the top toolbar.

If you want to go a step further with your email management, you can try these tips:

- After Outlook Express finishes sending your message, it doesn't hang up your Internet connection. However, you can set it up to do so. Choose Tools | Options. Click the Dial Up tab in the Options dialog box; then click to check the Hang Up

When Finished Sending, Receiving, or Downloading check box. If Outlook Express isn't dialing when you send messages, you also can check the Automatically Dial When Checking for New Messages check box. Click OK to close the dialog box and put your changes into effect.

- Outlook Express enables you to use stationery to decorate a message (assuming your recipient's email program can handle such decoration). To create a new message with stationery from the Outlook Express window, choose Compose | New Message Using to display a submenu of stationery choices. Click the stationery you want to use, and then address and send the message as usual. To apply stationery to a message in the message window, choose Format | Apply Stationery to display the stationery choices; then click the one you want to use. Figure 16.5 shows the message from Figure 16.4, this time with stationery applied.

FIGURE 16.5

Stationery applies an attractive background, and sometimes special font formatting, to a message.

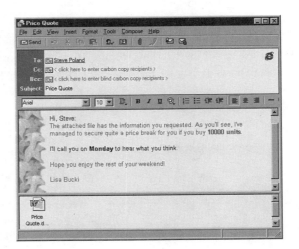

Reading and Responding to Messages

When you click the Send button to send a message, Outlook Express not only sends your outgoing messages but also checks your ISP's mail server for messages addressed to you and transfers any incoming messages to your Outlook Express Inbox folder. If you don't have a new message to send but want to check for incoming messages, click the Send and Receive button on the Outlook Express window's toolbar. Outlook Express connects to the Internet, if needed, and then transfers your incoming email and hangs up if you've set it up to disconnect automatically.

When you have new email, you'll see a little envelope icon in the system tray area at the right end of the Windows taskbar. In the Outlook Express window, a number in parentheses (all formatted in blue) appears beside the Inbox folder in the folder list at the left. The number indicates how many new, unread messages you've received in your Inbox.

To read your messages, click the Inbox folder in the folder list, or click the Read Mail icon at the right side of the Outlook Express window. A list of messages appears at the right side of the Outlook Express window, with the bottom message in the list selected. Information about who sent the selected message and its subject appears in the message header area just below the list of messages. Below that, the text of the message appears (see Figure 16.6).

FIGURE 16.6

The Inbox folder lists your new messages, so you can read each one in the Outlook Express window.

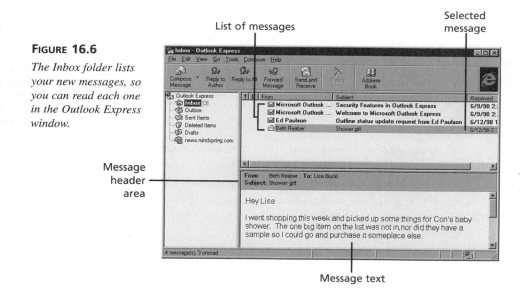

List of messages

Selected message

Message header area

Message text

You can use the scrollbar to the right of the message text to read the message. If the message includes one or more attachments, a large button with a paper clip on it appears at the right end of the header area above the message text. Click the button; then click the file you want to view in the list. Windows opens the file in the source application used to create it (such as Word for a Word file). To view another message, click it in the list of messages in the Outlook Express window.

To view a message in its own window, double-click the message in the list of messages. In the message window, message attachments appear in the bottom pane. Right-click an attachment; then choose the Save As command to display a Save As dialog box you can use to save the attachment.

To respond to a message and automatically address it, first select the message you want to respond to by clicking it in the list of messages. Then, click the Reply to Author button (to reply to the sender only), the Reply to All button (to respond to the sender plus everyone else who received the original message), or the Forward Message button (to send a copy of the message to someone who neither sent nor received it originally) on the Outlook Express toolbar. A new message window appears. You can specify a To address if you forwarded the message or additional recipients if Outlook automatically addressed the reply message. Type your responding text in the message area, above the Original Message line, attach any files you want to send, and click the Send button to send the response.

Working Offline with Multiple Messages

You can create messages without being connected to the Internet. It's also a good idea to read messages while you're offline, just to avoid burning up too much connect time.

To go offline, use these steps:

To Do: Working Offline

1. If you're prompted to connect to the Internet when you start Outlook Express, open the Select the Connection You Would Like to Dial drop-down list and select Don't Dial a Connection. Click OK to finish opening Outlook Express without logging on. Or, if you're already connected and working, hang up your connection as described in the section titled "Closing the Connection, If Needed," in Hour 14, but don't exit Outlook Express.

2. Choose File | Work Offline in the Outlook Express window to toggle Offline mode on.

Then, you can create or reply to messages as you normally would. When you click the Send button in the message window, Outlook Express places the message in your Outbox folder instead of connecting and transferring messages. You may find working offline particularly convenient if you need to send several messages in one session and want control over exactly when you're online.

To go back online, choose File | Work Offline to toggle off offline mode.

Then, to send any messages held in your Outbox folder, click the Send and Receive button on the Outlook Express toolbar to connect to the Internet and send the messages from your Outbox.

Both Outlook Express and Internet Explorer always either prompt you to connect to the Internet or reconnect automatically as needed, depending on what you're doing, even when you're working offline.

Setting Up for News

As for your Internet mail account, the Internet Connection Wizard should have prompted you for the information that Outlook Express needs to connect to your ISP's news server to download Internet newsgroups. Each newsgroup covers a particular topic and serves as a public message board where users can read and post messages.

If you later need to change newsgroup settings in Outlook to ensure that it can retrieve newsgroup information, choose Tools | Accounts. Click the News tab in the Internet Accounts dialog box; then click the name of your news server, as in news.mindspring. com, in the list. Click the Properties button to display a Properties dialog box for the connection. You can then change settings as needed. You'll probably need to change entries on the General, Server, and Connection tabs, changing entries such as the name or reply email address you want to use. (See "Creating Your Internet Connection" in Hour 14 to learn more.)

16

Using your real name and correct email address for Internet News is purely optional, and you might want to use an alias (or *handle*) to reduce the amount of junk email you receive. To use a nickname instead of your real name for newsgroup messages you post, enter the nickname in the Name text box of the General tab of the Properties dialog box for the connection. You also can use a fake email address to make it more difficult for other newsgroup posters to send you junk mail. In the Reply Address text box of the General tab of the connection's Properties dialog box, enter an email address that includes a dummy character or two somewhere in the address. Then instruct other users to remove that dummy character when replying to a posting of yours via email; the theory in this case is that the need to remove the extra character discourages those who want to send mass email or junk email, also called *spam*.

After you change the needed settings, click OK, and then click Close to resume working in Outlook Express.

Reading News

After you set up your secret newsgroup identity, you can start exploring the news. To do so, choose Go|News; click the icon for your news server in the bottom of the Outlook Express window folder list, or click the Read News icon at the right side of the Outlook Express window.

The first time you try to read news, Outlook Express displays a message telling you that you're not subscribed to any newsgroups, and asking if you want to do so. (See the next section, "Subscribing and Unsubscribing to Newsgroups," to learn why and how to subscribe.)

If you previously subscribed to newsgroups, Outlook Express displays its news window, and tools for reading news. You'll see the newsgroups you subscribed to listed under the News Server icon in the folder list at the left. You can jump ahead to "Transferring News and Opening a Newsgroup."

Subscribing and Unsubscribing to Newsgroups

Most news servers now list tens of thousands of newsgroups. You don't want to spend the time downloading all those newsgroups and the hundreds of messages each one might contain to your computer each time you read news. Subscribing to a newsgroup selects it for download. Then, when you read news, Outlook Express downloads only the newsgroups to which you are subscribed.

When you try to read news the first time, click Yes to tell Outlook Express that you want to subscribe to newsgroups. Outlook Express next asks if you want to connect to the newsgroup server. Click Yes to do so. Outlook Express dials your connection, if needed, logs onto the news server, and downloads the newsgroups. This takes several minutes or more, depending on your connection's speed.

After all the newsgroups download, they appear in the Newsgroups window. To display only newsgroups that might be of interest to you, type a few letters or a word to match in the Display Newsgroups which Contain text box above the News groups list. To subscribe to a newsgroup, click the newsgroup name in the News groups list; then click the Subscribe button at the right side of the window. Outlook Express copies the newsgroup name to the Subscribed tab and marks the newsgroup name with an icon on the All tab, as shown in Figure 16.7.

To redisplay the entire list of newsgroups on the All tab and the Subscribed tab, clear the entry in the Display Newsgroups Which Contain text box.

To unsubscribe from a newsgroup, click the Subscribed tab in the Newsgroups window. Click the newsgroup in the News Groups list; then click the Unsubscribe button at the right to remove the newsgroup from the list. After you finish choosing which newsgroups you want to be subscribed to, click the OK button to close the Newsgroups window. You should note, however, that Outlook Express must download message headers for subscribed newsgroups to your system, which can take quite some time. You should limit the number of groups to which you subscribe.

An entry here displays only newsgroups with matching characters

FIGURE 16.7

Use the Newsgroups dialog box to subscribe to and unsubscribe from newsgroups.

Indicates a subscribed group

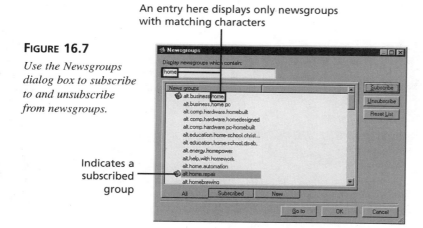

To redisplay the Newsgroups window at a later time when you're working with news, click the News Groups button on the Outlook Express toolbar. (This button appears only after you click the news connection icon in the folder list, click the Read News icon, or select Go | News.) You can work with your subscriptions as needed, or click the Reset List button to download an updated list of the newsgroups from the news server to Outlook Express.

Transferring News and Opening a Newsgroup

To proceed with reading news, you need to tell Outlook Express to transfer the headers (descriptions) of the new *articles* (messages or postings) in your subscribed newsgroups.

If you're not connected to the Internet, click the Connect button that appears in the Outlook Express toolbar after you display its news tools. Outlook Express dials your connection and connects to the news server.

After you're online (either the first time you're reading news or later), the list of newsgroups at the right might still not appear to be updated with new message headers. What you need to do is select a newsgroup to transfer its headers.

To select or open a newsgroup, click the newsgroup name below the news server name in the folder list at the left. If needed, Outlook Express transfers new headers from the news server to your system. A number in parentheses appears beside the newsgroup name in the folder list, to indicate how many message headers (for unread messages) the newsgroup holds. The Outlook Express window lists the message headers for the selected newsgroup in the upper-right pane. To transfer and display headers for another newsgroup, instead, click that newsgroup in the folder list.

Reading an Article

After you transfer the headers, you can simply scroll the message list to review the article (message) topics. To read an article, click its header in the message list. The text of the article appears below the header bar, as shown in Figure 16.8. You can use the scrollbar beside the article to read more of the article.

FIGURE 16.8

Click a header in the message list to read the article contents below.

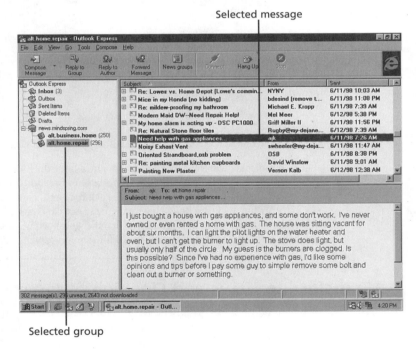

Selected message

Selected group

To read another article, click its header in the message list. You can scroll through the message list as needed to find other articles. After you read an article, Outlook Express removes the bold formatting from its header, so you can easily identify which articles you haven't read.

If you see a plus sign to the left of a message header, that tells you there's a *thread*, or series of responses to that message that others have posted. To display the headers for the thread, click the plus sign. Then click the header for any message in the thread to read that message.

A newsgroup can contain thousands of messages. If you want to see if your newsgroup has more messages in it, choose Tools | Get Next 300 Headers to transfer more headers.

Posting a Response

Sending a newsgroup message works almost exactly like sending an email message. The difference is in how Outlook addresses the message, depending on how you want to post the message. Here are your options:

- Post a completely new message to the selected newsgroup   Choose Compose | New Message. Outlook Express displays a new message addressed to the newsgroup, as in alt.home.repair. Sending the message sends it to the newsgroup, with its subject line that appears as the header in the message list.

- Post a message that responds to an existing message   Select the header for the message to respond to in the message list; then choose Compose | Reply to Newsgroup or click the Reply to Group button on the toolbar. The message is addressed to the newsgroup, and the header appears as part of the thread for the original message.

- Respond privately to a message author via email   Select the header for the message to respond to, and choose Compose | Reply to Author or click the Reply to Author button on the toolbar. This sends an email message to the author, but posts nothing to the newsgroup.

- Respond both to the group and the author   Select the message header to respond to; then choose Compose | Reply to Newsgroup and Author. As shown in the example in Figure 16.9, Outlook addresses the new message as both an email message and a posting.

After you use one of the previous methods to start your message, type the information you want to send or post in the body area of the message. Then click the Post button at the left end of the message window toolbar to post the message and send it via email, if needed.

Addressed to the newsgroup

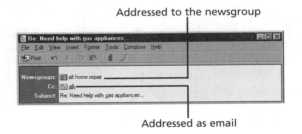

FIGURE 16.9

Outlook automatically addresses a posting or message.

Addressed as email

It may take a few hours for your article to appear on the news server. Log off for a while, and then log back on and transfer the message headers to find your message.

Summary

Now you know how to exploit the Internet to get in touch with other people—friends, family members, business associates, and other explorers like you who participate in online newsgroups. In this hour, you learned how to open the Outlook Express program and to use it to send, receive, and reply to email messages and read and post messages in newsgroups.

From here, you leave the online world to step into the money management world, seeing how to use Microsoft Money 99 to organize, track, and improve your financial picture.

Q&A

Q. What can I use Outlook Express for, and how do I start the program?

A. Outlook Express actually can help you manage and work with several types of information. This hour describes how you can use Outlook to send and receive email and read and post newsgroup messages. To launch Outlook Express, either double-click the Outlook Express shortcut on the desktop or click the Launch Outlook Express button on the Quick Launch toolbar on the taskbar.

Q. How do I send or read an email message?

A. Click the Compose Message button or choose Compose | New Message. In the message window, enter the To email address, a Subject, and the body of the message. Then click Send to transfer your email. You also can click the Send and Receive buttons on the Outlook Express toolbar to transfer messages. To read a message, click the Read Mail icon or the Inbox folder on the folder list; then click the message to read in the list of messages.

Q. How do I read news?

A. Click the Read News icon or the icon for your news server in the folder list. When prompted to do so, connect and download the newsgroups from the mail server. In the Newsgroups window, click a newsgroup in which you want to see messages; then click the Subscribe button. After you close the Newsgroups window, click the newsgroup name in the folder list (while connected) to transfer article headers, and then click the header for the article you want to read to display its contents in the bottom pane of the window.

16

PART IV

Your Evening Financial Workout with Money 99

Hour

HOUR 17

Setting Up Your Money File and Basic Accounts

You can use your home computer to get yourself organized once and for all, including gaining better control of your finances. Money 99 can help you take charge of your finances today. Use this financial management program to schedule your bill payments and print checks, perform online banking, monitor your investments and net worth, and set goals for tomorrow.

Before it can help you, you need to provide Money with information that enables it to track your finances. In this hour, take these initial steps with Money 99

- Start Money, and create Money files for your personal accounts.
- Create Money accounts to manage your checking and savings accounts.
- Create categories and subcategories to identify expenses and sources of income.
- Open an account to view its history or to update the account with new financial transactions.
- Exit Money 99 and back up your Money file.

Starting Money

After you start Money, you can use it to organize and update your financial information. The first time you start Money, you should have your bank statements, checking account register, and investment information available so you can begin setting up *accounts*— each Money account tracks the transactions you make in a real-world account. Follow these steps to begin working with Money 99:

To Do: Opening the Money Program

1. Click Start; point to Programs, and then choose Microsoft Money.

2. When the Money Home screen opens, you can set up your accounts or otherwise work in Money. The first time you use Money 99, it asks you to respond to a series of questions called your Personal Profile. After you enter or select your answers to all the questions, click the Done Answering Questions button. Money uses your answers to these questions (which cover areas such as your age, investments, and investment topics you'd like to learn more about) to provide you with helpful tips to get started. It also creates your first money file, called My Money, and sets up personalized links on your Money home page. The Money home page (see Figure 17.1) appears immediately when you subsequently start Money.

FIGURE 17.1

The Money home page appears after you start Money, so you can choose what you want to do.

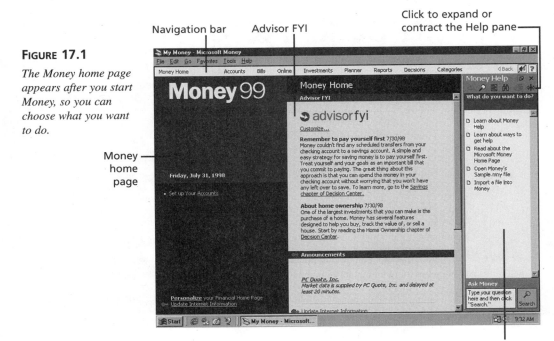

Navigation bar **Advisor FYI** **Click to expand or contract the Help pane**

Money home page

Money Help pane

The Money program offers two unique features. The first, the navigation bar, appears below the menu bar onscreen. You click the commands on the navigation bar to display different parts of the Money program.

The Money Help pane appears at the right side of the Money window. You can click one of the topics listed in the window to learn more about it. Alternatively, you can type a topic you need help with in the Ask Money text box near the bottom of the pane, and then click Search to display related help topics. To expand and contract the pane, click the button that looks like a double-headed arrow with a vertical bar. To close the Money Help pane, click its Close (X) button. To redisplay the pane, choose Help|Help Topics.

Note that the Money home page includes an area called Advisor FYI. The Advisor FYI oversees your activities to help you set priorities, prevent you from making mistakes, and keep you well informed. For example, you can customize Advisor FYI to alert you when your account balances are too low or high, when your spending has exceeded your plan, when important financial dates are approaching, or when investment values have reached critical prices. You also can choose what kind of information the Money home page displays, such as helpful information about debt management, investing, home and mortgage, and budgeting.

Think of Advisor FYI as a personal financial advisor, providing you with information that pertains to your financial situation. Say that you recently paid an insurance bill. Tracking that action, Advisor FYI might alert you to an article on how to save money on your insurance.

Working with Money Files

Money 99 stores the different types of financial information you enter in a file. The first time you start the Money program, it automatically creates the first file for you and names the file My Money. If you'll be the only one in your household using Money, you can start using the My Money file.

If more than one person will be using Money and each person's financial information needs to remain separate, then each user needs to create and name his own Money file. For example, if a household member named Kate wants to track her own finances, she could create her own file with any name she wants, such as Kate's File or Kate's Finances. You also might need to separate different sets of accounts, such as accounts related to your home versus accounts related to your business.

Creating a New File

Creating a new file in Money resembles the process of creating or saving a file in Works or Word. To make a new Money file, follow these steps:

To Do: Starting a New Money File

1. Choose File|New (Ctrl+N). The New dialog box appears.

2. (Optional) To save to a folder other than the default one (C:\My Documents), click the Up One Level button in the dialog box toolbar once or twice. (You also can click to open the Save In list, and click a folder higher on the tree to select it.) Then, double-click the folder you want to select in the list of folders that appears in the dialog box.

3. Type the name for the new file in the File Name text box, as shown in Figure 17.2.

FIGURE 17.2

Type a unique filename for your Money File in the New dialog box.

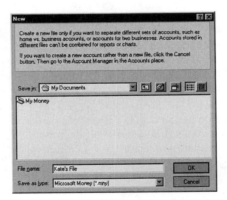

4. Click OK.

5. When you see the Back Up to Floppy dialog box, insert a blank floppy disk into your system's floppy disk drive. Then click Back Up Now to create a backup copy of the previously opened file, close the old file, and create and open the new file.

6. If Money displays the Personal Profile window (as it did when you started the program the first time), respond to each question as needed; then click Done Answering Questions.

If you previously used Quicken to track your finances, you can convert your Quicken file to Money 99 format by choosing File|Convert Quicken File. Money 99's Converter Wizard leads you through the process for converting the Quicken file.

Opening the File to Use

When you start Money, it opens the file you most recently used (or created). To work with the financial information in a different Money file, you need to open the Money file you want to use. These steps explain how to do so:

To Do: Opening a Money File

1. Choose File|Open. The Open dialog box appears.

2. If the file you want to open is not in the default folder, click the Up One Level button on the dialog box's toolbar once or twice. (You also can click to open the Look In list, and click a folder higher on the tree to select it.) Then, double-click the folder to select in the list of folders that appears in the dialog box.

3. Click the file you want to open in the list.

4. Click Open.

5. Insert a floppy disk in your floppy disk drive; then click Back Up Now to create a backup copy of the previously open file. Alternatively, if you choose not to make a backup copy now, click Don't Back Up. Money opens the file you selected in Step 3.

With your Money 99 file open, you can set up accounts, update account balances, personalize the Money home page, prepare reports, or use the many other tools Money 99 offers. However, the first step in using Money 99 is setting up accounts, which you learn about in the next section.

Creating Accounts

Accounts summarize financial transactions. In Money 99, you create an account for each real-world bank or investment account you have and enter the transactions you make for that account (deposits, checks or bills, and so on). Money calculates the current account balance based on the transactions you enter.

Entering all this information in Money 99 accounts enables you to track financial activity with greater accuracy, helping you make better decisions so you can build your net worth (the difference between your assets and debts). Accounts hold the information for reports and charts so that you can reveal spending habits, schedule upcoming bills, monitor your investment portfolio's performance, and quickly access income tax data when you need it.

You can set up these types of accounts in Money 99:

- Asset   Track things you own (and don't have a loan for), such as real estate, automobiles, antiques, and other items that have a measurable value.

- **Bank** Track the activity of any bank account that's not a checking or savings account.

- **Cash** Document money you hold for out-of-pocket expenditures and petty cash transactions, such as if you stop at a drugstore and pick up a magazine.

- **Checking** Manage checks you write and (typically) income you receive.

- **Credit card** Track transactions and purchases you make with credit cards or with a line of credit, as well as interest charges and your payments to the credit card company.

- **Employee Stock Option** Track employee stock option grants you have received from your employer.

- **House** Identify your home's value and how much equity (ownership) you've accumulated.

- **Investment** Track securities, including CDs, stocks, mutual funds, and T-bills.

- **Liability** Keep tabs on regular debts you owe, such as an insurance payment, personal loan, or any other obligation that's not an amortized loan.

- **Line of Credit** Document how much you spend and how much you pay off with regard to a line of credit from a bank, such as a home equity credit line.

- **Loan** Amortize car and student loans.

- **Mortgage** Amortize your home mortgage loan.

- **Other** Track income and expenses that don't apply to another account type.

- **Retirement accounts** Follow tax-deferred retirement plans, such as 401(k), IRAs, 403(b)s, SEP-IRAs, Keoghs, and RRSPs (a Canadian retirement plan that allows you to save on a tax-deferred basis).

- **Savings** Track all activity in a savings account at a bank or other financial institution.

> This book can't cover all the different Money accounts; it focuses on those you're most likely to use. Hour 18, "Working with Your Checking or Savings Account," covers bank (checking and savings) accounts. Hour 19, "Tracking Your Credit Cards and Debts," covers credit card and loan accounts. Hour 20, "Monitoring Your Investments," covers investment accounts.

Money's New Account Wizard helps you set up a new account in your Money file. You answer a series of questions the wizard asks and specify what type of account to open.

Although the overall steps are about the same for any account type, you can move on now to see how to set up two specific kinds of accounts: checking and savings.

Hour 21, "Creating Budgets and Reports," covers Money *reports*. Reports summarize your financial information to help you make decisions. Reports can't combine information from accounts stored in separate files. If you think you might want to use reports to compare information from certain accounts, make sure you create those accounts in the same Money file.

Setting Up a Checking Account

Most people handle the bulk of their financial business via a checking account. It's likely that you pay most of your bills and make charitable donations and gifts from your checking account. Via direct deposit, your employer deposits your salary into your checking account.

Automating your checking account with Money 99 makes it easier for you to track expenditures, pay your bills, and prepare for taxes. After you create a checking account in Money, you can enter a bill transaction into that checking account, and then print a hard copy (paper) check to pay each bill. Before you can begin working with your checking account, you must create and set up that account in the open Money file. You create new accounts in Account Manager, using the New Account Wizard.

To set up a checking account in Money 99, first get the last paper statement you received for the account. You'll need some information from that statement to create the account. Then, follow these steps:

To Do: Adding a Checking Account in Your Money File

1. Click Accounts on the navigation bar or choose Go|Accounts (Ctrl+Shift+A). The Account Manager appears.

If you perform Step 1 and you don't see icons for various accounts but instead see a register for an existing account, you must click the Account Manager button to the far right of the account name.

2. Click the New Account button at the bottom of the Account Manager screen. The New Account dialog box appears.

▼   3. Leave the Held At option button selected, and enter the name of your bank in the
         Held At text box (see Figure 17.3). Click Next.

FIGURE 17.3

*Enter the name of the
financial institution
where you have your
checking account in the
Held At text box.*

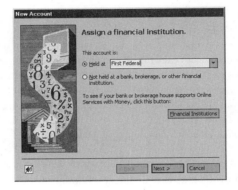

4. Leave Checking selected in the next dialog box; then click Next.

5. Edit the suggested account name in the Name text box, if needed, and then click
   Next.

6. Enter the account number in the text box in the next dialog box. Click Next.

7. Enter the closing balance of the account from your last statement in the What Is the
   Balance for This Account text box. Click Next.

8. Leave I Have No Other Accounts at This Institution selected and click Next.

▲   9. Click Finished in the dialog box that tells you Account Created.

When you finish setting up your checking account, an account icon and description
appear in the Account Manager, as shown in Figure 17.4.

> You need to be sure to synchronize the checking account balance you enter
> in Money when you create the account with the balance of your real
> account with your bank. To do so, work from your most recent, balanced
> checking account statement from your bank. Enter the ending balance from
> that statement (not the amount you calculated when you balanced it). Then,
> when you finish creating the account, you'll need to enter any transactions
> (recorded in your paper checkbook register) that you've made since the clos-
> ing date for the statement. When you reconcile the checking account, your
> Money checking account will have the same number of transactions as the
> paper statement. Hour 18 explains how to enter transactions and reconcile a
> checking or savings account.

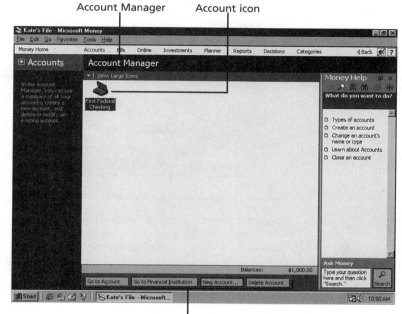

FIGURE 17.4

The Account Manager displays an icon for each account you create. Display the Account Manager to create and select accounts.

Buttons for working with accounts

Setting Up a Savings Account

Setting up a savings account works very much like setting up a checking account. Again, grab your most recent statement for the account; then follow these steps to create a corresponding account in Money:

To Do: Adding a Savings Account to Your Money File

1. Click Accounts on the navigation bar or choose Go|Accounts (Ctrl+Shift+A). If needed, click the Account Manager button to the far right of the account name. The Account Manager appears.

2. Click the New Account button at the bottom of the Account Manager screen. The New Account dialog box appears.

3. Enter the name of the financial institution where you have your savings account in the Held At text box, and then click Next.

4. Choose Savings (see Figure 17.5), and then click Next.

▼ **FIGURE 17.5**

Each time you add a Money account, specify what kind of account you want to create.

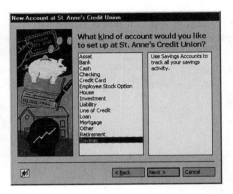

 Be sure to select Savings, not Bank. Bank accounts are for banking accounts other than checking and savings. For example, if you have a Certificate of Deposit or a Money Market Account at a bank, choose Bank.

5. Edit the suggested account name in the Name text box, if needed, and then click Next.

6. Enter the account number in the text box in the next dialog box. Click Next.

7. Enter the closing balance of the account from your most recent statement in the What Is the Balance for This Account text box. Click Next.

8. Leave I Have No Other Accounts at this Institution selected and click Next.

▲ 9. Click Finished in the dialog box that tells you Account Created.

 If you don't have your most recent statement on hand to enter the account number or ending balance for an account, you can edit the account later to update that information. Choose Go|Accounts. Right-click the account icon, and then click Go To Details. Change any entries as needed in the Account Details screen. Changing the Bank text box entry on the Account Details screen doesn't change the account name. To change the account name, click the Modify button. In the Modify Account dialog box, enter a new account name in the New Name text box. Avoid changing the account type (by choosing an option button in the Account Type area of the dialog box). Changing account types can really mess up previously entered transactions. Click OK to close the Modify Account dialog box. Then click the Account Manager button to the far right of the account name to return to the Account Manager.

Setting Up Categories and Subcategories

To master your budget, you need to understand where your money comes from and where it goes. In Money 99, you assign a *category* or *subcategory* to each transaction to identify how you made or spent the money involved. Then, you can use Money to generate reports totaling money you made (or spent) in each category or subcategory. Money offers predefined categories and subcategories. Categories define general income and expense sources, and subcategories fall within categories so you can identify an expense or income item even more specifically. For example, Money offers a Household category, which contains a Furnishings subcategory.

Money 99 comes with many common expense categories already set up and ready for you to use, but you can add your own category or subcategory to supplement the list. For example, if you employ a home cleaning service, you might want a Cleaning subcategory for the Household category. Money also assigns each category and subcategory to a *category group* for reporting purposes. When you create a category or subcategory, you tell Money which category group it fits into best. Your new Cleaning subcategory would fit best in the Household Expenses category group.

To create your own category or subcategory, follow these steps:

To Do: Adding a Category or Subcategory

1. Click Categories on the navigation bar, or choose Go|Categories & Payees (Ctrl+Shift+C). The Categories & Payees list appears.

2. To create a new subcategory, click a category in the list, as shown in Figure 17.6. Otherwise, don't click anything.

3. Click the New button at the bottom of the Categories & Payees list window. The New Category dialog box appears.

4. Choose the Create a New Category or Add a Subcategory to (Category) to create either a category or subcategory. If you clicked a category in Step 2, click the latter option button. Click Next.

5. If you're creating a new category, enter its name in the Name text box, and then click either the Income or Expense option button, as shown in Figure 17.7. For a subcategory, enter its name in the Name text box. Click Next.

6. In the list of category groups that appears in the next dialog box, click the category group your new category or subcategory best falls into. For example, for the new Dry Cleaning category shown in Figure 17.7, you could click the Clothing Expenses category group. Click Finish.

Click the New button at the bottom of the Categories & Payees list to create a new category or subcategory.

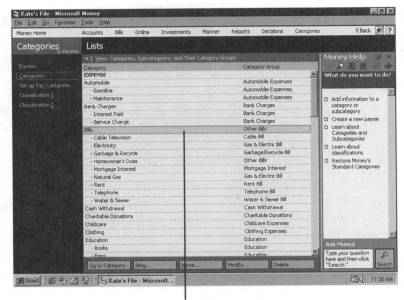

Click a category to which you
want to add a new subcategory

FIGURE 17.7

When you create a new category, you enter its name and then identify whether it's an income or expense. You only have to enter a name for a new subcategory.

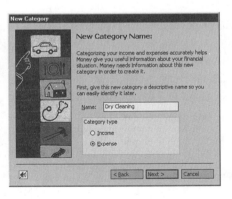

Every time you enter a transaction, create a new account, or make other changes to your Money file, Money 99 automatically saves your work. You don't need to do anything special to save your file as you work or when you exit.

Opening and Viewing Accounts

At any point, when you're ready to enter transactions into or otherwise work with an account, you need to use the navigation bar to return to the Account Manager. Then, you use the Account Manager to select an account and display its *Account Register*, the area where you enter transactions for the account. The Account Register looks a lot like your paper checkbook register, listing each transaction on a separate line.

However, you enter checks, deposits, transfers, withdrawals, and cash machine (ATM) transactions in the *transaction forms*, which look like a series of tabs at the bottom of the Account Register window.

Use these steps to open an account and view its register and other information:

To Do: Displaying an Account's Register

1. Choose Go|Accounts (Ctrl+Shift+A). Alternatively, click Accounts on the navigation bar. If needed, click the Account Manager button to the far right of the account name.

2. Double-click the icon for the account you want to open. Its register appears, as shown in Figure 17.8.

Click to view the
account register

Click to redisplay the
Account Manager

FIGURE 17.8

You view and enter transactions in an account's register, like the one shown here.

Click to edit
account details

Click to see a
running account
balance

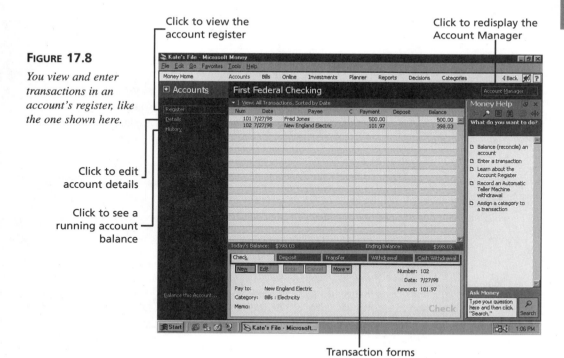

Transaction forms

3. To view and edit account information (the information you specified when you created the account), click Details at the left side of the screen.

4. Click History at the left side of the screen to view a chart showing a running balance of account expenditures.

5. Click Register at the left side of the screen to redisplay the transaction register for the account you selected in Step 2.

6. Click the Account Manager button to redisplay the Account Manager screen so you can open another account.

> After you add accounts to your Money file, your Money home page includes a Favorite Accounts area. You can click an account listed there to open the register for that account.

> If you don't see the transaction forms when you display the register, click the View drop-down list arrow below the account name, and then click Transaction Forms.

Backing Up Your Money File

Use Money 99's back up feature to ensure that you have a recent copy of your work in case your file is ever lost or damaged. By default, when you exit Money, the program creates a backup copy of the current file on your hard disk. It also checks to see the last time you backed up your Money file. If you last backed up more than 14 days ago, Money prompts you to back up the current file to a floppy disk.

You can also choose backing up a file at any time. Money gives you the option of backing up to your hard disk or backing up to a removable disk such as a standard floppy disk, an LS-120, Zip disk, or Syquest.

> It is recommended that you back up to your hard disk at least once a week and back up to a removable disk once a month. This dual backup path offers both convenience (it's faster to back up to the hard disk) and ample protection (the removable disk will be there if your hard disk fails).

Follow these steps to back up the open Money file:

To Do: Creating a Backup of Your Money File

1. Choose File | Back Up.

2. Specify where to create the backup file:

   - Removable disk   Click the Back Up to Floppy option button, and select the disk to back up to from the accompanying drop-down list. Also be sure to place a floppy or other disk in the removable drive you specified.

   - Hard disk   Click Back Up to Hard Disk (see Figure 17.9). To change the backup folder and filename, click the Browse button. Choose another folder using the Save In list, and type a name for the backup file in the File Name text box. Click OK.

FIGURE 17.9

This example illustrates creating a backup file on the hard disk.

3. Click OK. Money creates the backup file in the location you specified.

> If you want to change the way Money backs up your file, choose Tools | Options and choose the Backup tab. For example, if you want Money to prompt you to back up your file to floppy disk more often than every 14 days, you can change that to a lesser number of days.

When you need to use a backup file, you don't open it, you restore it. Use these steps to restore your Money information from the backup file you most recently created for it:

To Do: Restoring from a Backup File

1. Choose File | Restore Backup. The Restore Confirmation dialog box appears.

2. Leave the Restore from a Backup File option button selected, and then click Next.

3. Leave the Restore from Default Backup File option button selected in the Restore Backup dialog box, and then click Restore.

4. Verify that the Restore Target dialog box specifies the correct name and location for the restored file. (Otherwise, click the Browse button, specify another folder and filename, and then click OK.) Click Restore. Money restores the file and displays the Money home page.

Exiting Money

When you finish working with Money, exit the program to remove it from your display. Because Money 99 automatically saves your file as you make changes to the file (create accounts, enter transactions, and so on), you don't need to save your Money file when you quit the program. However, if you haven't backed up your file recently, Money might prompt you to perform the backup, and you can respond accordingly.

Follow these steps to shut down Money:

To Do: Finishing Your Work with Money

1. Choose File | Exit.

2. If you haven't backed up your file to a floppy or some other removable disk for more than 14 days, Money displays the Back Up to Floppy dialog box (see Figure 17.10).

FIGURE 17.10

*From here, you can cre-
ate a backup file on a
floppy disk.*

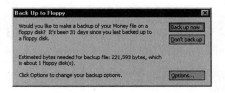

3. Insert a disk in your floppy disk drive, and then click Back Up Now. To skip the back up, click Don't Back Up Now. If you opted to create a backup, Money informs you as it creates the backup file. The Money program closes.

▲

Summary

Now you can start up Money 99 and set up separate Money files for different purposes. Within each file, you set up accounts such as checking and savings accounts to track different types of transactions. This hour also covered how to create categories and subcategories to precisely track income and spending. Finally, you learned how to back up your Money file and then leave the program. Move on to the next hour to learn more about how to work with your checking and savings accounts in Money 99.

Q&A

Q. What if I want to track my small business financial transactions and my personal finances? Do I create two separate files?

A. Yes. You can create a new file if you want to keep a separate set of accounts. For example, to maintain a set of accounts for your personal finances and another set for your small business, you can create two different files: My Personal and My Business. You might want to create two sets of accounts for two businesses that you operate; you can do that too! To create a new file, choose File|New and specify a filename and location for the new file.

Q. What's the difference between a new file and a new account?

A. A file holds a collection of accounts. Each account tracks some aspect of your financial affairs. Each account generally corresponds to a real-world account you have with a financial institution or brokerage, an asset you own, or a debt you owe. For example, your My Personal file could hold the My Checking account (to track checking account transactions) and the My Mortgage account (to track your home mortgage). You add a new account to your Money file in the Money Account Manager. Click Accounts on the navigation bar, and then click the Account Manager button at the far right, if needed. When you see the Account Manager (rather than a transaction register), click New Account to begin adding the new account.

Q. Should I keep saving my work as I am creating new accounts, entering transactions, and so on?

A. No. Money automatically saves the changes to your file as you make them. At any time, you can choose the File|Back Up command to create a backup file as an insurance policy against losing your work.

Q. How do I exit Money?

A. Choose File|Exit. If Money prompts you to back up your file, insert a floppy disk in your drive, and click Back Up Now.

17

HOUR 18

Working with Your Checking or Savings Account

Think of all your bills, deposits, withdrawals, and cash transfers. Your financial transactions like these affect your checking and savings accounts. For each transaction that occurs with regard to your real-world account, you need to enter a corresponding transaction. Then, Money can calculate the current account balance for you and even print checks. This hour covers how to enter key transactions in your Money checking or savings account and explains how to

- Review how to display the account register.
- Record checks (payments), transfers between accounts, and regular and ATM cash withdrawals.
- Set up recurring transactions.
- Print checks so you can pay your bills.
- Use Money 99 to balance your checking account.

Viewing the Register and Transaction Form

As you saw in Hour 17, "Setting Up Your Money File and Basic Accounts," the account register looks a lot like the paper register you received from your bank for your checking account. You should find the workings of Money's account registers familiar, if not intuitive.

Before you can enter transactions, you need to display the checking (or savings) account where those transactions apply. As you'll recall from the last hour, start by choosing Go|Accounts (Ctrl+Shift+A). Alternatively, click Accounts on the navigation bar. If needed, click the Account Manager button to the far right of the account name to display the Account Manager, which includes icons for the individual accounts. Double-click the icon for the account you want to open.

> To make sure a particular Money 99 account appears in the Favorite Accounts list on your Money home page, display the account's register. Click Details at the left side of the screen, and then click to check the Favorite Account check box.

While working in an account register, you can

- Enter transactions   You can enter transactions using the transaction forms found at the bottom of an account register screen. The next five sections in this chapter explain the different types of transactions you can enter into a checking (or savings) account.

- Balance your account   You can reconcile your Money 99 account balance with that of a financial institution statement while in the account register. See "Reconciling Your Account," later in this hour, to learn how to accomplish this task.

- Change the way you view transactions   You can sort the transactions in the register, so they appear in the order you prefer. Click the View drop-down list arrow below the account name. Then click Sort by Date, Sort by Number, or Sort by Entry Order (the order in which you entered the transactions) to choose the order you want.

Entering a Bill (Check)

You use a checking account to write checks to pay for things. Once or twice a month, you sit down with your checkbook and bills, write out checks (bill payments) longhand,

and write a corresponding transaction in your paper checkbook register. When you enter a check (bill) in Money and then use Money to print the check, you only have to enter the transaction once. Money records the check in the account register and correctly calculates the new *ending balance* (the amount of money you have left after deducting the check) before you print the check. You can then print the check on your printer, as described in the later section, "Printing Checks."

On the other hand, you don't have to print checks for bills and other payments from Money if you don't want to. You can write out the checks longhand, and then enter a corresponding check transaction. Money then calculates your balance accurately and categorizes your expenses and income.

Use these steps to enter each check transaction into the register for your Money checking account:

To Do: Entering a Check Transaction in the Register

1. In the register for the checking account you want to use, click the Check transaction form tab.

2. Edit the check number in the Number text box, if needed. For a check that you plan to print from Money, open the Number text box drop-down list and click Print This Transaction. Press Tab.

3. Click the drop-down list arrow beside the Date text box, and click the date for the check in the calendar that appears. You can postdate checks to any date that you want, so that you can enter and print several checks at a sitting rather than do the work on several different days. Press Tab to finish your date entry.

4. Enter a payee in the Pay To text box, and then press Tab.

> After you enter a payee the first time, Money stores the payee name and transaction information in its Categories & Payees list. Then, when you type the first few characters of the payee name in the Pay To text box, the rest of the name appears, and you can just press Tab to move to the Amount text box. Money automatically fills in the Amount, Category, and Memo text boxes using the information from the last check you entered for that payee. You can then edit any of the entries as needed.

5. Enter the check amount in the Amount text box, and then press Tab. The Category drop-down list opens automatically.

6. Click a category; then press Tab twice.

▼   7. Enter a description or note in the Memo text box. Your transaction now should look something like the one shown in the Check transaction form at the bottom of Figure 18.1.

Watch your Ending Balance to ensure
the account has adequate funds

FIGURE 18.1

The transaction form here shows an example, in-progress transaction entry.

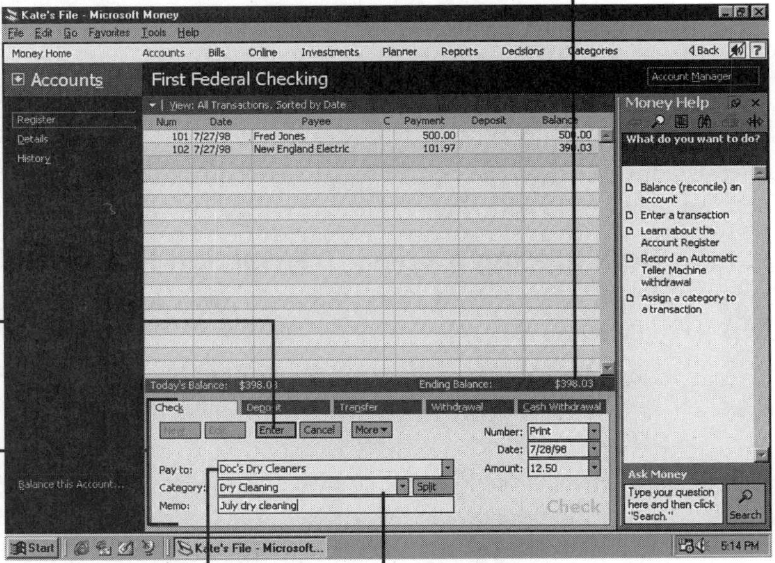

Click to finish
entering the
transaction

Check
transaction
form

Enter the check
recipient

Choose an Expense category to
identify how you spent the money

To cancel a transaction you've started, click the Cancel button on the Check
transaction form or press Esc before you click the Enter button.

8. Click the Enter button on the Check transaction form to add the check to the register.

9. After you enter the first check, click the New button on the Check transaction form
▲   to begin entering the next check.

If you specified Print This Transaction in Step 2, Money displays the Print Address dialog box after you click the Enter button to finish the transaction. You can enter payee address, phone, and account number information and click Done if you want to print that information on the check. Or, click OK without entering anything to skip the process.

If you don't like using the transaction forms or are a fast typist, you can enter transactions directly into the rows listed in the register. To hide the transaction forms, click to open the View drop-down list below the account name. Click Enter Transactions Directly into the Register. The transaction forms disappear. Click the first empty line in the account register. Type information directly into each field. Alternatively, click the down arrow that appears at the right side of the field, and then click a choice in the list. Press Tab to move between fields and finish the transaction. Open the View drop-down list and click Use Forms to Enter Transactions to redisplay the transaction forms.

Entering a Deposit

After you write a few checks, you may have depleted quite a bit of the money from your checking account. At some point, you'll need to deposit money into your checking account at your bank, and record that transaction in your checking account in Money. Similarly, if you receive an electronic payment, such as an automatic payroll deposit or interest payment, you need to enter the deposit in your Money checking account. Money calculates the new balance, so you'll know how much you have available for further checks.

The steps described here for making a deposit into a checking account also work for a savings or cash account you've created in Money. Display the account for which you want to enter a deposit transaction and click the Deposit transaction form tab to make the deposit.

You should enter deposits when you make them rather than wait until you receive your monthly bank statement. Money will let your checking account show a negative balance. If you haven't entered your deposits, you'll have to remember how much you deposited and not exceed that amount when you write checks. This makes you vulnerable to real overdrafts if you make a mistake. Entering the deposits as you make them prevents such a situation.

18

The bank doesn't necessarily add the deposit amount to your balance until the deposit clears, which can take two to three days. So, consider post-dating your deposits by two days or so, just to remind yourself that you may need to hold off on check writing. Also check your bank statement and update your deposit dates to match the statement dates.

Here's how to enter a deposit into your checking account (or other account):

To Do: Adding a Deposit Transaction

1. In the register for the checking account you want to use, click the Deposit transaction form tab.

2. Enter a notation such as DEP (for deposit) in the Number text box. Or, enter the number of the check that you're depositing. Press Tab.

3. Click the Date drop-down list arrow, and click the date you made the deposit or the expected electronic deposit date; then press Tab.

4. Enter a payer in the From text box, and then press Tab.

5. Enter the deposit amount in the Amount text box. Press Tab. The Category drop-down list opens.

6. Click a category from the Category drop-down list. Press Tab twice.

Make sure you assign an Income category, not an Expense category, to deposits.

7. Enter a description or note in the Memo text box. At this point, your deposit trans-action should resemble Figure 18.2.

8. Click the Enter button on the Deposit transaction form to add the deposit to the register.

9. After you enter the first deposit, click the New button on the Deposit transaction form to begin entering another deposit, if any.

From time to time, a wizard appears as you're entering a new transaction. Some wizards prompt you to set up recurring payments, or set up Money to track the taxes deducted from your pay deposits. You can read and follow the wizard screens to use the wizard to perform such tasks.

Previously entered check transactions

FIGURE 18.2

*Enter each deposit
transaction on the
Deposit transaction
form.*

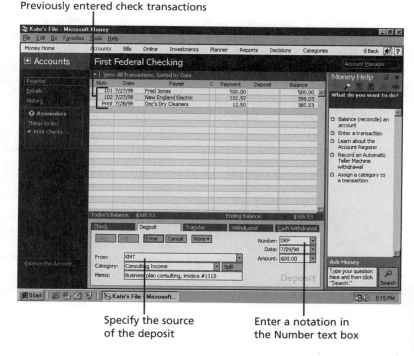

Specify the source
of the deposit

Enter a notation in
the Number text box

18

Entering a Transfer

Savings accounts pay interest and checking accounts typically don't. So, you earn the
most interest possible by maximizing the balance in your savings account and minimiz-
ing the amount you keep in checking. If your employer deposits your paycheck right into
your checking account, you might need to transfer money from your checking account to
your savings account. As with other transaction types, after you make the real transaction
at your bank or banks (or ATM, if both accounts are with the same bank), you need to
enter the transfer in your Money file. Money then calculates the new ending balance for
each account.

Use these steps to enter the transfer transaction, which actually enters a separate transaction in both accounts affected by the transfer:

To Do: Documenting a Transfer Between Accounts

▲ To Do

1. Display the register for the account from which you're transferring money.

2. Click the Transfer transaction form tab.

3. Enter a notation such as TRAN (for transfer) in the Number text box, if needed.
   Press Tab twice.

To open the register for one account directly from the register of another account, click the drop-down list arrow beside Accounts in the upper-left corner of the Register window. Then click the name of another account to display its register.

4. Click the Date drop-down list arrow and click the date you made the transfer. Press Tab. The To drop-down list opens.

5. Click the account into which you want to transfer funds. Press Tab.

6. Enter the transfer amount in the Amount text box. Press Tab twice.

The Pay To text box applies to electronic payments. You can perform electronic payments only if your bank enables you to use Money to initiate payments online, if the payee accepts online payments, and if the applicable accounts are set up for online banking. See Hour 22, "Handling Your Banking Online," to learn more about using Money online.

7. Enter a description or note in the Memo text box. Figure 18.3 shows a sample transfer transaction.

A previously entered deposit transaction

FIGURE 18.3

A transfer transaction documents when you move money from one account to another.

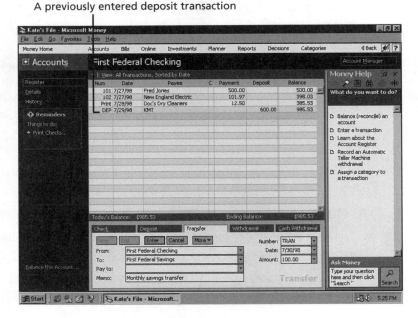

▼

▲

8. Click the Enter button on the Transfer transaction form to enter a transaction in the register for each of the accounts. In the account from which you transferred money, the transaction amount appears in the Payment column; Money deducts the amount from the Balance. The reverse occurs for the account into which you transferred funds; Money records the transaction amount in the Deposit column and adds the amount to the account balance.

Entering a Withdrawal

When you withdraw money from your bank using a withdrawal slip (rather than a check or ATM machine), you should enter that transaction as a withdrawal in your checking account (or savings account). You also can enter a withdrawal transaction for any unusual bank fees you incur, such as a bounced check fee. When you enter the withdrawal, you can assign a category and subcategory to identify how you spent the money, or even a specific payee, if you gave the cash to a particular person or entity such as a grocery story or dry cleaner.

Follow these steps to enter a withdrawal transaction in a checking or savings account:

To Do: Recording a Withdrawal Transaction

18

▼ To Do

1. In the register for the applicable account, click the Withdrawal transaction form tab.

2. In the Number text box, enter a notation such as WITH (for withdrawal), if needed. Press Tab.

3. Click the Date drop-down list arrow, click the date you made the withdrawal, and then press Tab.

4. If needed, enter a payee in the Pay To text box, and then press Tab. If you're just withdrawing cash for a miscellaneous purpose, you can enter Cash.

5. Enter the withdrawal amount in the Amount text box. Press Tab. The Category drop-down list opens.

6. Choose a category or subcategory from the Category drop-down list. Press Tab twice.

7. Enter a description in the Memo text box.

8. Click the Enter button on the Withdrawal transaction form to enter the transaction in the account register.

▲

Entering a Cash Machine Transaction

ATM machines make it easy to get cash from your bank account at any hour. One disadvantage of getting money from an ATM (as opposed to writing a check) is that you rarely take the time to document the purpose of the withdrawal. Such a practice can be a budget buster. After you make an ATM withdrawal, you should record the transaction in your account in Money 99 using the Cash Machine transaction form in the register. This practice helps document your spending habits and can even help you keep track of tax deductible expenditures, such as expenses your employer won't reimburse.

> If you withdraw cash from an ATM machine that charges you a fee, don't forget to include the fee in your ATM transaction or to later check your statement for fee amounts and enter those fees as withdrawals.

Be sure to keep your ATM receipts so that you can make the correct entries in Money 99. You might want to note the purpose of each ATM withdrawal directly on the ATM receipt. For example, if you withdrew cash to pick up a dinner check, write dining out on the receipt. That way, you'll be able to enter categories and subcategories for more ATM transactions, building a more accurate record of what you're spending money on.

Use this process to enter a transaction for each ATM withdrawal into your account register:

To Do: Entering an ATM Transaction

1. In the register for the account from which you made the ATM withdrawal, click the Cash Withdrawal transaction form tab.

2. Click the Date drop-down list arrow, click the date you made the withdrawal, and then press Tab.

3. Enter the ATM withdrawal amount in the Amount text box. Press Tab. The Category drop-down list opens.

4. Click a category or subcategory in the Category drop-down list. Press Tab twice.

5. Enter a description in the Memo text box.

6. Click the Enter button to enter the transaction in the account register. Figure 18.4 shows both an ATM (cash) withdrawal and regular withdrawal entered into a checking account's register.

▲ To Do

▼

▼ **Figure 18.4**

You can enter two types of withdrawal transactions, as shown here, in a checking or savings account.

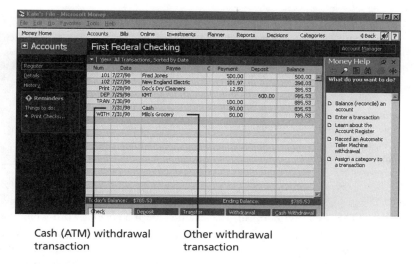

▲

Cash (ATM) withdrawal
transaction

Other withdrawal
transaction

Splitting a Transaction

Many times you'll spend cash from an ATM withdrawal, other cash withdrawal, or even a check on a variety of items. For example, if you write a check to pay a credit card bill, that credit card bill might include charges for gas, groceries, clothing, and more. In such an instance, you need to assign multiple categories to the transaction, called *splitting the transaction*.

You can split expenditures into multiple categories by clicking the Split button on the transaction form as you're entering the transaction. The Check, Deposit, Withdrawal, and Cash Withdrawal tabs each include the Split button. Rather than making a choice from the Category drop-down list, click the Split button to display the Split Transaction window, which appears with the Category drop-down list open for the first split row.

Click a category or subcategory in the drop-down list. Press Tab. Type a Description and press Tab. Then type an Amount that represents the portion of the transaction that falls under the category or subcategory you selected for the row. Press Tab, and repeat the process for each category or subcategory you need to specify for the transaction. Figure 18.5 shows a transaction for which two subcategories have already been assigned.

When the Unassigned amount reaches 0.00, click Done to finish entering the split information. Press Tab, type a transaction Memo, and then click the Enter button on the transaction form to finish entering the split transaction.

18

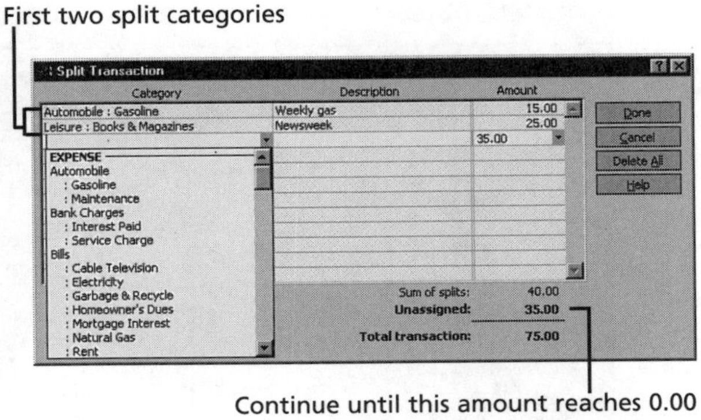

First two split categories

FIGURE 18.5

In the Split Transaction window, you apply multiple categories or subcategories to a single transaction and specify how much of the transaction amount Money should apply to each category.

Continue until this amount reaches 0.00

ATM (Cash Withdrawal) transactions merit a special word when it comes to split transactions. There are two ways to keep track of your cash expenditures from ATM withdrawals. First, you can simply split your ATM withdrawals and categorize what you spend the cash on. The second way to track ATM withdrawals is to create a cash account for just your ATM withdrawals. That method involves entering all your ATM withdrawals as transfers from whatever account you took the money from. You then transfer the money into your cash account and track it from there. Then each time you spend some of the cash from an ATM withdrawal, you enter a separate transaction in the cash account. (You can think of this almost as transferring money from a savings to a checking account and then writing multiple checks to spend the transferred amount.)

Financial planners recommend the second method to get a deep understanding of your spending habits. To do so, you have to keep detailed records of spending. Splitting transactions helps you keep very accurate records of all your expenditures.

Taking Advantage of Transaction Techniques and Shortcuts

You've now reviewed the basic techniques for entering transactions into a checking or savings account. You can save time and ensure the accuracy of your transactions by using the following techniques to enter and update transactions:

- Make changes   To edit any transaction, double-click it in the register. Make the changes you want on the selected transaction form tab at the bottom of the register, and then click the Enter button to accept the changes.

- Use the right mouse button   Right-click any text box on a transaction form to display a shortcut menu with applicable commands. For example, when you right-click Amount, the shortcut menu includes Previous Amounts. When you click Previous Amounts, the Amount entries for your last five transactions appear. Click the amount you want to enter.

- Use the plus sign (+) and minus sign (-) keys   You can increase or decrease the transaction number or date by moving to that text box and pressing the + or - key.

- Use AutoComplete+   When you enter a payee name you've used before in the Pay To text box and press Tab, AutoComplete+ automatically enters the Amount, Memo, and Category entries from the last transaction using the same payee name.

Creating a Recurring Transaction

Recurring transactions occur with a regular frequency. Monthly electricity, telephone, or similar bills are good examples. Rather than entering a check transaction for such a bill every month, you add a transaction into the Bills & Deposits list, which reminds you that the payment is due. When a recurring bill becomes due, usually a click of a mouse button can record a check transaction to cover the recurring payment into the register.

Money 99 gives you the ability to not only schedule recurring bills but also recurring investments. You may have heard a professional financial planner say "Pay yourself first." This means that right after you receive your salary, you should make an investment so you won't be tempted to spend all your money. You can set up a recurring transaction to pay yourself first, or remind you to transfer money from your checking to your savings account or make a deposit into a mutual fund investment account. You can also schedule recurring deposits such as a direct deposit of your weekly paycheck.

18

Follow these steps to set up an existing transaction as a recurring transaction:

To Do: Setting Up a Recurring Transaction

▼ To Do

1. Go to the account register containing the transaction you want to specify as a recurring transaction.

2. In the account register, right-click the transaction. A shortcut menu appears.

3. Click on Add to Bills & Deposits to display the first Create New Scheduled Payment dialog box.

4. If it is not already selected, choose the More Than Once, at Regular Intervals option button. Open the Frequency drop-down list and click the frequency at which the transaction will occur, such as Monthly or Twice a Month. Click Next.

▼

▼ 5. Open the Payment method drop-down list, and click to select the payment method. By default, the payment method is set to Write Check, but you might want to choose Printed Transaction for checks you want to print. Click Next.

6. If the bill is usually the same amount, click Yes, It's Typically the Same Amount. If the payment is not usually the same amount, choose No, The Amount Usually Varies and then enter an estimated amount. Click Next. Details about the transaction appear, as shown in Figure 18.6.

FIGURE 18.6

Money gives you the opportunity to change details about the recurring transaction.

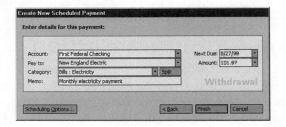

7. Enter or edit transaction details.

▲ 8. Click Finish.

When the recurring transaction is due, Money displays a reminder on the Money home page in the Bills area, as shown in Figure 18.7. Click the underlined transaction to display it under Upcoming Bills & Deposits in the Bills & Deposits list. Right-click the transaction, and click Record Payment at the top of the shortcut menu (or the corresponding command for that transaction type). In the dialog box that appears, edit any transaction information as needed, such as adjusting the Amount; then click the Record Payment button (or corresponding button) to enter the transaction into the register.

To see your list of recurring transactions, choose Go|Bills & Deposits (Ctrl+Shift+B). Right-click a transaction in the list and click Edit to make changes to it. Alternatively, right-click it and click Skip Transaction if you want to skip its next occurrence.

A Billminder icon in the tray area at the right end of the taskbar also appears when you have an upcoming recurring transaction. Click it, and then click Start Money to enter the transaction.

Recurring transaction reminder

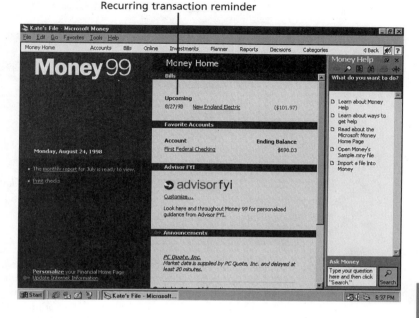

FIGURE 18.7

When you set up a transaction to recur at regular intervals, the Money home page reminds you the transaction is due.

Printing Checks

Printing checks from Money 99 saves you the trouble of handwriting them. When you enter your check transactions, you tell Money which check transactions to print by choosing Print This Transaction from the Number drop-down list. When you're ready to print, you choose a check format, and send the checks to the printer.

Money sequentially numbers the transactions (changes the Number text box entry) when you print more than one check. If the checks you want to print should not be sequentially numbered in the register (say you want to print checks 1203 and 1205, but want to print 1204 at a later time), print the checks one at a time. Also, before you mail your printed checks, double-check the printed check number versus the number assigned in the register to ensure that they match.

Follow these steps to print checks in Money:

To Do: Printing Checks

1. Choose File|Print Setup|Check Setup. The Check Setup dialog box appears.
2. Verify that the correct printer is selected from the Printer drop-down list. Choose a check format from the Type drop-down list, as shown in Figure 18.8. Also, if you want to always print the payee address on every check, make sure the Require Address for Payee when Printing Checks check box is checked. Click OK.

18

▼ To Do

▼ FIGURE **18.8**

Before you print checks, select the correct printer and check type.

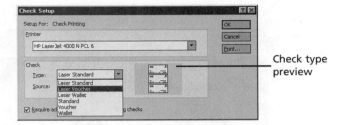

Check type preview

3. Choose File|Print Checks. The Print Checks dialog box appears.

4. To print all checks, leave the All Checks option button selected. To print only selected checks, click Selected Checks to display the Select Checks dialog box. Click each check that you do not want to print to remove the highlighting, and then click OK to return to the Print Checks dialog box.

Depending on what printer and check format you've selected, different options appear below the Number of First Check in Printer text box of the Print Checks dialog box. You'll want to change the settings here depending on how many checks you're inserting into the printer, and so forth. If you have doubts about how these settings will work, test them by inserting a blank page into the printer, clicking Print Test, and then comparing the results with your check format. Then, choose Print This Transaction from the Number drop-down list for any check transaction to reprint the check.

5. If needed, edit the entry in the Number of First Check In Printer text box (see Figure 18.9) to match the number of the first check you've placed in the printer.

FIGURE **18.9**

Make sure to adjust the number in the Number of First Check to Print text box to match the first check to print.

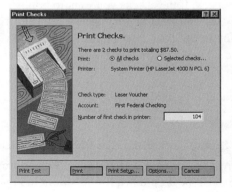

▼

6. Review and correct any other options as needed, and then click Print.

7. Make sure your checks printed correctly; then click Finish. Alternatively, click Reprint, click a check in the list to reprint, specify an entry in the Begin Reprinting Checks at Check Number text box. Click OK, and then click Finish.

Reconciling the Checking Account

Just as you have to synchronize your bank records and paper account register, you have to synchronize your bank records and your Money 99 checking account register (or other account register). This process is called reconciling or balancing your account. As soon as possible after you get your monthly statement from the bank or other financial institution, you should follow the reconciliation process described here, to keep your Money 99 account information as accurate as possible.

Account reconciliation ensures that your records are in agreement with those of the financial institution and that neither of you have created errors. Also, by reconciling accounts you gather new information that needs to be updated, such as fees and charges that need to be deducted and interest and dividend earnings that need to be added to your register.

> After you reconcile the account, cleared transactions display an R in the C column, and the lower-left corner of the register screen displays the date you last balanced the account.

Follow these steps to reconcile an account:

To Do: Reconciling Your Account

1. With your bank statement handy and with the register for the checking account (or other account) to reconcile open onscreen, click the Balance this Account choice in the lower-left corner of the Account Manager.

2. Click Next in the Balance (Account) dialog box that appears.

3. Specify the statement date using the Statement Date drop-down list.

4. Verify that the Starting Balance matches the statement starting balance. Enter the statement ending balance in the Ending Balance text box.

5. Enter any service charge listed on the statement in the Service Charge text box. (This should not include ATM withdrawal charges or bounced check fees, which

18

▼

you should enter as withdrawal transactions.) Optionally, choose a subcategory from the right Category drop-down list. Money enters a transaction for this service charge.

6. Enter any interest listed on the statement in the Interest Earned text box. Figure 18.10 shows the Interest Earned and other entries. Click Next.

FIGURE 18.10

As you start the reconciliation process, enter basic information that appears on your bank statement.

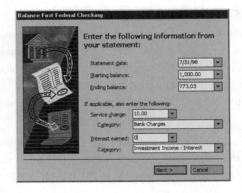

7. To clear each transaction that appears on the statement, click to place a C in the C column (see Figure 18.11).

FIGURE 18.11

Click each transaction to mark it as cleared.

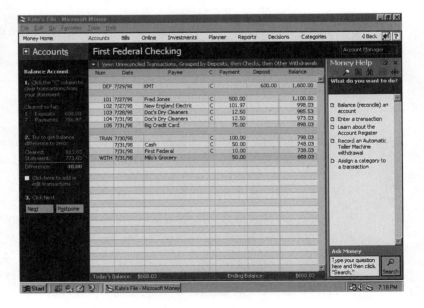

▼

▼   8. When you've cleared all the transactions that appear on the statement or when the
            Balance Difference at the left reaches 0, click Next.

        9. If you fail to properly clear all your transactions or there's some discrepancy, a
            Balance (Account) dialog box appears to inform you that the account hasn't bal-
            anced and that there may be an error. You can do one of the following:

            • Click Go Back to Balancing the Account and click Next to double-check the
              transactions you marked.

            • Click Use AutoReconcile to Help Find the Error, and then click Next for help
              finding the error.

            • Click Automatically Adjust the Account Balance, specify a Category, and
              then click Next.

▲   10. Click Finish at the dialog box that informs you you've balanced your account.

Summary

In this hour you learned to work with account registers and transaction forms for checking and savings accounts. The skills you learned here apply to other account types, as
well. You learned how to use Money 99 to pay your bills, print your checks, move money
between accounts, and keep track of your ATM transactions. You worked with another
powerful and hassle-reducing Money feature—reconciling your account balances with
those of your financial institution. Now move on to Hour 19, "Tracking Your Credit
Cards and Debts," where you learn how to manage your debts using Money 99.

18

Q&A

Q. Where do I enter a transaction?

A. Display the register for the account where you want to enter the transaction. Click
the transaction form tab for the type of transaction to enter: Check (payment),
Deposit, Transfer, Withdrawal, or Cash Withdrawal (for ATM transactions). Fill in
the transaction information, and then click the Enter button. To edit a transaction,
double-click it in the register to return it to the transaction form, where you can
make changes and click Enter.

Q. How do I use Money to print checks?

A. Start by selecting Print This Transaction from the Number drop-down list when you enter the check transaction. Use the File|Print Setup|Check Setup command to choose the correct type of check to print. Finally, choose File|Print Checks to start the check printing process.

Q. If I am diligent in keeping my accounts up-to-date and reconcile my accounts in a timely manner, what kind of useful data or information will be available to help me be successful?

A. At a minimum, you can use your accounts to prepare a budget. The best strategies for wealth accumulation and financial security begin with controlled spending and spending in line with your goals. If you click Reports in the navigation bar, you see a list of reports that help you see where your money goes, what your monthly cash flow looks like, and how well you are doing staying within your budget. To start the reconciliation process, click Balance This Account in the lower-left corner of the account register window.

Hour 19

Tracking Your Credit Cards and Debts

Money can help you keep track of your credit cards and debts. In tracking credit cards and loans, you store important financial details that can help you estimate your net worth, prepare budgets, and monitor your cash flow. Debt information can help you plan to reduce your debt burden, consolidate your debts, lower your cost of debt, and refinance your loans.

This hour focuses on credit card and loan accounts, teaching you to

- Create a new credit or charge card account to keep track of purchases, payments, and credits.
- Reconcile your credit card account register balances with those from the credit card issuer.
- Create loan accounts to track payments of principal and interest over the life of the loan.
- Reconcile your loan account records with those from the lender.

Creating the Credit Card Account

Estimates indicate that more than 75% of adults have at least one credit card. Banks and other financial institutions generate revenues by lending money, and credit cards are one very profitable way to lend money. Credit card offers for pre-approved lines of credit flood mailboxes daily. For consumers with decent credit records, credit is easy to get but not always so easy to control. That's where Money 99 can help. By using Money 99 to record and store your credit card purchases, payments, and cash advances, you can have a more clear picture of what you're charging to a credit card, so you can later take steps to regulate credit card spending.

The starting point for tracking your credit card transactions in Money is setting up a credit card account. Gather up your most recent credit card statement, and follow these steps to create the account:

To Do: Adding a Credit Card Account in Money

1. Choose Go|Accounts (Ctrl+Shift+A) or click Accounts on the navigation bar. If needed, click the Account Manager button to the far right of the account name to display the Account Manager.

2. Click the New Account button near the bottom of the Account Manager. The New Account dialog box appears.

3. Enter the name of the bank or financial institution that issued the credit card in the Held At text box.

> You don't have to enter the financial institution name if you have already set up another account from that institution. For example, if you have a First Bank and Trust credit card and already have a Money checking account set up for that bank, simply select First Bank and Trust from the Held At drop-down list.

4. Click Next to display the next New Account dialog box.

5. Click Credit Card in the list of account types at the left, and then click Next.

6. Enter a name for the account in the Name text box. For example, if it is a VISA, you could enter First Federal VISA. Click Next.

7. Enter the account number in the text box of the next dialog box; then click Next.

8. Enter the amount you owe on the credit card in the How Much Do You Owe on This Credit Card text box (see Figure 19.1). Click Next.

▼ **FIGURE 19.1**

Enter the current balance for the credit card from your credit card statement.

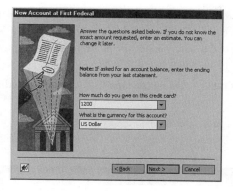

9. Leave Credit Card selected. Click Next.

Credit cards (VISA, MasterCard, or retail store card, for example) charge interest and allow you to carry a balance from month to month as long as you make the minimum payment. Charge cards like American Express require you to pay the entire balance each month and typically charge no interest.

10. Enter the interest rate for the account in the top text box of the next dialog box. If that rate you entered is a special introductory rate, also check the Introductory Rate Is in Effect check box; then specify the Date of Rate Change (when the permanent rate takes effect) and the Permanent Rate. Click Next.

Be wary of low "teaser" credit card rates. Creditors offer teaser rates (introductory rates sometimes as low as 3.9%) to entice you to transfer your credit card balances to the teaser card. After a brief period of time, the teaser rate is raised to a much higher rate, such as 16 to 18 percent, that may be even higher than the rate you previously paid.

11. Enter the credit limit (the maximum amount you charge) in the What Is the Total Credit Limit on This Account text box in the next dialog box. Your most recent account statement should show your current credit limit. Click Next.

12. Leave Keep Track of Individual Credit Charges selected to keep details of each charge you make, such as assigning an expense category to each transaction. Click Next.

▼

▼   13. To have Money remind you each month to pay the credit card bill, leave Yes,
        Remind When the Bill Is Due selected. Enter the Estimated Monthly Amount and
        the Bill Is Due Next On date. Select the account to use to pay the bill from the Pay
        Bill from Account drop-down list. Click Next.

    14. Leave I Have No Other Accounts at This Institution selected, and then click Next
        again.

    15. Click Finish. As Figure 19.2 shows, the credit card account icon appears in the
        Account Manager screen.

FIGURE 19.2

*Account Manager
includes an icon for the
newly created credit
card account.*

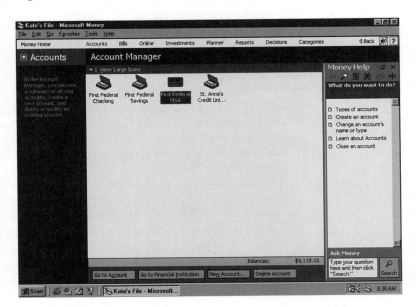

▲

Even if you decide you don't want to carefully track all your credit card activity, at least
enter all the account information, such as the name of the issuer, account number, current
balance, credit limit, and so on. This information is critical if the cards are stolen or lost
or if your statements are destroyed or lost. In addition, you should periodically update
the account balance for your credit card account so Money can accurately calculate your
net worth.

Money 99 doesn't track all key credit card information, so you should keep
your own list (with your other important papers) of credit card information.
For each card, record the name, address, and phone number of the issuer;

account number; and expiration date. Also record any 24-hour toll-free phone number for reporting a lost or stolen credit card. If the card is lost or stolen, you have no liability if you report the loss prior to the fraudulent use. The maximum liability under U.S. law is $50, no matter how long after the fraudulent use you report the loss. If you are not planning to use a credit card, leave it home in a safe place until you need it. If you are traveling, carry one or two major credit cards and traveler's checks.

Entering Credit Card Transactions

If you double-click the icon for a credit card account in the Account Manager, it displays a register (see Figure 19.3) much like the checking (or savings) account register you saw in Hours 17 and 18. A credit card account register not only shows the balance but also the credit limit. The register shows charges (purchases or cash advances) and credits (returns of merchandise) and payments (which you create as a transfer) you enter and calculates a running balance. The credit card account register includes three transaction form tabs: Charge, Credit, and Transfer.

FIGURE 19.3

Double-click a credit card account icon in the Account Manager to see its register, where you enter transactions for the credit card account.

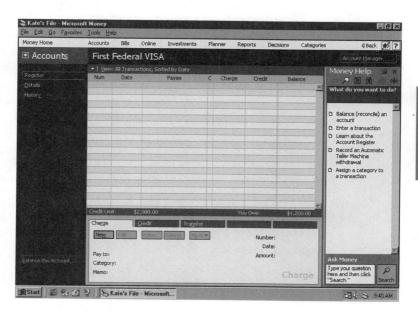

19

> If you want to enter your credit card transactions directly into the account register lines (rather than use the transaction forms), hide the form tabs by opening the View drop-down list below the account name and choosing Enter Transactions Directly into the Register.

Most often, you'll be entering your charges (purchases) in the credit card account register. Follow these steps to do so:

To Do: Entering a Charge (Purchase)

1. In the credit card account register, click the Charge transaction form tab, if needed. Otherwise, simply click the New button on that tab.

2. Click the drop-down list arrow beside the Date text box, and click the charge date. Press Tab to finish your date entry.

> For the most part, you can ignore the Number text box on the Charge transaction form. That text box would only apply if you were transferring money electronically between a credit card account and a bank account.

3. In the Pay To Text box, enter the name of the entity from which you purchased the item or service. Press Tab.

4. Enter the charge amount in the Amount text box. Press Tab. The Category drop-down list opens automatically.

5. Click an Expense category, and then press Tab twice.

6. Enter a description or note in the Memo text box. Your transaction now should look something like the one shown in the Charge transaction form at the bottom of Figure 19.4.

7. Click the Enter button on the Charge transaction form to add the charge to the register. Money automatically increases the account balance to reflect the greater amount you owe.

8. After you enter the first charge, click the New button on the Charge transaction form to begin entering the next charge.

What you owe, you must pay at some point. When you make a payment to your credit card company, you generally do so by check. Enter a credit-card payment using the Transfer transaction form tab. Doing so tells Money to enter a transaction crediting the credit card account and a transaction deducting the check from the checking account you use to pay the credit card.

FIGURE 19.4

Enter charges in the Charge transaction form of the credit card register.

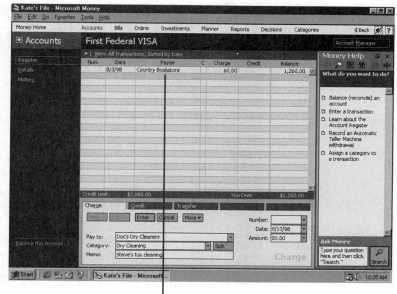

Previously entered charge

Follow these steps to enter a payment you make on the credit card account:

To Do: Recording a Payment to the Credit Card Account

1. In the credit card Account Register, click the Transfer transaction form tab.

2. Enter the number of the handwritten check you used to pay the credit card in the Number text box. Alternatively, open the Number drop-down list and click Print This Transaction if you intend to print the payment check from your Money checking account. Press Tab.

3. Open the From drop-down list and select the checking account that you're using to pay the credit card bill. Press Tab.

4. Click the drop-down list arrow beside the Date text box, and click the payment date. Press Tab to finish your date entry. The To drop-down list opens automatically.

5. Click the name of the credit card account. Press Tab.

6. Enter the payment amount in the Amount text box. Press Tab.

7. Select the name of the credit card account again from the Pay To drop-down list. Press Tab.

8. Enter a description or note in the Memo text box. Your transaction now should look something like the one shown in the Transfer transaction form at the bottom of Figure 19.5.

To Do

19

FIGURE 19.5

Use the Transfer transaction form to enter a credit card payment.

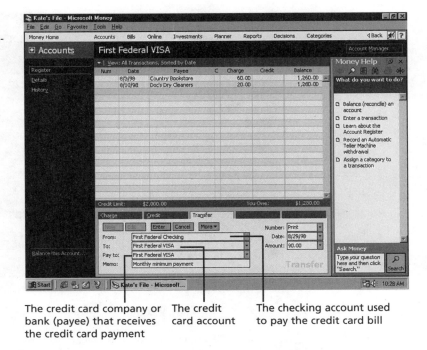

The credit card company or bank (payee) that receives the credit card payment

The credit card account

The checking account used to pay the credit card bill

9. Click the Enter button on the Transfer transaction form to add the payment to the register. Money automatically decreases the account balance to reflect the lesser amount you owe.

10. If the Print Address dialog box appears, enter the address information for the check recipient (the bank or credit card company) and click OK.

11. If Money tells you the transaction matches a recurring payment (if you opted to have Money tell you when payments are due in Step 13 of the account setup process under "Adding a Credit Card Account in Money,") click Yes to have Money mark the bill as paid. Click Yes again if Money asks whether you want to record changes to that recurring transaction.

Don't forget to display your checking account register and print and mail the check for the credit card payment. To move quickly to another account, click the Accounts drop-down list arrow to the far left of the account name displayed at the top of the register, and click the account you want to view in the list that appears.

> You also can initiate payments to your credit card accounts through your checking account. Also use the Transfer transaction form in your checking account register to enter a credit card payment.

One of the expert system features of Money 99 is the Advisor FYI alerts. Figure 19.6 shows an example of the alert displayed when your credit card payment appears to be a relatively low one. This type of alert can help you rethink your debt management. The alert in Figure 19.6 shows that by making a relatively low payment, it will take more than a year to pay off the account (even assuming you make no more charges) and that you will pay $127.97 in interest expenses. Knowing these facts, you might opt to pay a bit more in the short term to save money in the longer term. Click the Dismiss button to close the alert.

FIGURE 19.6

Advisor FYI alerts you when a credit card payment seems low, so you can decide whether to pay more.

19

When you return an item you've previously charged, you need to apply that credit to the balance of your credit account by entering a credit transaction. You can enter a credit transaction immediately after you make the return, or later when you receive your account statement. Use these steps to enter a credit transaction:

To Do: Recording a Credit to a Credit Card Account

▼ To Do

1. In the credit card account register, click the Credit transaction form tab.
2. Click the drop-down list arrow beside the Date text box, and click the credit date. Press Tab to finish your date entry. The To drop-down list opens automatically.
3. Open the From drop-down list and click the name of the company returning credit to your account. Press Tab.
4. Enter the credit amount in the Amount text box. Press Tab. The Category drop-down list opens automatically.

▼

▼   5. Click the Expense category you want to use. Make sure to select the same category
       you used when you entered the original purchase transaction. Press Tab twice.

    6. In the Memo text box, enter a note, such as the reason for the credit and the name
       of the particular returned item.

    7. Click the Enter button on the Credit transaction form to add the credit to the regis-
▲   ter. Money adjusts the account balance accordingly.

Reconciling Credit Card Accounts

Similar to balancing your checking account, reconciling your credit card account
involves making sure that your records (your Money credit card account information)
agree with the account statement from the credit card company or bank. You resolve any
differences you find in an appropriate manner. Be sure you have the most recent credit
card account statement on hand, and then use these steps to reconcile the account:

To Do: Reconciling a Credit Card Account

1. Open the register for the credit card account and enter any transactions that appear
   on your statement that you haven't yet entered.

2. Click the Balance this Account choice in the lower-left corner of the Account
   Manager.

3. Specify the statement date using the Statement Date drop-down list.

4. Verify the previous month's statement balance in the Total Amount You Owed Last
   Month text box. (If the previous balance from your statement does not agree with
   the Total Amount You Owed Last Month entry, you might have forgotten to balance your account one month. Be sure to reconcile the previous month's statement
   before moving forward with this reconciliation.) Enter the new ending balance
   from the credit card statement in the Total Amount You Owe This Month text box.

5. Enter any charges listed on the statement in the Service Charge and Interest Charge
   text boxes. (Your service charge is usually any annual fee you pay for the card.
   Enter cash advance fees as transactions in the register, instead.) Money enters
   transactions for the service and interest charges. Figure 19.7 shows how your
   entries look at this point. Click Next.

6. The Balance Account area appears at the left side of the screen. To clear each
   transaction that appears on the statement, click to place a C in the C column of the
   register.

▼   7. When you've cleared all the transactions that appear on the statement or when the
       Balance Difference at the left reaches 0, click Next.

▼ **FIGURE 19.7**

Enter basic information that appears on your credit card statement.

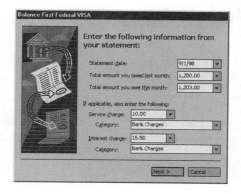

8. If you fail to properly clear all your transactions or there's some discrepancy, a Balance (Account) dialog box appears to inform you that the account hasn't balanced and that there may be an error. You can do one of the following:

   - Click Go Back to Balancing the Account and click Next to double-check the transactions you marked.

   - Click Use AutoReconcile to Help Find the Error and then click Next for help finding the error.

   - Click Automatically Adjust the Account Balance, specify a Category, and then click Next.

9. If you haven't paid your bill and want to do so, click Pay Bill Now at the dialog box that informs you you've balanced your account. Otherwise, click Pay Bill Later and enter the payment transaction later.

▲

19

You can get yourself into dire financial straits by abusing credit cards. Personal financial planners say that as a general rule, monthly payments on all loans and credit cards (except home mortgage) should not exceed 20 percent of available cash flow (salary, wages, and so on). If you get overwhelmed by credit card debt or believe there must be a more efficient way to borrow, you can use the Debt Reduction Planner. The Debt Reduction Planner can help you devise a strategy to pay down your credit card and other high interest debt. The planner can show you effective tactics like the impact of making an extra monthly payment. To go to the Debt Reduction Planner, click Planner on the navigation bar, and then click Debt Reduction Planner.

Creating a Loan Account

Why create a loan account? After all, the bank or other lender will provide you with a loan statement and a year-end summary. Well, here are some reasons:

- By amortizing the loan using Money, you provide a double-check on the lender's system.

- Comparing your lender's statements with a loan account helps you verify that your payments are being applied to principal and interest properly and that any fees charged for late payments or service are legitimate and correct.

- Money can remind you of upcoming loan payments.

Creating a loan account is similar to creating a credit or charge account. Again, you use the Account Manager to step you through the loan account setup, using these steps:

To Do: Setting Up a Loan Account

1. Choose Go|Accounts (Ctrl+Shift+A) or click Accounts on the navigation bar. If needed, click the Account Manager button to the far right of the account name to display the Account Manager.

2. Click the New Account button near the bottom of the Account Manager. The New Account dialog box appears.

3. Enter the name of the bank or financial institution that issued the loan in the Held At text box.

4. Click Next to display the next New Account dialog box.

5. Click Loan in the list of account types at the left, and then click Next. Also click Next after reading the first New Loan Wizard dialog box and the General Information that appears in the next dialog box.

6. Leave Borrowing Money selected. Click Next.

7. Enter a descriptive name in the Loan Name text box, and enter the lender name in the Make Payments To text box. Click Next.

8. Select Adjustable Rate Loan (ARM) or Fixed Rate Loan. If you are not sure whether your loan is an ARM or a fixed rate loan, check the promissory note or loan agreement. Click Next.

9. If you have made payments on the loan already, leave Yes, Payments Have Been Made selected. Money then gives you the option of tracking the previously made payments. Otherwise, click No, Payments Have Not Been Made. Click Next.

These steps assume that no payments have been made and that it's a fixed rate loan.

10. Enter or select the Due Date for the first payment. Click Next, and then click Next again after reading the Calculate Loan information.

11. Open the Paid How Often drop-down list and select from the drop-down box how often loan payments are due. Click Next.

12. In the next dialog box, click the option that describes how interest is calculated on your loan. You might need to check your loan agreement or call your bank to answer this question. Click Next.

13. Enter the amount (original amount of the loan) in the Loan Amount text box. Click Next.

14. Subsequent dialog boxes prompt you to enter the Interest Rate, Loan Length, Principal+Interest (the total amount you'll pay, a figure your lender is required by law to disclose to you), and Balloon Amount (one-time balance payment at the end of the loan term) for the loan. Enter values in all prompts except Principal+Interest. When you are prompted to enter Principal+Interest, press Next to have Money insert a calculation tag. After selecting Next for Principal+Interest, you will notice that Money has inserted the "Calculate" tag. Clicking Next after the Balloon Amount will then prompt Money to calculate the Principal and Interest. (Money calculates the remaining value for you.)

15. Money displays a dialog box with the calculated payment amount. Click OK to verify the amount and display the calculation summary (see Figure 19.8). Review the information, and click Next.

19

FIGURE 19.8

Money summarizes the loan information you entered.

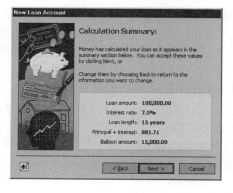

▼ 16. Review the next information about managing payments, and then click Next.

17. Select a category or subcategory to apply to the interest portion of the mortgage payments from the Interest Category and Subcategory drop-down list. (Choose Bills: Mortgage Interest for a home mortgage.) Click Next.

18. If the loan is for a home mortgage, click Yes. If not, select No. Click Next.

19. If the Interest on this particular loan is tax deductible, click Yes. Otherwise, leave No selected. Click Next.

20. If there are any other costs associated with the loan, such as insurance and taxes, assign those costs to expense categories by clicking Other Fees, entering a Category, Description, and Amount for each fee, and clicking Done. Click Next.

21. To have Money remind you to make the loan payment, click Yes, Remind Me. Choose Next Payment Due Date and Pay from Account entries. Click Next.

22. Review the Summary information to ensure its accuracy. If you want to make changes, click the Back button. Otherwise, click Next.

23. If you have an asset associated with the loan, such as an automobile that you pledged to get the loan or a home (as in the case of a home mortgage or an equity loan), click Yes and click Next. Money asks you to select an asset or house account from a drop-down list. (Just enter an account name to have Money automatically create one.) Click Finish and Next. Enter the asset value in the What Is the Asset's Current Value text box, and then click Finish. Click Finish again. If there is no asset associated with the loan, click No, click Finish, and click Finish again. The
▲   loan account icon and name will be added to the Account Manager.

Entering Loan Transactions

Just like a checking account register and the credit card register, a loan register enables you to keep track of activity in the account. The loan register lets you see how many payments you have made, how much interest and principal you have paid, and how much you owe on the loan. Use the loan register to make a regular loan payment by following these steps:

To Do: Making a Regular Loan Payment

1. Choose Go|Accounts (Ctrl+Shift+A) or click Accounts on the navigation bar. If needed, click the Account Manager button to the far right of the account name to display the Account Manager. Double-click the icon for the loan account to open it.

2. Click the New button in the transaction form area near the bottom of the window. A message dialog box appears.

▼ 3. Click Make a Regular Loan Payment and then click OK. The Edit Transaction dialog box appears. It offers many of the same options that you've seen for transaction forms in other account registers.

4. Enter or edit the payment information, including the Number (check number or Print This Transaction), Account (checking account you're using to make the payment), Date, Pay To (the mortgage company), Amount, Category, and Memo. (The Pay to, Amount, and Category entries should already be correct if you set up the mortgage account correctly.)

5. Click OK. If the Print Address dialog box appears, enter the mortgage company address information; then click OK. Money enters the payment transaction in the loan account, and a transaction for a check to make the payment in the checking account you specified. Remember to print that check from the checking account, if
▲ needed.

If you are interested in refinancing a particular loan, open the register for that loan and click Consider Refinancing in the lower-left part of the Account Manager screen. The Loan Planner Worksheet appears. You can use this Money 99 feature to compare the costs of two loans (the loan you have now and the one you would use to refinance).

Any time you want to review the payment terms of a loan (loan amount, remaining balance, rate, monthly payment, and so on), with the loan account register open, click Payment Terms in the upper-right part of the screen (under Accounts). Money displays loan calculation data and bill details.

19

Reconciling the Loan Account

You have to reconcile a loan account just as you'd reconcile any other account. Although most loans seem to run on autopilot, you might have forgotten to record a loan payment or a late fee charged by the lender. Sometimes the lender can make a mistake and post a payment to the wrong account. If your loan account register balance doesn't agree with the statement balance, first enter any missing transactions you identify, such as missing loan payments. If the amounts still don't agree, you need to reconcile the Money account to enter an adjustment in the register. That adjustment can account for a service charge or other type of charge, depending on the category you assign.

To reconcile your loan account, click the Balance This Account choice near the lower-left corner of the loan account register. The Adjust Loan Balances dialog box appears. Enter the ending balance shown on the statement from the lender in the New Ending Balance text box. Specify the statement date using the As of Date text box. Choose a category or subcategory to assign to the adjustment from the Category for Adjustment drop-down list, and then click OK. Money enters the transaction to reconcile the account.

Summary

Money 99 can help you monitor your payments on credit cards and loans. In the last hour, you've learned to set up a credit card and loan account, enter transactions in those accounts, and reconcile them to double-check the information on your bank statement. Move on to Hour 20, "Monitoring Your Investments," to learn how to monitor your investment accounts with Money.

Q&A

Q. Can Money help me maintain or improve my credit rating?

A. Yes. If you create accounts for your credit cards and loans, Money can remind you of upcoming payments so you make them on time. Good credit histories don't just happen. They come about because people have been diligent in creating a track record of timely payments and effectively managing debts. In addition to reminding you of upcoming debt obligations, Money and the Debt Reduction Planner can help you create and implement strategies to reduce credit card balances and refinance high interest debts.

Q. How do I get started with creating a credit card or loan account?

A. Choose Go|Accounts (Ctrl+Shift+A) or click Accounts on the navigation bar. If needed, click the Account Manager button to the far right of the account name to display the Account Manager. Click the New Account button near the bottom of the Account Manager. Enter the name of the bank or financial institution that issued the credit card or loan in the Held At text box, and then click Next. Click Credit Card or Loan in the list of account types at the left; then click Next. Follow the onscreen instructions and enter requested account information to establish the account.

HOUR 20

Monitoring Your Investments

Monitoring your investments begins with some housekeeping work. Before you can use Money 99 to download quotes, update your portfolio values, prepare allocation charts, and track the performance of the S&P 500 against your investments, you need to set up investment accounts. Then you need to enter the details about each of your investments, such as quantity of shares (or units), purchase and sale dates, prices, and so on.

Just as when you set up other types of accounts (such as your checking, savings, and debt accounts), you need to gather up source data—statements from your broker, mutual funds, banks, and insurance companies—so that you can enter accurate starting information. With detailed investment account information in place, you are on your way to monitoring and helping your investments grow with Money 99.

This hour covers these key issues in Money:

- Understand the workings of an investment account and the types of assets to track in such an account.

- Set up investment accounts and the details of the investments held by those accounts.
- Add investments to accounts and enter buy transactions into an account.
- Update an investment account when you sell an investment.
- View the associate cash account of any investment account.
- Learn to monitor investments, gather financial data, educate yourself on investment opportunities and strategies, and watch the financial markets.

Understanding Investment Accounts

You purchase an investment with the expectation and hope that the asset will generate income and grow in value over time. Investments pay interest, or dividends, or offer the potential of capital gains. Typical investments include the following:

- Stocks (common and preferred)
- Bonds
- Mutual funds
- Certificates of Deposit
- Money market funds

You set up investment accounts for groups of investments you hold in a brokerage account or in other financial institution accounts. A rule of thumb is to create an investment account for every statement you receive from a financial institution that tracks such investments as stocks, bonds, and mutual funds that you own. After you have set up an investment account, you can do the following:

- Add individual investments as you acquire them.
- Track the value of investments in the account.
- Track investment income, such as dividends and interest earned.

If you have accounts for your IRA, SEP-IRA, 401(k), 403(b), or other types of retirement plans that hold various investments, create a retirement account to hold those investments in Money as opposed to a Money investment account.

Setting Up an Investment Account

Just as you create a separate Money 99 account for each checking or savings account you have, you need to create a separate Money 99 account for each mutual fund or stock investment account you have. Because you have to track some different information when you track investments, such as share prices and dividends, the process for setting up an investment account differs from the process of setting up checking and savings accounts.

To create your investment account, gather up your investment account statements and follow these steps:

To Do: Creating an Investment Account in Money

To Do

1. On the navigation bar, click Investments.

2. If it is not already selected, click Holdings View at the left side of the Investments screen.

3. At the bottom of the screen, click the New button. The New dialog box appears.

4. Leave A New Investment Account selected and click Next. The New Account dialog box appears.

5. Enter the name of the bank or financial institution where you have the investments in the Held At text box, and then click Next.

6. In the list at the left, click the type of investment account that you want to set up. Choose Investment for a typical brokerage or mutual fund account. If the account is a retirement account, such as an IRA, 401(k), Keogh, 403(b), profit sharing, or company pension plan, click Retirement. Click Next.

> If you have invested in unexpired stock options—not options given to you as part of a company benefit plan—they should be put in an investment account as opposed to an Employee Stock Option Account.

20

7. Use the Name text box to enter a name for the account or simply accept the default name. Click Next.

8. Choose No if the investments in the account are taxable. If the investments are taxable (such as fixed and variable annuities) or tax-free (such as Municipal Bonds, choose Yes. Click Next.

▼   9. Enter the estimated value of the investments in the text box near the top of the next dialog box, but do not include any cash balance (uninvested funds such as money in a cash account at a brokerage house). If you're starting an investment account from scratch (that is, you've deposited cash in it, but haven't placed any securities trades), enter zero as the estimated investment value and the amount of deposited cash as the current cash value in Step 11.

 As you enter the estimated value of the investment account, do your best to enter the current market value. With actively traded stocks, bonds, and mutual funds, you can update the values shown on your account statement by using the current day's financial section of the newspaper or by using the online quote services of a Web-based broker. If the investments are not actively traded, such as is the case with the stocks and bonds of obscure companies and municipalities, call your broker for help. For investment contracts, such as annuities, call the insurance company that issued the contract.

10. Leave Yes selected if the account includes an account that holds uninvested cash. If there is no associated cash account in the investment account, then select No. Click Next.

11. If you chose Yes in Step 10, you need to enter the cash balance in the account in the How Much Do You Have in the Cash Account text box. Click Next.

12. Click Finish. As Figure 20.1 shows, Money displays the new account in your Portfolio.

▲ 13. Repeat Steps 3-12 to add other accounts, as needed.

You can also create a new investment account by opening the Account Manager and clicking the New Account button at the bottom of the screen. To redisplay the Account Manager, double-click the Accounts button on the navigation bar. Alternatively, choose Go|Accounts (Ctrl+Shift+A), and then click the Account Manager button from near the upper-right corner of the account register.

Money doesn't prompt you to enter an account number when you create the investment account, but you can add it later. Right-click the account icon in the Account Manager, and then click Go To Details. Enter the number in the Account Number text box, and enter any other details you deem necessary; then click the Register choice at the left to work with the account register.

Investment account   Account market value

FIGURE 20.1

The Portfolio shows each new account you add and its current market value.

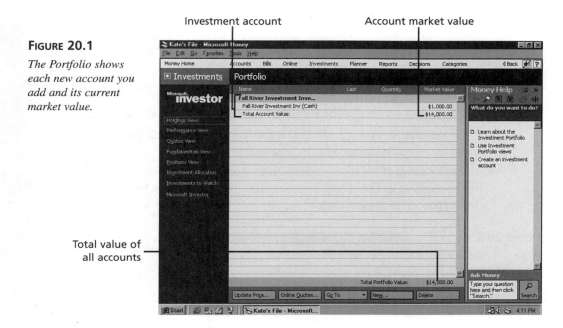

Total value of all accounts

Adding an Investment to the Account

After you create your investment account, you need to tell Money which investments the account holds. For example, if the account already holds 10 shares of Microsoft stock, you have to enter information about Microsoft in the account, specify how many shares the account holds, and specify the present value of each share.

 The steps in this section show a stock investment. Obviously, you'll want to choose the right Investment type (stock, mutual fund, and so on) and Activity (buy, sell, dividend deposit, and so on) for each of your transactions, and then enter any additional information that's not specifically covered here.

20

Follow these steps to identify each investment in an account and specify how many shares the account presently holds:

 ## To Do: Entering a New Investment and Your Initial Holdings

1. Open the register for the investment account. To do so, double-click the Accounts button on the navigation bar to redisplay the Account Manager. Then, double-click the icon for the investment account.

> If you set up a cash account component for the investment account, make
> sure you select the Investment Account icon, not the Cash Account icon. The
> Investment Account icon looks like two certificates.

2. In the transaction form at the bottom of the register, click the New button.

3. Click the drop-down list arrow beside the Date text box; click the date for the purchase in the calendar that appears, and then press Tab.

4. Enter the name of the investment (such as a company name in the case of stock) in the Investment text box, and then press Tab. The Create New Investment dialog box appears (see Figure 20.2).

FIGURE 20.2

*When you enter a new
investment name,
Money asks you to
verify the investment
type.*

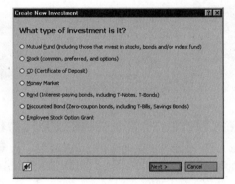

> Steps 4 through 6 apply only if you haven't previously entered a transaction
> for a particular investment (a particular stock or mutual fund, for example).

5. Click the investment type, and then click Next. Another dialog box appears so that you can enter information about the investment.

6. Specify any details you want about the investment. For example, for stocks and mutual funds, you can enter the ticker symbol in the Symbol text box. Click Finish. The Activity drop-down list opens by default.

> If you don't know the symbol for your investment, you can connect to
> `investor.msn.com` to find the symbol by clicking the Find Symbol button in
> Step 5.

▼   7. In the Activity list, click Add (Shares). You select the Add (Shares) option if you don't have investment purchase records available, if the investment was gifted to you, or if you bought the investment in several lots and don't want to enter the history of purchases. If you have your investment purchase records or are making the purchase now, select Buy as the activity. (See the next section, "Entering a Buy Transaction.")

8. Enter the Quantity (number of shares) and Price (per share or unit), and press Tab after each entry. Money calculates the Total for you, as shown in Figure 20.3.

FIGURE 20.3

Use the transaction form to add an investment and the initial shares owned to an account.

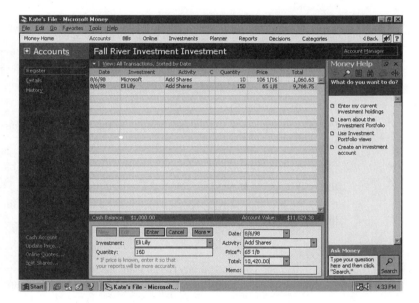

9. Press Tab again, and type a memo, if needed.

▲   10. Click the Enter button on the transaction form to enter the stock transaction in the register.

After you enter each investment, Money adjusts the account value to reflect the actual value of the investments you enter, if that amount differs from the estimate you specified when you created the account.

Entering a Buy Transaction

Each time you buy or sell stock, mutual fund shares, or other investments or receive a dividend or other distribution that's deposited into your real-world investment account, it's a transaction. You need to enter each transaction into the register for the investment account in Money 99. Entering an investment account transaction is similar to entering a checking account transaction, but you need to provide even more information, as described in this task.

This section shows how to enter a stock purchase (buy) as an example. To do so, follow these steps:

To Do: Entering a Buy Transaction

1. Open the account register for the investment account holding the investment that was sold.
2. Click New in the transaction form at the bottom of the screen (below the register).
3. Use the Date drop-down list to specify the date you made the purchase. Press Tab.
4. Open the Investment drop-down list and click the name of the investment that you bought. Press Tab. The Activity drop-down list opens automatically.
5. Select Buy from the Activity drop-down box. Press Tab.
6. Enter the number of shares you bought in the Quantity text box. Press Tab.
7. Enter the price you paid per unit or share in the Price text box. Press Tab.
8. Enter the fee you paid in the Commission text box. Press Tab.
9. Press Tab again. If needed, select the account from which the funds you used to make the buy have been or will be deposited from the Transfer From drop-down list. Press Tab.

> When you enter a buy or sell transaction, you can specify the account from which you withdrew cash to place the buy, or the account into which to place cash resulting from a sale. If your brokerage account includes the capability to store cash (that is, you specified that the investment account includes a cash account), Money automatically suggests that account in the Transfer From (for a buy) or Transfer To (for a sell) entry in the transaction form.

10. Type a Memo, if needed, and then click the Enter button on the transaction form.

If you enter a sell transaction in the Investment account register, Money might display the What Shares Should I Use dialog box (see Figure 20.4). If you want to specify a certain lot of shares as the ones sold, choose Yes; then click Next, and follow the instructions. Otherwise, click No. (No is the default and should already be selected.) Money allocates the shares on a first in, first out (FIFO) basis. Then click Finish. If you want Money to always use the FIFO basis, check the I Want All My Investment Sales To Be Tracked as FIFO check box in the What Shares Should I Use dialog box.

FIGURE 20.4

Specify how Money should do the accounting for shares you sell in this dialog box.

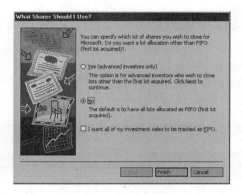

Each block of shares you buy is a *lot*. If you buy 100 shares of a particular company's stock, that's the first lot. If you buy another 20 shares, that's the second lot, and so on. The IRS has rules about whether you need to track stock sales by lot or on a first in, first out basis. So, check with your accountant or tax preparation professional to verify which method you need to use.

Displaying the Account Cash

Investment accounts can have cash accounts. This is where idle, uninvested cash sits while you decide what to invest in next. If your investment account includes a cash account, you told Money that when you set up the investment account. Money then created the cash account, which is linked behind the scenes to the investment account to handle cash transfers for buy and sell transactions.

To review the register for the cash account of your investment account, use one of these techniques:

- In the register for the investment account, click Cash Account in the lower-left part of the screen.
- Double-click Accounts on the navigation bar, and then double-click the Investment Account Cash Account icon (a Cash Investment Account icon has a certificate with a stack of money in front of it) in the Account Manager.

20

Adding to an investment cash account from your checking account works just like adding cash to your savings account from your checking account, with the cash account register displayed. Click the Transfer tab; click New, and complete the transfer form.

Using Money to Watch over Your Portfolio

Money 99 offers a number of features that help you monitor your investment portfolio and make good investing decisions. Figure 20.5 shows the Microsoft Investor screen which you can display by clicking Investments on the navigation bar and then clicking Microsoft Investor at the bottom of the list at the left.

FIGURE 20.5

Use the Microsoft Investor screen choices to learn more about investments.

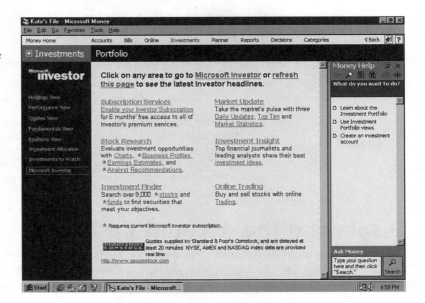

Many of the links here launch your Web browser, connect you to the Internet, and display the Microsoft Investor Web site. You can monitor the markets, read informative investment-related data and articles, and analyze financial fundamentals and charts. In addition to using the Microsoft Investor screen to connect with the live information on the Internet, you can look at different *Portfolio views* to find out more about your portfolio and other investments. Here's a summary of what each view offers, so you can begin to explore:

- Holdings View   Latest price, quantity, and market value of your investment holdings.
- Performance View   Performance data for your investments, such as dollar gain, percentage gain, and annual return.

- Quotes View   Latest market data for your investments, such as last price, change, high, low, and volume.

- Fundamentals View   Price information, P/E Ratios, and volatility ratings for your investments.

- Positions View   Price, quantity, and market value for your individual investments.

- Investment Allocation   A pie chart of your holdings by investment type.

- Investments to Watch   Tracking information for investments and indexes that you specify. You can add investments that you don't own but are interested in watching for possible investment.

Summary

In this hour, you learned how Money 99 helps you track and manage your investment portfolio. You learned to start out by creating an investment account to which you can add specific investments and transactions. You also learned how to view the Microsoft Investor page in the Portfolio and how to use other Portfolio views to evaluate investment performance. The next hour builds on the theme, showing you how to view reports about your financial information and budget for the future.

Q&A

Q. Do I need just one investment account for all my investments?

A. No. You should create one investment account for each investment relationship you have with financial institutions and others. For example, if you have a brokerage account, an investment account with your bank, an account with an insurance company, and some investments that you hold in a safe deposit box, you should set up a separate Money investment account for each one of those situations.

Q. Can I enter transactions in an investment account's cash account?

A. Yes. Your broker might pay interest on money swept into a cash account, or even allow you to write checks from that cash. So, you'll need to enter a transaction for each interest deposit or check in the cash account's register, which you display by clicking Cash Account in the lower-left corner of the window for the investment account itself.

20

Q. **If I "invest" in collectibles such as baseball cards, antiques, or oriental rugs, do I enter those assets in an investment account?**

A. Because the term investments usually implies financial assets as opposed to tangible assets (such as baseball cards, antiques, and oriental rugs), you should use the Asset account type to track collectible investments. Money recommends that you use Asset accounts for property you own, such as a car or art collection. Use an investment account for such items as stocks, bonds, and mutual funds (financial assets).

HOUR 21

Creating Budgets and Reports

This hour presents creating and managing a budget. You can work on these skills:

- Generate a budget using AutoBudget.
- Create a budget by telling Money about your income and expenses.
- Define an amount of money you want to put aside for occasional unexpected expenses.
- Monitor your budget progress.
- View and print reports and charts to track budget progress.

Using Money's Financial Planning Tools

Microsoft Money's Budget Planner is a tool for planning long-term savings. The Budget Planner Wizard prompts you for information on your income and expenses and helps you figure out how you can cut your expenses and build up savings.

Another powerful tool in Money's budget control arsenal is AutoBudget. AutoBudget calculates your budget based on your existing spending and income patterns.

Both the Budget Planner and AutoBudget can help you adopt a more conscious plan for controlling your expenses and saving money. After you define a budget, Money 99 provides reports and graphs to monitor your progress toward your financial goals. In Figure 21.1, budget progress is reflected in one of Money's charts.

FIGURE 21.1

Money makes it easy to compare budgeted income and expenses with actual income and spending.

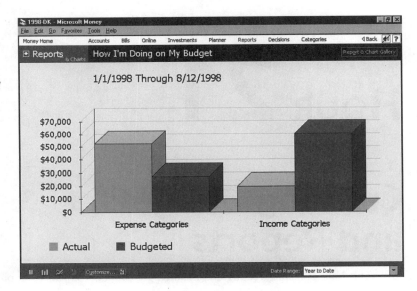

Setting Up Your Budget

Money provides two basic ways to define your budget. You can let Money generate a budget based on your existing spending and income patterns, or you can create your own budget.

AutoBudget generates a budget for you. Alternatively, you can use a wizard to supply Money with the information needed to generate a budget.

Using AutoBudget

Money can generate a budget plan for you automatically *if* you have been using Money for at least one month, and *if* you have been assigning categories to your expenses. The longer you've been using Money, the more transactions there are to use for AutoBudget calculations.

Money calculates your AutoBudget based on the income and spending activity you have already recorded in the accounts you set up. If you are just beginning to use Microsoft Money, you can use the Budget Planner Wizard to project a budget. The Budget Planner Wizard is discussed in the next To Do, "Calculating a Budget."

Follow these steps to let Money calculate your budget:

To Do: Calculating a Budget

1. Select the Planner view from the navigation bar.
2. Click the Expenses link on the left side of the Planner view. An expense log appears, as shown in Figure 21.2.

FIGURE 21.2

The Expenses view in the Budget Planner shows your spending record.

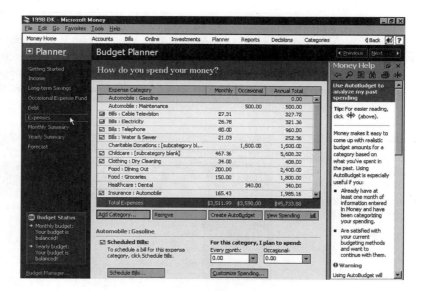

3. Click the Create AutoBudget button on the left side of the Budget Planner window. The AutoBudget dialog box appears.
4. In the AutoBudget dialog box, you can deselect expenses that you don't want included in your calculated budget. By default, all your expense categories are selected. You can deselect an item by clicking the check box to remove the check mark from that item. Figure 21.3 shows all budget items selected. After you have reviewed the expenses that will be used to generate your AutoBudget, click the OK button in the dialog box.

21

FIGURE 21.3

*Money uses your exist-
ing spending habits to
calculate your budget.*

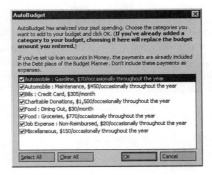

To maintain the integrity of the budget, you should leave all the expenses
checked.

5. After you generate your AutoBudget, you can check your budget status in the
lower-left corner of the Budget Planner window. The Budget Status box indicates if
your budget status is OK (you're spending falls within your income). Additionally,
you can click links to see your monthly and annual income projection. Figure 21.4
shows a monthly budget calculation.

FIGURE 21.4

*Based on your income
and expenses, Money
99 projects your
account balances.*

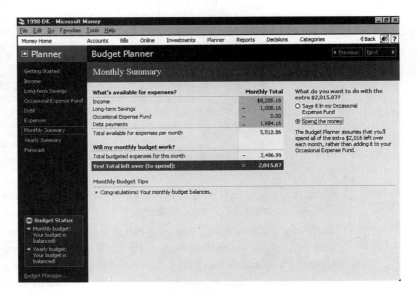

6. If your budget shows a surplus, you can select the Save It in My Occasional Expense Fund radio button in the Monthly Summary view to assign this money to a special savings fund that can be assigned to a vacation, an education fund, or some other savings goal.

7. After you have reviewed your projected monthly and annual account balances, you can see a graph of your projected balances by clicking the Forecast link on the left side of the Budget Planner window. The graph shows your projected balances and your projected savings if you assigned money to an Occasional Expense Fund in the previous step. Figure 21.5 shows that graph.

FIGURE 21.5

You can see your projected account balances graphed for the next year.

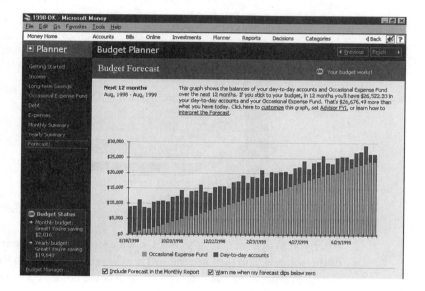

Entering Budget Information

If you haven't been using Money long enough to create a spending and income pattern, or if you want to define income and expenses manually, you can use the Budget Planner Wizard to enter expenses and income. Money then creates projected account balances for you based on the information you enter.

> If you are new to Money 99, and using the Budget Planner to project your income, you'll want to prepare by collecting your income and expenses. Take some time to gather your bills, paychecks, and other budget information before you start the wizard. Your budget projections are only accurate if you provide Money with a complete picture of your finances.

21

To define a budget, follow these steps:

To Do: Defining a Budget

1. Click Planner in the navigation bar, and click the top link on the left side of the window to see the Budget Planner view.

2. Click the Next button in the upper-right corner of the window to see the Where Does Your Income Come From screen. If you have already entered some income sources in Money, those display. If you have additional income categories, click the Add Category button. When you do, the Add Category to Your Budget dialog box appears. Select an income category from the Category and Subcategory drop-down menu, as shown in Figure 21.6.

FIGURE 21.6

Adding income categories to be calculated into your budget.

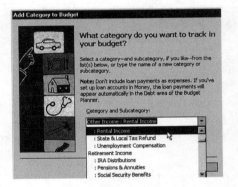

3. After you assign income categories, click each of them in the ledger on the top half of the window, and then use the In This Category I Expect to Receive fields to assign an amount to that category. If the income comes every month (like rental income or child support), use the Every Month field. If the income is occasional (like bonuses from work or gifts), use the Occasional field.

4. Click the Schedule Deposits button if you want to add this income item to your list of regularly scheduled deposits at the same time that you define it as a budget expense. A wizard then guides you through the process of entering this income item as a regularly scheduled income item that is automatically added to a selected account.

5. When you finish defining all your projected income, click the Next button in the upper-right corner of the window.

6. The next window prompts you to enter "What Do You Put Into Long-Term Savings information. Your existing savings contributions are already here. You can use the New Contribution, Edit, or Remove buttons at the bottom of the window to add,

change, or delete savings contributions. After you enter your savings contributions, click the Next button.

7. The What Do You Set Aside for Occasional Expenses" window prompts you to enter a budget category for money you set aside for unexpected expenses. Use the Edit button to define how much you want to set aside, as shown in Figure 21.7. After you define your contribution, click the OK button in the Customize Contribution dialog box, and click the Next button.

FIGURE 21.7

Setting aside a monthly contribution to occasional expenses.

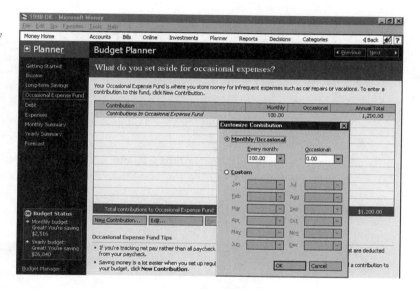

8. The Review Your Debts and Loans window shows loan payments you set up. Review your loan payments and click the Next button.

> You learned to set up loan payments in Hour 19, "Tracking Your Credit Cards and Debts."

9. The How Do You Spend Your Money window shows your scheduled payments. Use the Add Category button to add new expenses. You learned to schedule payments in Hour 18, "Working with Your Checking or Savings Account." These expenses are calculated into your budget.

10. The last three screens in the wizard show a monthly and annual summary of your projected account balances and graphed budget forecast.

21

Viewing Budget Reports and Charts

After you define your budget (or let Money do that for you using AutoBudget), you can look at your budget status in report or chart form. Refer to Figure 21.1 at the beginning of this hour to see a chart that compares actual income and expenses to budgeted income and expenses.

Money's Report view has two reports that are custom-tailored to report on your budget and your budget progress.

Creating and Printing a Budget Report

To view a report reflecting budget progress, follow these steps:

To Do: Viewing Budget Reports

1. Select the Reports view in the navigation bar.

2. Click the Spending Habits link on the left side of the screen to see a list of reports that reflect your budget.

3. In the list on the right side of the window, select the My Budget Report, as shown in Figure 21.8. Then click the Go to Report/Chart button at the bottom of the window.

4. Use the vertical scrollbar on the right to see your entire budget report.

FIGURE 21.8

Selecting a budget report.

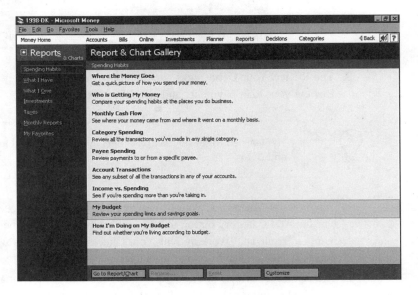

You can print any report. Before you do, you might want to select File | Print Setup | Report and Chart Setup from the main menu bar. In the Report and Chart Setup dialog box, you can define paper size and orientation, as shown in Figure 21.9. Landscape orientation (sideways) often works best for reports with many columns.

FIGURE 21.9

Preparing to print a budget report.

When you have defined your print setup, you can follow these steps to print your report:

To Do: Printing Your Report

1. With the budget report in your current view, select File | Print from the main menu bar.

2. Click OK in the Print dialog box.

Viewing Your Budget Progress in Report and Chart Form

The How I'm Doing On My Budget report can be viewed as a report, or as a chart. The chart form works well for providing you with a quick summary of your projected income and expenses as opposed to your actual income and expenses.

The following steps display a chart of your Budget progress:

To Do: Displaying a Chart of Your Budget Progress

1. Select the Reports view from the navigation bar.

2. Click the Spending Habits link on the left side of the window, and click the How I'm Doing On My Budget report on the right side of the window. Select a date range from the Date Range drop-down menu.

3. Click the Go to Report/Chart to see your Actual and Budgeted Income and Expenses.

4. Click the Customize button at the bottom of the window to fine-tune your report. To consolidate small income and expense categories into a few, combined large

21

▼ categories, click the Rows & Columns tab, and enter 10% (or some other percentage) in the Combine All Values Under field, as shown in Figure 21.10.

5. Click the OK button in the Customize Report dialog box, and view your report. Actual and budgeted amounts for different expense and income categories are compared for the selected Date Range.

FIGURE 21.10

Use the Customize Report dialog box to consolidate budget categories.

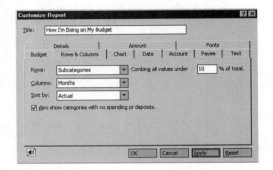

You can use the Columns drop-down menu in the Rows and Columns tab of the Customize Report dialog box to display figures by total, by quarter, or by other time increments instead of by month.

6. Select File | Print and OK in the Print dialog box to print your report.

7. Click the Bar Chart icon at the bottom of the Report window to view your Budget progress in graph form. You can point with the plus sign (+) cursor at any bar on the chart to see details for that budget item, as shown in Figure 21.11.

8. You can fine-tune your graph by clicking the Customize icon at the bottom of the window and selecting chart options in the Chart tab of the Customize Report dialog box. Figure 21.12 shows the dialog box, with 3D display and a legend at the bottom of the chart selected.

9. You can print your chart by selecting File | Print and then clicking the OK button in
▼ the Print Chart dialog box.

FIGURE 21.11

Checking up on budget progress graphically.

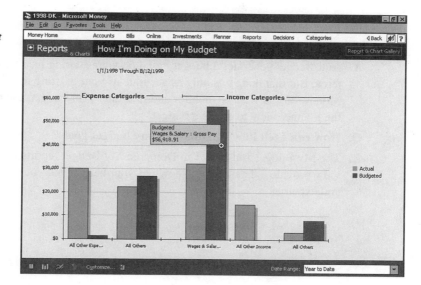

FIGURE 21.12

Defining chart options for a budget graph.

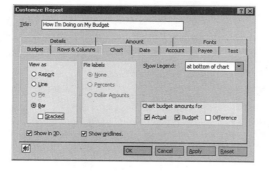

Summary

Microsoft Money makes it easy to consciously budget your income and expenses. You can let Money generate a budget for you, using AutoBudget, or you can define your own budget. Then, you can monitor your budget progress using Money's budgeting reports.

21

Q&A

Q. Can I just let Money create a budget for me?

A. AutoBudget generates a budget based on your existing income and spending patterns. But that budget is only as accurate as your existing records. If you are new to Money, or you want to monitor and fine-tune your budget, use the wizard in the Planner view to create a budget.

Q. How can I tell how I'm doing on my budget goals?

A. The My Budget and How I'm Doing on My Budget reports in the Reports view provide a detailed breakdown of your budget and your actual income and expenses.

HOUR 22

Handling Your Banking Online

This hour presents online banking. You can work on these skills:

- An overview of what online banking is all about.
- Signing up for online banking privileges with your bank or financial institution.
- Carrying out online transactions with Microsoft Money.
- Transferring money between online accounts.

What Online Banking Does

Online banking means that you can handle financial transactions with your bank or other financial institution (like investment institution) over the Internet. Microsoft Money meshes smoothly with online banking, enabling you to make payments, check balances, and record bank transactions directly from your PC.

Different financial institutions provide different levels of support for online banking. Some offer account balances only, whereas others offer online payments, transfers and other features. Figure 22.1 shows an electronic payment, written and ready to be transferred over the Internet to a financial institution.

FIGURE 22.1

Making payments directly over the Internet through online banking.

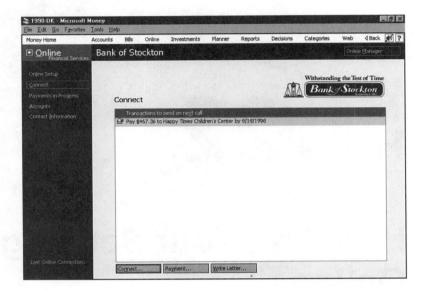

You need two things to do your banking online: a connection to the Internet and a bank or other financial institution that provides online banking. In Hour 14, "Preparing to Go Online," you learned how to connect with the Internet. In this hour, you learn to use that connection for online banking.

If your bank does not support online banking with Microsoft Money, it may still provide its own Web site and online banking features. In that case, you might be able to see your balance online, or even make payments online, but you won't be able to do that through Money. And you'll have to record those transactions separately in Money.

Making Online Banking Arrangements

The first step in online banking is to find out what online banking features your bank provides. You can ask your bank what online services they support with Microsoft Money. Or, later in this hour, you will learn to look up this information online using Microsoft Money.

If your bank supports online banking with Money, then you can sign up for an online account.

Just because you have an account with a bank does not mean you are signed up for online banking. Some banks let you sign up for online banking over the Internet. Others require that you complete an application and mail it in using snail mail (not email). In any case, you need to apply for online banking privileges with your bank. This is similar to the way you have to sign up for auto-teller privileges along with your bank account.

22

Find Out What Online Services Your Bank Provides

Not all banks support online banking with Money. But Money helps you find out what services are provided for online banking by your financial institution.

Follow these steps to find out what financial services your bank offers online through Microsoft Money:

To Do: Discovering Whether Your Bank Supports Online Banking

1. Select the Online view by clicking on Online in the navigation bar.
2. Select an account for the bank you want to learn about, and then click the Go To button at the bottom of the Online Manager.
3. A new view appears with your bank's page. Click the Investigate Offerings button.
4. If you are not currently logged on to the Internet, a Direct Services Setup dialog box appears. If you have set up an Internet connection, select the Use My Existing Internet Connection check box, and click the Next button.

If you need to set up an Internet connection, you can refer to Hour 14 in this book.

5. The name you assigned your financial institution when you set up the account may not be exactly the same as the name the bank uses for online banking. In the Enter the Name of Your Financial Institution dialog box, click the Financial Institutions button and select your bank, as shown in Figure 22.2. If your bank doesn't appear on the list, type its name in the field in the dialog box.
6. After you enter the name of your bank, click the Next button and wait while Money looks up your financial institution. The final dialog box tells you what services your bank provides. Figure 23.3 shows a report from a bank that provides a full menu of online banking features.

Figure 22.2

Selecting your bank from the list of available online banking institutions.

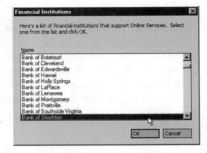

Figure 22.3

Money tells you what online financial services are available from your bank.

Your bank may not support online banking. It's possible that your bank offers online banking, but has set it up in a way that doesn't let you enter online transactions through Money. Figure 22.3 shows a description of the financial services for one of the banks in that category. Your only options are to find a bank that does work with Money, or to forgo online banking with Money until these services are offered by your bank.

Signing Up for Online Banking

Just because your bank offers online banking doesn't mean you have online banking privileges. Before you can start to do online transactions, you need to get a pass code and (sometimes) other information from your bank.

After you have determined that your bank supports online banking, with Money, you should find out the details. Some banks charge fees for online banking, and you should learn what they are before you sign up. Then, you can apply for an online account with your bank.

Follow these steps to find out online banking details:

To Do ## To Do: Investigating Your Bank's Online Banking Services

1. If your bank provides online banking in conjunction with Microsoft Money, you'll see Steps 3, 4, and 5 after you check out their online banking features. Figure 22.4 shows a screen with these steps.

FIGURE 22.4

If your bank offers support for online banking with Money, you can learn the details about online banking fees.

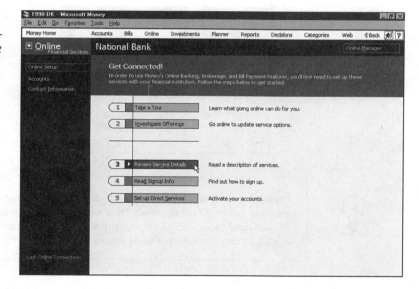

2. Click Step 3 in the window to read the service details for your bank's online banking.

3. After you review and print the description of your bank's online banking features, click the Finish button in the dialog box that describes those features. You're now ready for Step 4: signing up for services.

> Read the description of online banking carefully for your financial institu-
> tion. In most cases, online banking is not free. You may be able to get a free
> trial period, or a certain number of free transactions, but there are usually
> fees involved somewhere along the line. These fees may be well worth the
> cost, but you should print out the description of services and fees and con-
> sider them carefully before signing up for online banking.

4. Click Step 4, Read Signup Info. Here, you might find a link to your bank's Web
   site, where you can fill out an application for online banking (see Figure 22.5).

FIGURE 22.5

*Some banks let you
sign up for online
banking over the
Internet.*

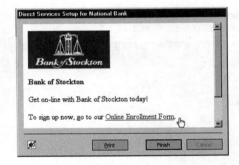

> Most banks will send you a pass code and other information you need
> through snail mail, or by email. They won't give out a pass code when you
> fill out your application. This is to prevent someone from fraudulently sign-
> ing up to conduct Internet transactions on your account.

5. When you finish gathering all the information your bank requires for online banking (and this will probably take some time), you can click Step 5 in the Online
   Setup window. Here, a wizard prompts you for account number and other information required by your bank to process transactions online. After you enter this
   information in Step 5, you're ready to start conducting online transactions in
   Money.

Setting Money Up for Online Banking

After you set up one or more online accounts, you need to assign specific payments, transfers, and so on to those online accounts.

Follow these steps to assign transactions to online accounts:

To Do: Assigning Transactions to Online Accounts

1. Select the Bills view by clicking Bills in the navigation bar.
2. Click an unpaid bill that you want to pay online.
3. Click the Record Payment button at the bottom of the Bills view.
4. In the Record Payment dialog box, select a bank that supports online banking from the Account drop-down menu.

> Before you can pay checks through online banking, you must sign up for an online account, as described earlier in this hour. Accounts that have online banking set up have a small blue lightning bolt next to them in the Account menu.

5. Select Electronic Payment (Epay) from the Number menu in the dialog box. When you have selected an online bank and Epay, as shown in Figure 22.6, click the Record Payment button.

FIGURE 22.6

Recording an electronic (Internet) payment.

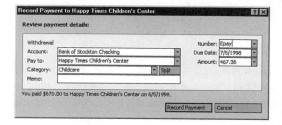

> Most banks have a time delay before they can process online payments. If, for example, you attempt to make an electronic payment for the current date, you may see a dialog box warning you that your bank can't process online payments that quickly. You then receive notification of the earliest date that your transaction can be recorded.

22

▼ 6. After you record an electronic payment, you're prompted for an address and
account number for your payment. Enter this information in the Online Payee
Details dialog box and click the OK button.

7. If you are making an online payment to a payee for the first time, Money prompts
you with the Modify Future Payment Details dialog box. Here, you can click the
Yes button, as shown in Figure 22.7. If you select Yes, you modify your payments
to this payee, so that in the future they are processed online.

FIGURE 22.7

*You can modify a
recurring payment so
that in the future it is
made online.*

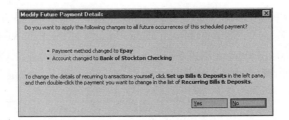

8. After you enter an online payment, click Online in the navigation bar, and click the
Connect link on the left side of the window. Then click the Connect button at the
bottom of the right side of the window to process the payment online. You see a
list of electronic payments ready to process (refer to Figure 22.1). You're prompted
for a PIN (personal identification number) assigned by your bank. Enter that num-
▲   ber, and click the OK button.

Transferring Online Banking Information

You can make an electronic transfer between accounts if both accounts are with the
same bank.

If you want to transfer money from one account to another, you can make a regular electronic payment from one financial institution to another. That process is the same as if
you were making an electronic payment to your utility or for your home loan. You
learned how to do this in the previous section of this hour.

To transfer money between online accounts, follow these steps:

To Do: Transferring Money Between Online Accounts

1. Select Accounts in the navigation bar, and double-click the account from which
you want to transfer money.

2. Pull down the To drop-down menu, and select an account to which you are making
an online transfer.

22

▼ 3. Pull down the Number menu and select electronic transfer (Xfer).

4. Click the Enter button at the bottom of the Account window.

▲ If both your accounts are set up for online banking, you can complete your transfer.

Summary

Online banking is offered by many banks. Some, but not all, of those banks provide online banking services that can be accessed from within Microsoft Money.

After you sign up for online banking, you can make payments and transfer money online.

If your bank does not support online banking with Microsoft Money, your bank may still provide its own Web site with online banking features.

Q&A

Q. I already have an account with my bank. Can I start making online transactions from that account?

A. Not until you sign up, separately, for online banking from your account.

Q. What's the downside to online banking?

A. Banks that do provide online banking usually charge for online transactions in some form or other, so you should investigate what those charges are before signing up.

Q. If my bank doesn't support online banking with Money, what are my options?

A. Unless you wield a whole lot of influence with the bank's board of directors, you might have to find a bank that does support online banking with Money.

Part V
Finishing Your Day with Other Applications

Hour

HOUR **23**

Creating Greeting Card Projects with Graphics Studio Greetings 99

Works Suite 99 comes with an easy-to-use program that helps you design and print greeting cards, invitations, stationery, and more. Microsoft Graphics Studio Greetings 99 is a specialized program for creating all kinds of greeting card items and anything else you can think of to print. Combine it with a color printer, and you practically have your own print shop at home. Even without a color printer, there are plenty of projects you can create.

In this hour, you'll learn all the basic steps for using Graphics Studio Greetings 99 to create all kinds of greeting cards and other projects. The highlights of this hour include

- Starting and exiting the Greetings 99 program
- Navigating the program window
- Creating a greeting card

- Adding a picture or photo to your project page
- Learning how to add shapes and lines
- Changing the project background
- Printing and saving your project

Starting and Exiting Greetings 99

Before you get started, insert your Greetings 99 CD into your computer's CD-ROM drive. You won't be able to use the program without the CD.

> Unlike other programs that copy all their files onto your computer's hard disk drive when you install them, many of the Microsoft Greetings files remain on the CD. That's because most of the files are graphics, pictures, and illustrations. These image files would take up too much room on your hard disk drive; instead, they remain on the CD. For that reason, you'll need the Greetings 99 CD inserted every time you use the program.

To open the program, click the Start button on the Windows taskbar and choose Programs | Microsoft Greetings; then select Microsoft Greetings again.

You can also start the program using the shortcut icon on the desktop. When you installed Greetings 99, the installation program placed a shortcut icon for the program on your Windows desktop; double-click the icon to open the program.

Figure 23.1 shows the Greetings 99 main program screen. Greetings 99 looks a lot different from the other Works Suite programs. Of course, the familiar title bar and menu bar appear the same, but everything else is radically different. Each program feature is represented as a tab on the left side of the screen. To activate a tab, click on it. As you create each project, you'll have the opportunity to save it to use it again.

> To see a short demo of the program, click the middle graphic on the Introduction tab. This opens a series of dialog boxes that demo the program's features and give you an idea of the types of projects you can create.

Most of the projects you create with Greetings 99 revolve around cards—greeting cards, invitations, announcements, and so on. You can create paper-based cards, print them, fold them, and give them to friends or family. Look for these project types on the Paper Projects tab and on the Occasions tab.

FIGURE 23.1

Welcome to Graphics Studio Greetings 99, a program that taps into Hallmark designs and messages and lets you turn them into your own.

Tabs—

Click here to start a demo

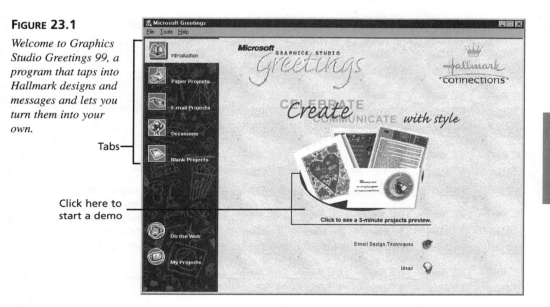

23

Do you conduct most of your correspondence using email? You can create electronic cards, most of which use animation and sound effects, and send them via email. You'll find a large selection of email greetings on the Email Projects tab.

You can also create stationery, such as letterhead, or buy all kinds of specialized papers for stationery projects at your local Hallmark store to use with the program. You can find stationery projects on the Paper Projects tab.

Greetings 99 comes with all kinds of designs, ranging from funny to serious, and you can also use your own creations, including photographs you've scanned in and saved on your computer. You can add your own personalized photos to any project. Look for photo projects on the Paper Projects tab.

When you installed Greetings 99, Microsoft's Picture It! program was also installed; you'll see a shortcut icon for it on the Windows desktop. You can use Picture It! to help you work with photos you scan in. If you have a scanner hooked up to your computer, there's no end to the personalized cards you can create. For example, you can design your own family Christmas cards with a group photo to send to all your relatives. Be sure to check out the Picture It! program and see what it can do.

In addition to all the great designs that come with Greetings 99, you can also log onto the Internet and download add-ons (collections of additional projects and designs), some of which are free.

As you can see, there's a lot you can do with Greetings 99.

Although you're not ready to quit the program just yet, when the time comes, you can exit the program by clicking the Close (X) button in the upper right corner of the program window, or choose File | Exit.

You should definitely check out the Graphics Studio Greetings Web site for all kinds of goodies, including add-on packs. To access the Web site, you must have an Internet account. Click the On the Web button main program window and log onto your account; then click the Add-On Packs link. Continue following the links to find the correct program version and see what add-ons are available for downloading.

Designing a New Project

Most applications open a blank file for you. Greetings 99 doesn't quite work that way. Because the types of projects you can create in Greetings 99 vary so dramatically, you have to tell the program what kind of project (file) you want to create. Each project you choose opens a different series of dialog boxes that walk you through the process of creating a design. The steps can include selecting artwork, adding a saying or other text, choosing a paper size, and so on.

Use the following steps to create a greeting card. (Make sure your Greetings 99 CD (labelled Disc 3 in the Works Suite CD set) is inserted before starting.)

The tasks in this hour depict creating a greeting card. The specific steps for different types of projects vary. However, the techniques you learn for working with text and pictures apply to any project you create.

Click the Ideas link on the Greetings 99 main program window to open a series of dialog boxes offering great ideas for using the program.

To Do: Creating a Greeting Card

1. Click the Paper Projects tab from the main program window.
2. Click the Greeting Cards link, shown in Figure 23.2.

FIGURE 23.2

Select a paper project from any of the options on this tab.

23

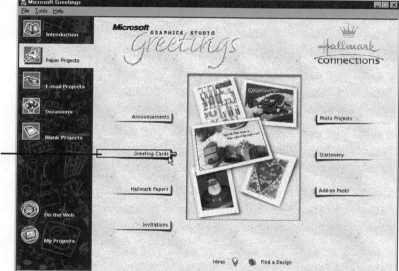

Click here to start a greeting card

3. The first dialog box you see, shown in Figure 23.3, asks you to select the type of card you want to create. Click the one you want to use; then click Next.

Choose a card type

FIGURE 23.3

Start by choosing the type of card you want to make.

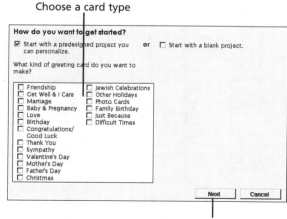

Click here to continue

▼   4. Next, choose a recipient from the list (see Figure 23.4). Use the scroll arrows to
         scroll through the entire list. After selecting the one you want, click Next.

FIGURE 23.4

*Use this dialog box to
select a recipient.*

5. The next dialog box, shown in Figure 23.5, has three options. First, choose a mood,
    such as Cute, Funny, or Serious. Then click a design. (Use the scroll arrows to see
    more designs.) As soon as you do, a third option appears for previewing the card's
    message, both inside and outside the card. Click the Select arrow button to change
    the card's message. Click Next to move on to the next dialog box.

> To find out what kind of paper fold the design uses, hover your mouse
> pointer over the design image and a ScreenTip appears describing the paper
> fold.

FIGURE 23.5

*Use this dialog box to
choose a mood, choose
a design, and preview
a message.*

Click a design

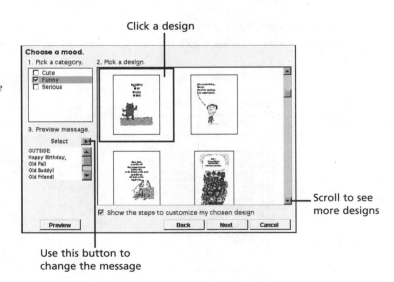

Scroll to see
more designs

Use this button to
change the message

▼

Any time you see a message or tip bubble in Greetings 99, you can click anywhere in the bubble to close it.

6. Use the next dialog box to personalize the message on the front of the card (see
   Figure 23.6). Click inside the text box shown on the card and edit the existing message, or type a new one. You can edit the text the way you do in a word processing
   program. When finished, click Next.

23

Here's an FYI about   Edit the text directly
the inside message   on the card

FIGURE 23.6

*Customize the front of
the card any way you
want.*

Click here to select
another message

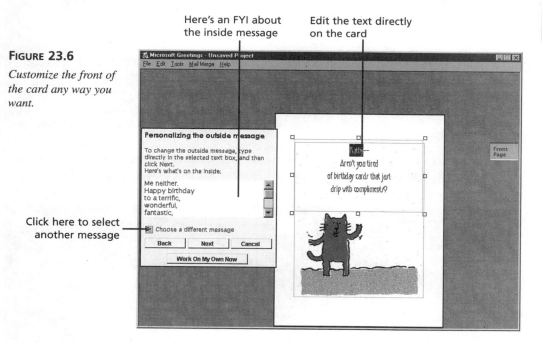

At any time during the creation of a project, you can click the Work On My
Own Now button to continue without all the dialog boxes. You can also
cancel a project by clicking the Cancel button, or return to a previous screen
by clicking the Back button.

7. Now you're ready to customize the inside of the card (see Figure 23.7). Click
   inside the text box and edit the existing text as needed, or type a new message.
   When finished, click Next.

FIGURE 23.7

The next step is to customize the inside of the card.

Look here to see your
card's front message

Personalize the inside message.

Change the inside message by typing
directly in the text box, and then clicking
Next.

To compare, see the outside message below.

Stacey–
Aren't you tired
of birthday cards that just
drip with compliments?

[Back]   [Next]   [Cancel]

[Work On My Own Now]

Me neither.
Happy birthday
to a terrific,
wonderful,
fantastic,
good-looking,
simply marvelous
friend!

Inside
Right

8. Last, but not least, customize the back of the card. Click inside the text box, as
   shown in Figure 23.8, and personalize the text. Click Next when finished.

FIGURE 23.8

Finally, customize the backside of the card.

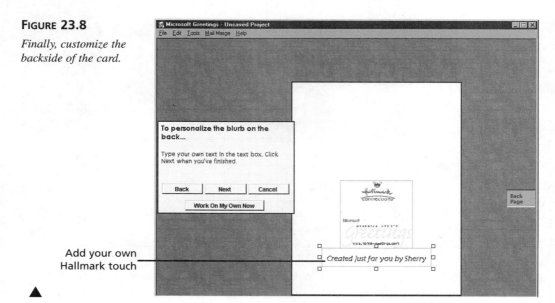

To personalize the blurb on the back...

Type your own text in the text box. Click
Next when you've finished.

[Back]   [Next]   [Cancel]

[Work On My Own Now]

Hallmark
Connections

Microsoft
GREETINGS STUDIO
Greetings
www.1618-greetings.com

Add your own
Hallmark touch

Created just for you by Sherry

Back
Page

When you've completed the card, or any other project you might have chosen, Greetings 99 displays the project in the program window, as shown in Figure 23.9. From here, you can print the project, save it, make changes to it, and edit it any way you want.

FIGURE 23.9

Greetings 99 displays your project in the program window along with various tools for editing each element.

Options box

Toolbar

Page buttons

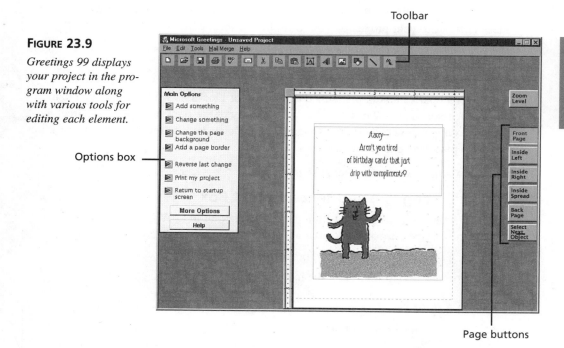

The page buttons along the right edge of the screen let you navigate to the different pages or parts of the project. For example, to edit the inside of the card, click the Inside Right button. Use the page buttons to display project pages.

Use the Zoom Level button to change your view of the project. For example, you can switch between viewing the whole project or zooming up close for a detailed look.

Fine-Tuning Your Project

After you design a project, you can use the Greetings 99 tools to fine-tune the project. For example, you can do any of the following:

- Add new text blocks.
- Insert pictures or photos.

- Turn text into shapes.
- Add lines and shapes.

You can use the Greetings 99 tools to do these things on your own, or you can select from any of the options listed in the Options box. In this section, you'll learn how to make changes to your project on your own, for the most part, using each of the techniques in the previous list.

Working with Text Blocks

Greetings 99 places text in predefined text boxes, or blocks. If you've edited text in a word processor such as Word 97, you can use many of the same techniques in Greetings 99. For example, you can use the Backspace and Delete keys to remove text and click the cursor in place and enter new text.

To edit existing text in a text box, use these steps:

To Do: Editing Existing Text in a Text Box

1. Click in the text box to position the insertion point in it. When you click inside a text box, the Formatting toolbar automatically appears.
2. Drag over text to select it, and press Delete to delete it.

 3. Type new text to insert it at the insertion point.

> The toolbar at the top of the Greetings 99 program window offers Cut, Copy, and Paste buttons to move or copy text. These buttons work just like those in Word.

To add another text box to your project, follow these steps:

To Do: Adding Text Boxes to Projects

1. Click the Add New Text Box button on the toolbar. A box appears on the project page with placeholder text and the Formatting toolbar appears, as shown in Figure 23.10.

> Placeholder text is dummy text that stands in for the real text you'll enter later. Of course, it's up to you to enter the actual text. The placeholder text is simply there to show you the default font and size used.

Click here to start
a new text box

Formatting
toolbar

FIGURE 23.10

*You can easily add a
new text box and for-
mat it as you please.*

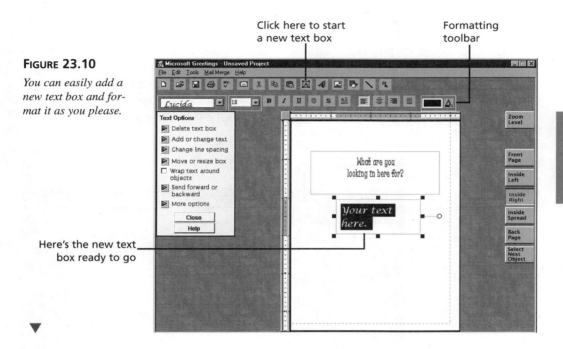

Here's the new text
box ready to go

2. Begin typing your own text.

3. To format the text, select it and then apply any of the options on the Formatting toolbar. These options are similar to the ones you use in Word or the Works Word Processor tool to format text. (Learn more about formatting options in the next section.)

> Like the other Works Suite programs you've learned about, you can quickly find out what a toolbar button does in Greetings 99 by simply hovering your mouse pointer over the button. A ScreenTip appears displaying the name of the button.

4. To move the text box, move the mouse pointer over a border around the text box until the pointer takes the shape of a four-sided arrow with the word MOVE next to it. Then click and drag the text box to a new location on the project page.

5. To resize the text box, move the mouse pointer over a corner of the selected text box until it takes the shape of a double-sided arrow with the word RESIZE next to it. Click and drag the corner to resize the text box.

Formatting Options

Each text box in the project you create uses text formatting meant to compliment the design you selected for the project. That doesn't prevent you from doing your own thing, though. For example, if you enter very little text in a text box, you might want to make the text larger. To do so, click the Change Font Size button, as shown in Figure 23.11, and choose another size. You can use the buttons on the Formatting toolbar to make all kinds of formatting changes to the text.

Click here to display a list of font sizes

FIGURE 23.11

Use the buttons on the Formatting toolbar to change the appearance and position of the text.

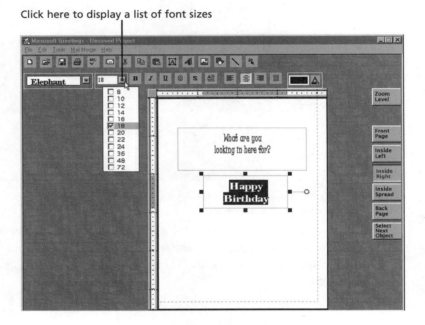

To format text, click the border of the text box to select the whole box and display the Formatting toolbar; then choose any of these formatting options:

- To change the font, click the Change Font Type drop-down arrow and click a new font for the text.
- To change the font size, click the Change Font Size drop-down arrow and select another font size to use. When you make text larger, the text box holding it automatically expands.
- To toggle Bold, Italic, Underline, or Outline on or off, click the button for that effect.
- To add a shadow effect to the text, click the Shadow button.

- To make the first letter a large initial capital, click the Big First Letter button.
- To change the alignment of the text, click an alignment button (Left Align, Center, Right Align, or Justify).
- To choose another text color, click the Change Color button; then click a new color in the palette that appears.

Inserting a Picture

23

The Works Suite programs call the predrawn pictures you can insert *clip art*. Greetings 99 calls its predrawn images *pictures*. Most project designs include one or two pictures, but not necessarily on each page. For example, a greeting card typically includes a picture on the front, but may not include a picture on the interior page with your message. You can add a picture to that message page to make it even more colorful and interesting.

Follow these steps to insert a picture:

To Do: Inserting a Picture

1. Display the project page where you want to insert a picture.
2. Click the Add New Picture button on the top toolbar. This opens the Clip Gallery dialog box where you can select a picture to use (see Figure 23.12).

FIGURE 23.12

Use this box to select a picture. Start by choosing a category.

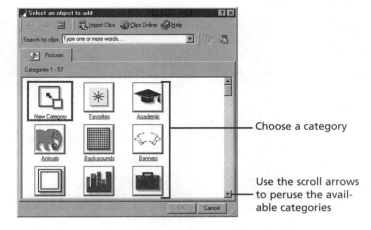

Choose a category

Use the scroll arrows to peruse the available categories

3. Click a category (use the scroll arrows to see the entire list) to open a list of related pictures.
4. When you find a picture you like, click it, and then click the Insert Clip button, as shown in Figure 23.13.

Use the navigation buttons to
move in and out of categories

FIGURE 23.13

*Select the picture you
want to insert.*

Click here to insert
the picture

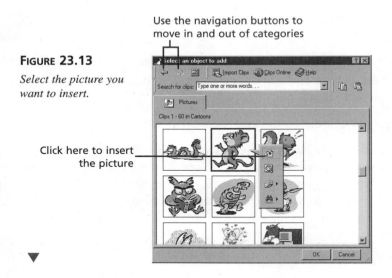

5. The picture is inserted onto your card (see Figure 23.14). It might need to be
moved or resized to fit. To move the picture, point to the picture border until you
see the MOVE pointer; then drag the picture to a new location. To resize the picture, point to a corner handle on the picture border until you see the RESIZE pointer; then drag the corner to resize the picture.

FIGURE 23.14

*Resize or move the pic-
ture to fit exactly
where you want it.*

Selection handles

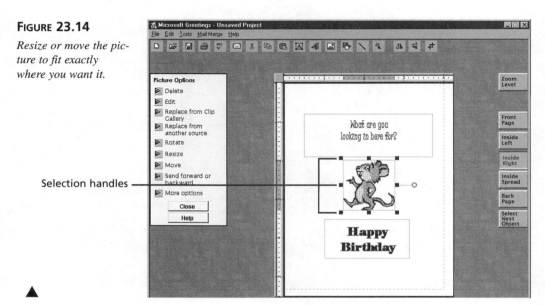

Inserting Photos

Are you the lucky owner of a digital camera? Digital cameras enable you to store pictures on disk rather than film. You can then print these images with your color printer. To personalize your projects in Greetings 99, you can insert a photo of your child or pet that you've snapped with your digital camera. Greetings 99 also considers graphics you've drawn in a program such as Windows Paint as photos. In fact, you can insert any "photo" in the .BMP, .PCX, .TIF, or a number of other graphics formats into a Greetings 99 project.

Even if you don't have your own digital camera, many local and national photo development companies will scan your photos and provide them on disk. For example, Seattle FilmWorks (1-800-FILMWORKS or www.filmworks.com) sells 35mm film that it will develop and provide as prints, slides, on disk, or all three. Seattle FilmWorks also provides image editing software, so you can touch up the scanned photos or convert them to another digital format, if needed. You might want to check with a local quick printer if you need to scan only a photo or two.

If the photo you want to insert is on a floppy disk, make sure you insert the disk in the drive or copy the image to your hard disk before starting this process so that Greetings 99 can find the photo.

The best way to use a photo is to select a project that's designed especially for photos. Click the Paper Projects tab and click the Photo Projects option. Follow the previous set of steps for creating a greeting card to walk you through creating a photo project. When you've completed your design, double-click the Place Photo or Other Design Here text. This opens the same dialog box you use to insert clip art pictures.

If the photo file is saved elsewhere, click the Import Clips button at the top of the dialog box to open yet another dialog box (see Figure 23.15) you can use to locate the photo file.

FIGURE 23.15

Use this dialog box to help you locate the photo file you want to use.

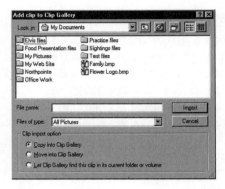

Use the Look In drop-down list to navigate to the disk and folder that holds the photo you want to insert, and then click on the photo filename. From the Clip import options in the lower section of the dialog box, choose an option, such as Copy, into Clip Gallery. Click the Import button. (You may have to assign a description for the photo; enter a name and click OK.) Now the file appears as part of the available pictures. Select it and click the Insert Clip button.

You can easily resize or move the photo just like you learned to do with pictures.

> To delete any picture or photo from a page, click it to display a black border with selection handles. Press Delete.

Inserting WordArt

If you completed Hour 4, "Formatting Pages," you already know about using Microsoft's WordArt utility to turn regular text into a special effect. You can use this same miniprogram to add text effects to your Greetings 99 projects.

Follow these steps to use WordArt in a project:

To Do: Using WordArt

1. Display the project page where you want to insert WordArt text.
2. Click the Add New Shaped Text button on the top toolbar. This inserts a text box onto the project page and opens a dialog box where you can enter the WordArt text (see Figure 23.16).

Type your text here   WordArt text box

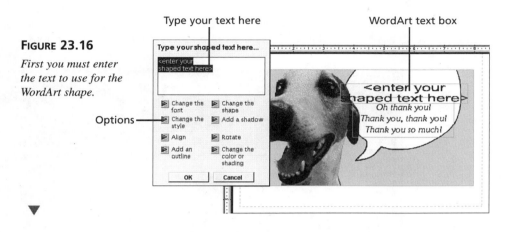

FIGURE 23.16

*First you must enter
the text to use for the
WordArt shape.*

Options

3. Click the Change the Shape option to display a palette of shapes you can use (see Figure 23.17).

Click a shape

FIGURE 23.17

Choose a shape to use.

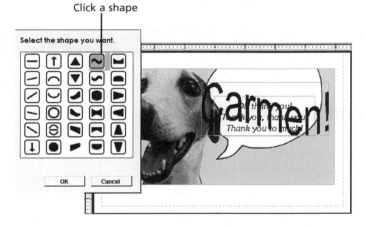

4. Click a shape. The WordArt text conforms to the shape you select. Continue selecting shapes until you find the one you want; then click OK.

5. To change the color of the WordArt text, click the Change the Color or Shading option.

6. Select a color and click OK.

7. Continue exploring the other WordArt options available. When the WordArt is exactly the way you want it, click OK.

You can now move and resize the WordArt text box as needed, as shown in Figure 23.18. To edit the effect at any time, double-click the text box and reapply the available options.

FIGURE 23.18

You'll probably have to resize and move the WordArt text to fit into your project.

WordArt

Adding Lines and Shapes

In addition to adding pictures, photos, and WordArt, you can also experiment with a few rudimentary drawing tools that come with Greetings 99. You can use these tools to create basic lines and shapes to place on the project.

To add a shape to your project page, first open the page using the appropriate page button. Next, click the Add New Shape button on the top toolbar. This opens a palette of available shapes, as shown in Figure 23.19.

Click the shape you want to use. As soon as you do, it appears on your project page, as shown in Figure 23.20. You can now move and resize the shape just like any other text or graphics object on the page. Notice new toolbar buttons appear when adding a shape. The buttons can be used to change the outline color, fill the shape with color, or switch to another shape entirely. Experiment with the buttons to create the effect you want.

Click the Add New Shape button

FIGURE 23.19

Use the Add New Shape button to display a palette of shapes.

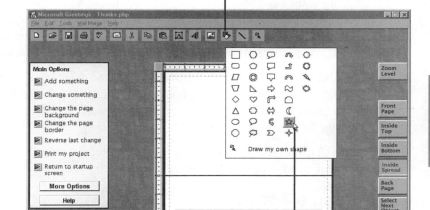

Select a shape from the palette

New toolbar buttons

FIGURE 23.20

You can resize and move the shape as needed.

Use this option to layer the shape

Shape

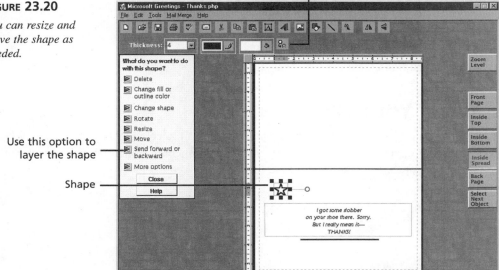

23

To place the shape behind a text box or picture, select the shape, and drag it into position. Choose the Send forward or backward option in the Options box. Select an action and click OK. You can use this layering option to create different effects with the various project elements. For example, you might place a large shape behind a photo, or place a text box on top of a circle shape. Again, experiment to create just the right effect.

Adding lines is as simple as adding shapes. Click the Add New Line button on the toolbar (beside the Add New Shape button). Immediately a line is added to the project page. You can resize it or move it like any other object or text box. Use the toolbar buttons to change the line thickness and color.

Like the shape feature, you can control the size, direction, or layering of the line. Keep experimenting until you get just the right line effect you're looking for.

Adding a Border

As if adding text, pictures, photos, WordArt, lines, and shapes weren't enough, you can also add special touches to your project page, such as adding a border.

To add a page border, click the Add a Page Border option in the Options box. (Be sure to deselect any text or graphic boxes you were working with on the page.) Select a category from the category drop-down list. You can choose from a variety of categories, ranging from Business to Nature, to Classical or Modern. The category you select affects the borders listed in the list box.

After choosing a category, select a border (see Figure 23.21). As soon as you make a selection, the border appears on the project page. You can continue selecting borders to see how they look on the page. You can also adjust the border thickness using the Set the Border Width To text box and arrow buttons.

When you find the border you want, click OK.

Saving Your Work

Saving a project in Greetings 99 resembles saving a project in other applications. When you save it, you name the project file and specify where to store it on disk so that you can later open, edit, and print it as needed.

Click here to display a list of categories

FIGURE 23.21

Add a border to the project page to really set things off.

Use these buttons to change the border width

Border

To Do: Saving a Project

1. Click the Save Project button located on the top toolbar. This opens the Save Project As dialog box, as shown in Figure 23.22.

FIGURE 23.22

Use this dialog box to assign the project a name and a folder to store it in.

2. If needed, use the Save In list to choose another disk and folder in which to save the file.

3. Click inside the File Name text box and enter a name for the project file.

▲ 4. Click the Save button.

After you save and name your project file, click the Save Project button to save your recent changes. You should resave the project every 10 minutes or so.

Reopening a Project

Any time you're using Greetings 99, you can stop what you're doing and open a project you worked with earlier. After you open the project, you can make changes to it, save it, and print it.

If you just started Greetings 99 and you're at the opening screen where you choose a new project to create, you can click the My Projects button. This opens the box shown in Figure 23.23 where you can choose to open an existing project file.

FIGURE 23.23

Select the project file you want to open.

To Do: Reopening Your Projects

1. Click the Open Project button. This opens the dialog box shown in Figure 23.23.
2. Click the name of the project to open.
3. Click the Open button.

Printing Your Project

Printing your project enables you to give copies to other people, or in the case of posters and banners, display it with pride.

Use these steps to print any project:

To Do: Printing a Project

1. Click the Print Project button on the toolbar. This opens the box shown in Figure 24.24.

FIGURE 24.24

Use this box to control how your project prints.

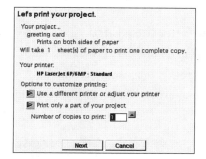

FIGURE 24.24

Use this box to control how your project prints.

23

2. If your computer has more than one printer connected to it, click the Use a Different Printer or Adjust Your Printer option. If you're using the default printer, skip to Step 5.

3. Select the printer to use from the Name drop-down list, and then click OK.

> The correct orientation—Portrait (tall) or Landscape (wide)—varies depending on the project type. You can't change this choice in the Print Setup dialog box unless you choose another printer. Then, the option button for the recommended orientation appears grayed. If you click the other choice, the only way to return to the recommended orientation is to cancel printing by clicking the Cancel button twice and then restart the steps for printing.

4. Click the Number of Copies to Print up arrow button to increase the number of copies to print.

5. Click the Next button, and the project is sent to your printer.

6. When the printout is complete, click Printed OK.

Creating an Email Project

Although most of the projects you create with Greetings 99 follow similar steps, email projects work a bit differently, enough to warrant a brief discussion on the topic. For starters, the greeting cards you send via email are animated and have other multimedia effects, such as sounds. You can also choose to send the card directly from the Greetings 99 program window.

Click the Email Design Techniques link on the Greetings 99 main program window (on the Introduction tab) to open a Help dialog box offering ideas and tips for using the feature.

To Do: Make an Email Greeting Card

1. Click the Email Projects tab on the main program window.
2. Select the type of email project you want to create.
3. From the Select Design dialog box, shown in Figure 23.25, choose a card design to use. Click Next to continue.

FIGURE 23.25

Use the Select Design dialog box to choose an email greeting card design.

4. The project opens onscreen, as shown in Figure 23.26, and you can begin editing the text or graphics as needed. Use the options listed in the Main Options pane to control how you edit and work on the project. Each option opens a list of other options you can use.
5. To select a page to view, click the page number at the bottom of the Main Options pane.
6. It's a good idea to preview your greeting before and after making changes. To preview your greeting, click the Preview project option, and then choose Entire project from the submenu.

Send button

FIGURE 23.26

When viewing email projects, the graphics are often animated onscreen.

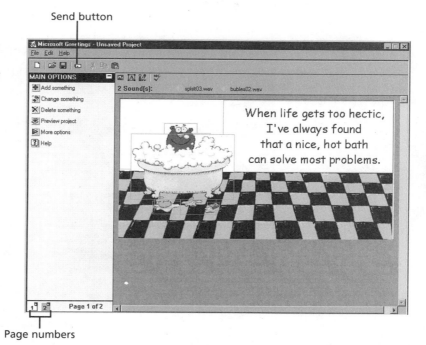

23

Page numbers

7. This runs the greeting in preview mode, including all the sounds and animation assigned to the greeting. To return to the previous window, click the Close Preview button.

8. To send the greeting, click the Send button on the toolbar (see Figure 23.26). You'll be prompted to save your work; click Yes and give the project a name, or click No and save it later.

9. The next dialog box asks you if you want to preview the greeting in the browser window. To skip this, click Next.

10. The next dialog box lets you define how you want to send the greeting. If your email program is listed, select it; then click Next.

11. A message box opens for you to fill in the email recipient and a message to accompany the greeting (see Figure 23.27). Follow the directions in the message box to complete the message.

Enter the recipient's   Attached greeting project
email address

FIGURE 23.27

Fill out the email mes-
sage box; notice the
greeting card is an
attachment.

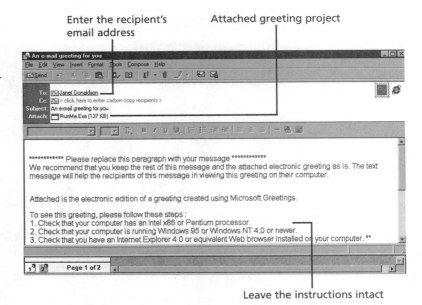

Leave the instructions intact

12. When you're ready to send the message, click the Send button. Log onto your
    Internet account (if you're not logged on already) and send the message.

There's just not enough room in this book to show you all the great things you can do
with Greetings 99, but you can explore all the options on your own. For example, you
can change the sound effects used with email greetings, add reminders about upcoming
events for which you need to make cards, or download more designs from the Web, as
explained in the note below.

> Greetings 99 comes with some wonderful designs and art, but even more
> good stuff is out there that you can download it from the Web, some of it
> free. The goodies are called *add-on packs*. All you need is a modem, an
> Internet account, and Internet Explorer. On the main screen of Greetings 99,
> click the On the Web button (the picture of the telephone). Internet
> Explorer opens and a connection box appears; click Connect and after a few
> seconds, the browser window displays the product home page. Click the
> Add-On Packs hyperlink. Now follow the links to find just the right add-on
> pack you want to download.

Summary

This hour reviewed how to create greeting cards and other projects using Microsoft Greetings 99, another super program that's part of the Works Suite 99 collection. In the next hour, you'll learn how to look up encyclopedia articles using Encarta.

Q&A

23

Q. Do I have to use the message suggested by the program?

A. No. You can type any message you want. Many people find it helpful to have pre-set messages, but if you're more creative, feel free to enter your own messages. That's the beauty of using a program like this: You get to be as creative as you want to be.

Q. Can I change colors in the card?

A. Some card objects let you change color or line thickness. You'll see special controls for these options on the toolbar when you select the object you want to change. Obviously, if you don't see the controls for changing color or line thickness, you can't pursue these options for that particular object.

Q. I only have a black-and-white printer. Will I not get full use out of the program?

A. Instead of brilliant colors, you'll see shades of gray and black in your printed projects. Your images will print just as nicely as color images, only without all the colors. Keep in mind that you can color your projects after you print them using colored pencils, markers, paint, and so on.

Hour **24**

Finding Facts with Encarta 99

Works Suite 99 suite of programs comes with Microsoft Encarta Encyclopedia 99, a dynamite encyclopedia program that you and your entire family can use. In this hour, you'll learn how to use Encarta to look up all kinds of information. The highlights of this hour include

- Starting and exiting the Encarta program
- Looking up topics and articles
- Playing multimedia clips
- Trying your hand at Encarta's interactive features
- Exploring the encyclopedia by categories
- Finding more encyclopedia information on the Internet

What Is Microsoft Encarta?

Microsoft Encarta 99 is an electronic version of a set of encyclopedias. Unlike book encyclopedias, however, Encarta offers much more than just text and pictures. With Encarta, you can look up topics and view video clips, sound clips, and more.

Encarta is basically a giant database of information, including multimedia items. You can access the information in a variety of ways.

- Encyclopedia articles   This is the equivalent of turning to an encyclopedia page in a book. Encarta's articles include text and pictures, as well as links to related articles.
- Multimedia clips   Many articles found in the encyclopedia's library include pictures, video clips, and sound clips. You can run a sound or video clip to see or hear more about a particular topic.
- InterActivities   Just as the name implies, this feature provides interactive learning tools for exploring more about a topic or concept.
- Categories   Rather than look up specific topics, you can also explore the encyclopedia by categories using Encarta's Explore feature.

Starting and Exiting Encarta

To begin using Encarta, click the Start button on the Windows taskbar; then select Programs | Microsoft Reference | Encarta Encyclopedia 99. The first thing you see is a prompt box, shown in Figure 24.1, telling you to insert the Encarta CD.

FIGURE 24.1

You'll be prompted to insert the CD when starting Encarta with the Programs menu.

You'll need the Encarta CD-ROM to use the program. The disc houses a vast library of information that would take up far too much room on your computer's hard disk drive.

Another way to start the program is to simply pop Disc 1 into your CD-ROM drive. If auto insert notification is turned on, Encarta starts automatically.

If inserting the Encarta CD doesn't immediately open the program, your computer's auto insert notification option might be turned off. To turn it on, click the Start button on the taskbar and choose Settings | Control Panel. Double-click the System icon to open the System Properties dialog box. Click the Device Manager tab, double-click CD-ROM, and then double-click the icon for your specific CD-ROM drive. Click the Settings tab and select the Auto Insert Notification option box. Click OK twice to exit the dialog boxes, and then close the Control Panel.

After you start Encarta, your screen will look like Figure 24.2. The Encarta home page is your home base for using the program. You can start Encarta's main features from this page. You'll also notice a title bar at the top of the program window and a menu bar for accessing commands.

24

FIGURE 24.2

Encarta's Home screen is a jumping-off point for using the program's features.

Title bar   Menu bar

Links to Encarta's features   Program window controls

When you're ready to exit Encarta, simply click the Close button in the top-right corner of the program window.

Looking Up a Topic

The library of encyclopedia articles is the largest part of Encarta. Click the Find link on the home screen (refer to Figure 24.2) to open the Pinpointer pane shown in Figure 24.3. Encarta's Pinpointer Search tool can help you look up articles, multimedia items, and more.

Enter the topic you want
to search for here

Scroll through the list of topics and
select the one you want

FIGURE 24.3

*You can look up ency-
clopedia articles using
the Pinpointer pane.*

Pinpointer pane

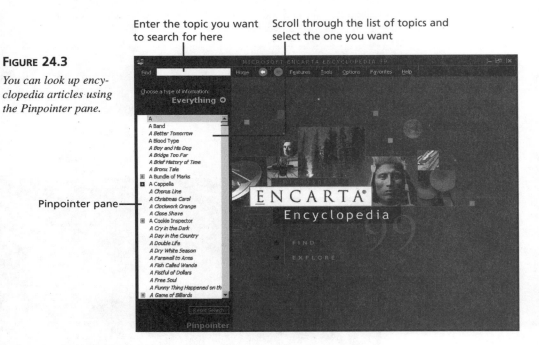

To open a topic in the Topics list, click the topic. Notice in Figure 24.3 that some topics have icons next to them. For example, a plus sign next to an entry means there are more topic articles and media items to list. Click the plus sign icon to display the items.

The other icons represent other types of media associated with the topic. Table 24.1 explains the icons you encounter in the Topics list. These icons are found throughout Encarta and you can use them at any time to play a multimedia clip or view a picture or chart.

TABLE 24.1 MEDIA ICONS

Icon	Media type
⊞	Lists more topics
▣	Opens a picture image
▣	Starts a video clip
◆	Starts an animation clip
◀»	Starts an audio clip
⇨	Begins an InterActivity (interactive tasks that help you explore a topic or concept)
▣	Displays a collage
◉	Opens a map
◈	Lets you change your view 360-degrees
▬	Opens a chart or table

24

The example used in the following steps walks you through the procedure for looking up the topic "dinosaur" using the Pinpointer pane, viewing a Contents page for dinosaur, and then viewing a related article. Follow along with the steps to view the article on your own computer.

To Do: Looking Up a Topic

1. From the home screen, click Find, if you have not already done so. This opens the Pinpointer pane (refer to Figure 24.3).

2. Click inside the Find text box at the top of the Pinpointer pane and type the topic for which you want to search. As you type, the list box scrolls alphabetically to the topics. For example, if you type dinosaur, the list displays the topics shown in Figure 24.4.

3. To view an article or Contents page, click the topic. For example, if you click the Dinosaur topic shown in Figure 24.4, the Dinosaur Contents page opens, as shown in Figure 24.5.

4. If you click the Prosauropod link in Figure 24.5, the article detailing the topic appears, as shown in Figure 24.6. Use the scrollbars to help you read the article.

FIGURE 24.4

Typing words in the Pinpointer box narrows down the list of topics displayed.

Type a topic   Click here to open a Contents page or article

Media bar

FIGURE 24.5

A Contents page has links to related articles and a media bar for viewing images and multimedia clips.

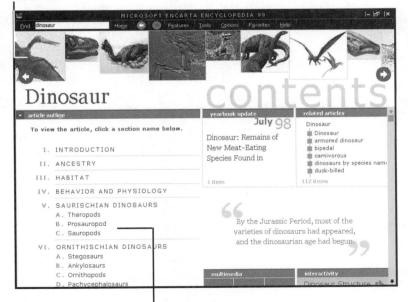

Click a link to display the article

▼ 5. To return to the previous page you were viewing, click the Back button (the left-pointing arrow) on the Menu bar button (see Figure 24.6).

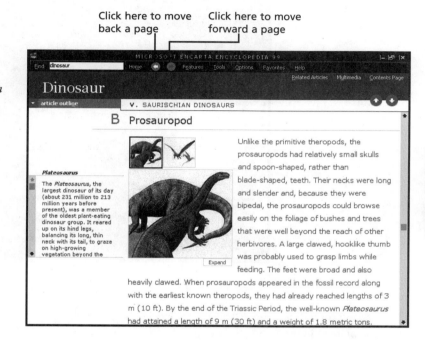

Click here to move back a page   Click here to move forward a page

FIGURE 24.6

An article might include pictures and a scrollable sidebar.

24

6. To look up another topic, click inside the Find text box on the menu bar and enter a new topic.

▲

You can also look up a specific type of media. By default, the Pinpointer pane is set to look up all media forms. To look up only one kind, click the Choose a Type of Information Everything arrow, as shown in Figure 24.7. This opens a menu where you can select a particular media item. Click the one you want and the Topics list box displays such items for the topic you entered into the Find text box.

Working with an Article

When the article you want is displayed, you can scroll through and read the information. Use the vertical scrollbar on the right side of the article page to scroll up or down the article. A click on the Article Outline drop-down arrow, located on the far-left side of the article page displays an outline of the topic's related Contents page with links to other related articles.

Click here to display the menu

FIGURE 24.7

You can look up specific kinds of media items.

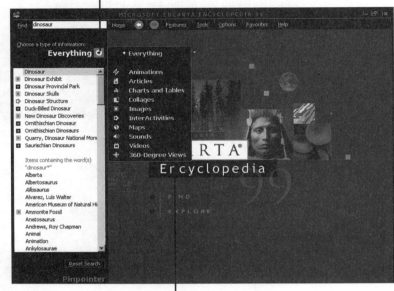

Click the media type you want to list

In addition to reading articles, there are a couple of things you can do with the article, as explained in the following sections.

Copying an Article

You can copy all or part of the article into your word processor so you can save it.

To Do: Copying an Article into a Word Processor

1. To copy just a certain portion of the article text, select it first. Click your mouse in front of the first line of text, and then hold down the left mouse button and drag to select the text you want. If you're planning to copy the entire article, you don't have to select the text.

2. Open the Options menu and choose Copy. The Copy dialog box appears, as shown in Figure 24.8.

3. If you selected text in Step 1, click Selected Text. If you didn't, click Whole Article. The text is copied to the Windows Clipboard.

4. Next, open your word processing program. You don't have to close Encarta; just click the Start button on the taskbar and open the program using the Programs menu.

FIGURE 24.8

Use the Copy dialog box to copy the article to the Windows Clipboard.

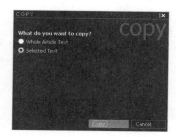

▼

▲

5. From the word processor window, open the Edit menu and choose Paste. The ency-clopedia material now appears in the word processor document for you to work with. (To return to Encarta, click the Microsoft Encarta button on the Windows taskbar.)

24

Printing an Article

You can print part or all of the article. If you want to print only part of it, select that part first. Otherwise, just go ahead and open the Options menu and choose Print. A Print dia-log box appears, as shown in Figure 24.9, with four options: Whole Article Text, Whole Article with Pictures, Selected Text, and Selected Text with Pictures. Click the one that describes what you want to print, and click Print.

FIGURE 24.9

Use the Print dialog box to print portions of the article.

Working with the Media Clips in an Article

Many of the encyclopedia articles have at least one media item (a picture, a video, a sound, and so on); others have numerous media items to explore. Encarta media clips include sound, video and film clips, tables, maps, photos, and collages (which can include several of the other media clip types). Look at the United States of America arti-cle to examine several of the media items you might encounter.

When you open Contents pages, any media items pertaining to the topic are displayed on the Media bar at the top of the page. The right side of the page details all media ele-ments, if available, and how many of each can be found for the topic. Figure 24.10

shows the United States of America Contents page, which has an extensive collection of media links. To locate the page, type United States of America in the Find text box; then click the United States of America topic in the Topics list. This opens the Contents page shown in Figure 24.10.

If the media links are extensive, as they are in Figure 24.10, you may see arrow buttons on the Media bar at the top of the window. Use these to move back and forth to view the available clips.

Use the arrow buttons to see the list of media links

FIGURE 24.10

This Contents page has a large variety of media items.

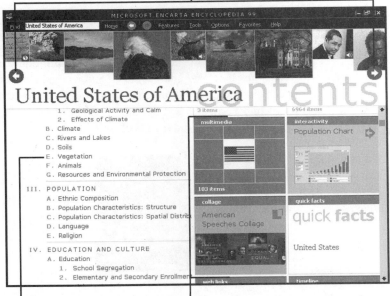

Click to display the related article

You can also click any of these media links

Playing Sound Clips

Most computers today have speakers for hearing sound files. Encarta 99 takes full advantage of this by offering all kinds of sound files with its articles.

To open a sound clip feature, click the media item containing a sound clip icon (see Table 24.1 for an exhaustive list of media icons). For example, a click on the moose photo on the Media bar in Figure 24.10 opens an article about land and resources, as shown in Figure 24.11.

FIGURE 24.11

After the article opens onscreen, click the media clip.

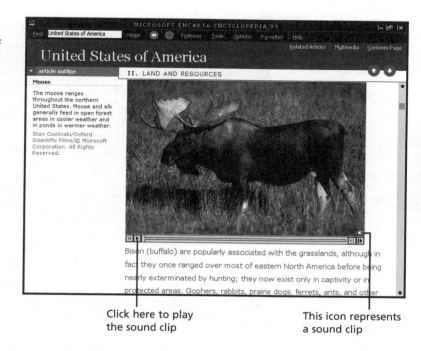

Click here to play
the sound clip

This icon represents
a sound clip

To play the sound clip, click the Play button shown in Figure 24.11. (You may need to expand the media item before seeing a Play button; to do so click the media icon.)

> The controls for playing video clips are almost the same as those for playing sound clips. Just click the Play button to begin the video.

Viewing Map Media

To view a map media item, click the second media item in the Media bar with a map media icon. (You can see the item in the upper-left corner of Figure 24.10.) When selected, an article opens with a map media item. Click the map to open Encarta's World Maps tools. When you move your mouse pointer over the map, it becomes a magnifying glass. Click to zoom in closer to the map. Figure 24.12 shows a view of the midwestern United States.

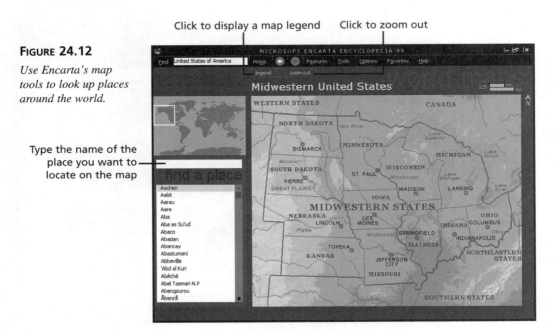

FIGURE 24.12

Use Encarta's map tools to look up places around the world.

Click to display a map legend   Click to zoom out

Type the name of the place you want to locate on the map

To zoom out again, click the Zoom Out button at the top of the map screen. Use the Find a Place tools on the left side of the map screen to search for a specific place on the map.

To return to the article screen, click the Back button on the menu bar.

To find all the maps available in Encarta, open the Features menu and select World Maps. This opens the World Maps feature with a global view of the world.

Viewing Collages

Like its name implies, a collage is a visual presentation of information. Collage media clips are actually a grouping of related media items, such as sound clips, articles, essays, and photos pertaining to an historic or contemporary event or topic. To view an example of a collage, scroll down the United States of America Contents page, as shown in Figure 24.13, and click the American Speeches Collage.

FIGURE 24.13

Collages are a combination of multimedia items.

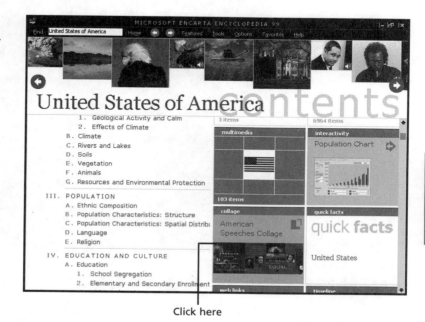

Click here

As you move your mouse pointer over the collage elements, you can click to view information, whether it's in the form of text or a media clip. Figure 24.14 shows the American Speeches collage.

To return to the previous page, click the Back button on the menu bar.

To find other Collage features in Encarta, open the Features menu and select Collages. This opens a central page listing links to all the topics containing collages.

If you like collages, you might like Encarta's Timeline, too. Open the Features menu and select Timeline. This opens the Timeline you can scroll through. To view an article, click the item on the Timeline.

Use these buttons to scroll left and right in the collage of images

FIGURE 24.14

This collage has photos, music, text links, and more.

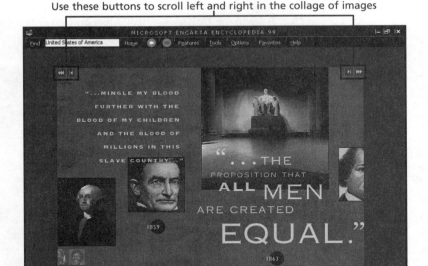

Working with InterActivities

Encarta's InterActivities feature is an interactive article that's a learning tool and an information resource. Depending on the topic, the activity may be a chart you can make changes to, a diagram you can build, or more. As with other media links, click an InterActivity to open the feature. Use the following steps to check out a dinosaur-related InterActivity.

To Do: Exploring an InterActivity Feature

1. Start by typing the word dinosaur in the Find text box.

2. Click the Choose a Type of Information arrow located below the Find text box and select InterActivities from the menu list.

3. Encarta lists the Dinosaur Structure topic in the Topics list box. Click the topic to open the InterActivity feature shown in Figure 24.15.

4. Follow the instructions for assembling the dinosaur skeleton. You can also read about the topic.

5. When finished, click the Back button on the menu bar to return to the previous screen.

Encarta has all kinds of InterActivities you can explore; some involve selecting various types of data from drop-down lists, manipulating graph data, performing science experiments, and more.

FIGURE 24.15

Use this InterActivity to build a dinosaur skeleton.

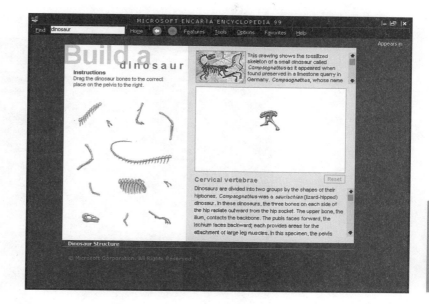

24

To explore solely InterActivity features found in Encarta, open the Features menu and select InterActivities. This opens a central page listing links to all the topics containing InterActivities.

Exploring by Category

Another way to use Encarta is to explore the encyclopedia by categories. Click the Home button on the menu bar to return to the Home page; then click the Explore link. You can also open the Features menu and select Encarta Explorer. Either method opens the Explore screen, shown in Figure 24.16.

Click the category you want to explore. This displays another screen like Figure 24.16, this time detailing more categories (subcategories) you can choose from. Continue selecting the category you want to explore, each time narrowing your topic. Finally, when the topic category is narrowed, a Contents page displays. From here you can read topic articles and explore media items.

Click a category

FIGURE 24.16

You can explore your electronic encyclopedia via categories.

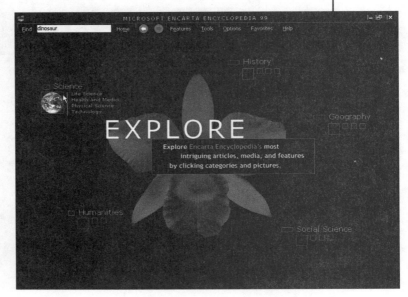

Going Online with Encarta

Even with Encarta's entire CD filled with information, you might find that you need more information on a topic. Perhaps you are looking up some obscure town that Encarta has only a paragraph or two about, or maybe you want up-to-the-minute info and your copy of Encarta is several months old. Whatever the case, you will want to check out the online component to Encarta.

You can get at these online features in several ways. You can open the Help menu and select Microsoft on the Web | Encarta Online. This opens your browser window and an Internet Connection dialog box for connecting to your Internet account. Click the Connect button to log on.

After you are connected, you'll see a page similar to the one shown in Figure 24.17.

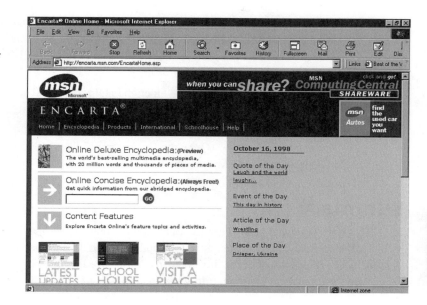

Here's a quick rundown of the other online features available (and which menus to find them on), all of which you should have no trouble at all exploring on your own:

- Yearbook   Open the Features menu and select Yearbook. Use this to manage updates to Encarta to keep your copy up-to-date. Encarta comes with the latest 99 update pre-installed.

  To get more updates, click Downloads, and then click Update Encarta. (Note that this is not a free service; you must buy a subscription for $19.95 a year to be entitled to updates. Full information appears when you click Update Encarta.)

- Downloads   Open the Tools menu and select Downloads. Doing so is the same as clicking Yearbook and then Downloads.

- Web Links   Open the Features menu and select Web Links. This is an assortment of links to Web pages with more information on them about selected topics. Select a link to follow; then click Connect to This Site. (The Links list can also be updated with a download if you have a Yearbook subscription.)

- Encarta Online   Open the Help menu and select Microsoft on the Web. This opens Internet Explorer and displays the Microsoft Encarta Web site (refer to Figure 24.17), where you can look up additional articles using the Microsoft Concise Encyclopedia (the free version).

- Technical Support on the Web   Open the Help menu and select Microsoft on the Web. Use this option to access Microsoft's technical support site when you're having trouble with Encarta.

- Microsoft Home Page   Open the Help menu and select Microsoft on the Web. Use this option to access Microsoft's home page on the Web.

Summary

This hour reviewed how to use the Encarta electronic encyclopedia. You learned how to look up articles, play media clips, copy and print articles, and look up topics by category. This concludes the hours in this book. You now have the skills necessary to tackle each Work Suite program and put it to work for you.

Q&A

Q. Can I copy articles to my other Works Suite programs?

A. You can copy text from the Encarta articles and place it in a document you create using Microsoft Works or in a document you create using Word 97. After you paste the data into the document, use the program's formatting tools to revise the text.

Q. Can I turn off the sounds that accompany every button click?

A. Yes. Open the Options menu and choose Settings. This opens the Settings dialog box. Deselect the Play Menu and Button Sounds check box, and then click OK to exit.

APPENDIX A

Using Expedia Streets 98

On-the-go users will appreciate the addition of Microsoft's Expedia Streets 98 to Works Suite 99. If you're traveling by car, bus, plane, or train, you'll find getting there is easier with Streets 98. Expedia Streets 98 is a detailed electronic road atlas that maps more than 5 million miles of U.S. roads. The program can help you plan routes, locate points of interest, look up specific addresses, book hotel rooms on the Internet, and more. In this bonus hour, you'll learn how to use Streets 98 to do any of the following:

- Look up specific addresses anywhere in the U.S.
- Locate businesses, restaurants, and hotels, including addresses and phone numbers.
- Plan a route around town or across the country.
- Look up restaurants using the ZAGATSURVEY Restaurant Guide.
- Look up hotels using the Expedia Hotel Directory.

As you'll quickly learn, Streets 98 can help you find anywhere you want to go.

Starting and Exiting Expedia Streets

Before opening Expedia Streets 98, make sure the Streets 98 CD is inserted into your CD-ROM drive. You'll need the CD in order to use Streets 98. If your computer's Auto Insert Notification feature is turned on, the Streets 98 program will start immediately when you insert the CD. If not, you'll need to start the program using the Start button; click the Start button on the Windows taskbar, and then select Programs | Microsoft Expedia | Streets 98.

Auto Insert Notification, when activated, automatically detects CDs inserted into the CD-ROM drive and opens any auto-start or Setup program automatically. If Auto Insert Notification is turned off, follow these steps to turn it on. Click Start | Settings | Control Panel. Double-click the System icon, and then click the Device Manager tab. Click the plus sign next to the CD-ROM drive, and then double-click the CD-ROM drive name. In the Properties dialog box, click the Settings tab and select the Auto Insert Notification check box. Click OK to exit, and then click OK again. You can now close the Control Panel.

There are far too many maps on the Streets 98 CD to install onto your computer's hard drive; the information would take up too much space. When you install Streets 98, only the crucial files for running the program are loaded onto your hard drive. All the maps and graphics remain stored on the CD.

When you first start Expedia Streets 98, a map opens onscreen and the Start Screen dialog box appears, as shown in Figure A.1. You can use the Start Screen to begin looking up an address, a place, or consult the ZAGATSURVEY Restaurant Guide or Hotel Directory. Click the Close button to exit the dialog box. After you exit, you can return to the Start Screen at any time by opening the Help menu and choosing Start Screen.

ZAGATSURVEY is the name of a popular survey guide that rates restaurants in cities across the country. You can use the guide to look up restaurant reviews, locations, and even phone numbers to call and make reservations.

FIGURE A.1

Welcome to Expedia Streets 98. The Start Screen offers a jumping-off point for using the program.

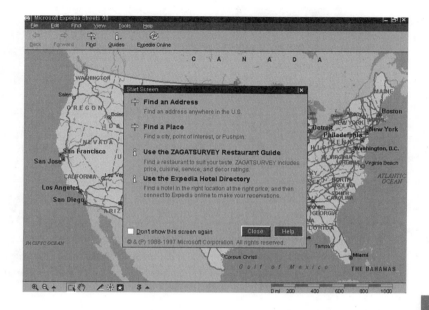

If you don't like the Start Screen and prefer to jump right into the Expedia Streets 98 program as soon as you open it, consider turning off the Start Screen. Click the Don't Show This Screen Again check box on the Start Screen and it won't be back to bother you (if you do want to see the dialog box again, choose Help | Start Screen).

Table A.1 explains each of the Start Screen options. To select an option, move your mouse pointer over the appropriate button and click. Each of these options on the Start Screen are also available through tools and menus in the program window.

TABLE A.1 START SCREEN OPTIONS

Option	Description
Find an Address	This option lets you find an address on the map based on portions of the address you enter, such as street name or city.
Find a Place	Use this option to look up a city, a business, or a particular place on the map.
Use the ZAGATSURVEY Restaurant Guide	Locate a restaurant based on price, location, service, and food.
Use the Expedia Hotel Directory	Look up hotels and lodging that meet the criteria you're looking for. You can even go on the Internet and make reservations.

When you're ready to exit the program, use any of these methods:

- Click the program window's Close button.
- Choose File | Exit.
- Press Alt+F4 on the keyboard.

Use Streets 98's help features any time you need additional help with the program. Choose Help | Contents to look up help with specific parts of the program.

Navigating the Streets 98 Program Window

Before jumping in and using the program, take a moment and acclimate yourself to the program window (see Figure A.2). It looks a bit different than the other Works Suite programs you've covered in the previous hours. Here's an explanation of each onscreen element:

- Title bar   This bar displays the name of the program.
- Menu bar   Use the menu bar to access the Street 98 commands. To display a menu, click its name; to select a command, click the command name.
- Navigation toolbar   The buttons on this toolbar help you navigate the map.
- Map area   The middle portion of the program window shows the map, which you can zoom in and out for more or less detail.
- Toolbar   The buttons on this toolbar are shortcuts to common Streets 98 commands or features. To activate a command, click the icon.
- Program window controls   Use these buttons to minimize, maximize, or close the program window.

The mouse is the easiest way to navigate the Streets 98 window; simply click on the feature or element you want to view. If you prefer using mainly the keyboard, you'll find plenty of shortcut keys to use to get around. For example, to display a menu, press the Alt key and the underlined letter of the menu name. To select a menu command, type the underlined letter in the menu command.

Working with the Streets 98 Toolbars

Expedia Streets 98 has two toolbars you can use. The Navigation toolbar, located at the top of the program window (see Figure A.2) has five buttons for navigating the map and program features. Strangely enough, the Navigation toolbar duplicates many commands found in the menu bar's menus. Table A.2 explains how to use each toolbar button.

FIGURE A.2

The default map shows the entire United States (except for Alaska and Hawaii).

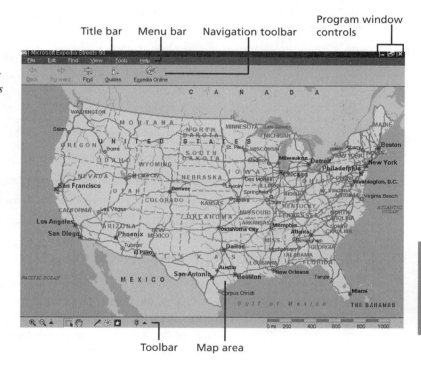

Title bar   Menu bar   Navigation toolbar   Program window controls

Toolbar   Map area

A

TABLE A.2 NAVIGATION TOOLBAR BUTTONS

Button	Description
Back	Click this button to move back to the previous view or undo an action you just did.
Forward	Click this button to move forward to the next view (but only if you used the Back button to move back) or redo your most recent action.
Find	Opens the Find drop-down menu with commands for locating places on the map.
Guides	Opens the Guides drop-down menu for looking up restaurants and hotels.
Expedia Online	Opens a dialog box with links that connect you to the Expedia online information Web site.

The toolbar at the bottom of the Streets 98 window contains useful shortcut keys to commonly used commands. Table A.3 explains each toolbar button's function. You learn how to use these buttons in the sections to come.

TABLE A.3   TOOLBAR BUTTONS

Button	Description
	Click this button to zoom the map view out.
	Click this button to zoom in.
	Use the Zoom Slider button to open a slider control for zooming your view in and out.
	Use this tool to zoom in on a particular area of the map.
	Use this button to drag your view of the map in any direction.
	Use the Route Highlighter to outline a route you draw on the map.
	Click this button to mark a spot on the map with a highlighted circle.
	Click this button; then click on the map to locate points of interest.
	Click this button to mark a spot on the map with an electronic pushpin. Click the drop-down arrow to display a palette of symbols you can use.

Moving Around the Streets 98 Map

There are several ways to move around the map display. If you move the mouse pointer to any edge or corner of the map area, the pointer takes the shape of a large arrow icon. When the pointer is a large arrow, click the mouse button to shift the map in the appropriate direction. For example, if you're pointing at the right edge of the map, the large arrow shape points east. If you click the mouse button, the map shifts to the left.

If you hold down the left mouse button, your view moves very quickly. This is the same principle involved in scrolling around a document page; use the arrows to scroll around the map.

Another way to move around the map is to use the Hand tool. Click the Hand button , and then drag it on the map in the direction you want to move.

Zooming In and Out

Streets 98's zoom features are invaluable for viewing the map. There are several zoom features to choose from, and each is represented by a button on the toolbar at the bottom of the program window.

To Do: Using Expedia Streets Zoom Features

▼ To Do

1. To zoom in your map view for a closer look at a particular area, click the Zoom In button on the toolbar.
2. To zoom out, click the Zoom Out button .

> You can click the Zoom In or Zoom Out button as often as you need to zoom your view of the map.

3. To select a zoom percentage, click the Zoom Slider button ![] to display the slider, and then drag the arrow down to zoom in or up to zoom out (see Figure A.3). You can also click the arrow buttons at the right edge of the Zoom Slider to zoom in or out.

FIGURE A.3

Use the Zoom Slider tool to zoom in or out.

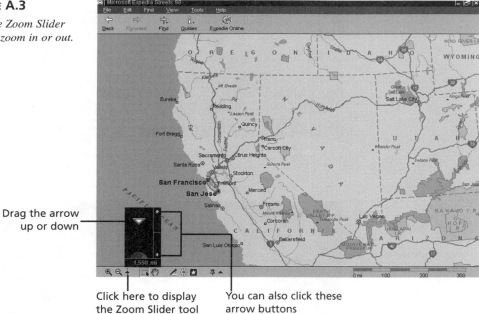

Drag the arrow up or down

Click here to display the Zoom Slider tool

You can also click these arrow buttons

To zero in on a particular area of the map, use the Selection button ![]. Click the button, and then draw an outline on the area of the map you want to zoom in on, as shown in Figure A.4.

After drawing the outline, the mouse pointer takes the shape of a magnifying glass with a plus sign in the middle. Next, click inside the outline and your view is zoomed to the dimensions of the outline you drew, as shown in Figure A.5.

Figure A.4

Use the Selection tool to draw an outline of the area you want to view.

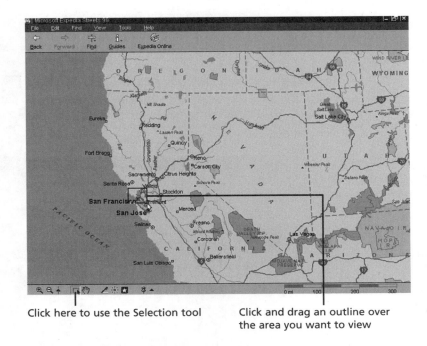

Click here to use the Selection tool   Click and drag an outline over
the area you want to view

Figure A.5

Use the Zoom Box tool to draw an outline of the area you want to view.

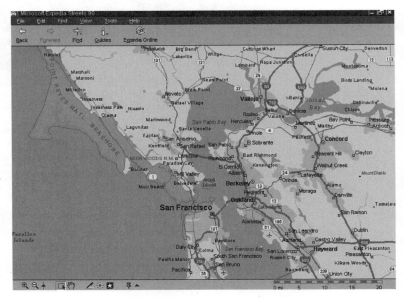

> If you right-click over an area of the map, a pop-up menu appears with zoom options. To quickly return to the default view of the 48 states, right-click and choose Zoom | To 48 States. To see all 50 states, right-click and choose Zoom | To Entire U.S.

Changing the Map Display

You can control what you see on your map using several tools. For example, to see the topography, such as mountain ranges and other natural terrain, open the View menu and select Display Terrain (this view is the default, so it may already be selected). To see points of interest on your map, such as museums, restaurants, libraries, and so on, choose View | Show Points of Interest. This opens the Show Points of Interest dialog box, shown in Figure A.6.

FIGURE A.6

Use the Show Points of Interest dialog box to specify exactly what points of interest categories you want to appear on the map.

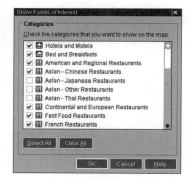

A

Select the categories you want to see on the map, and then click OK. Resist the impulse to select everything or your map will become too cluttered. Once selected, Points of Interest appear as icons on the map, as shown in Figure A.7.

> Regardless of how many categories you select in the Show Points of Interest dialog box, you won't see any Points of Interest icons on the map until you're zoomed in enough for the icons to be visible.

Each point of interest category is identified by an icon. To see a legend of all the icons, choose Tools | Map Legend. To close the legend, click its Close (X) button.

FIGURE A.7

Points of Interest appear as icons on the map.

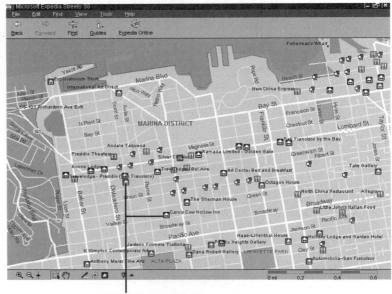

Points of Interest icons

Another way to change the map display is to use the Locator Map tool. Choose Tools | Locator Map. When selected, this feature opens a small window on top of the map that gives you a zoomed out view of the map area you're currently viewing—sort of a bird's eye view. You can click and drag inside the Locator Map to change your view of the larger map beneath. Figure A.8 shows an example of the Locator Map feature in use.

To close the Locator Map, click its Close (X) button located in the right corner.

If you're looking for geographic mapping information, such as latitude and longitude, display the Location Sensor tool. Choose Tools | Location Sensor. This opens the Location Sensor dialog box, as shown in Figure A.9. The dialog box shows the state, latitude, longitude, and time zone of the map area you're viewing.

To close the Location Sensor tool, click its Close (X) button.

Locator Map

FIGURE A.8

Use the Locator Map feature to put the current map view you're using in context with a larger area of the map.

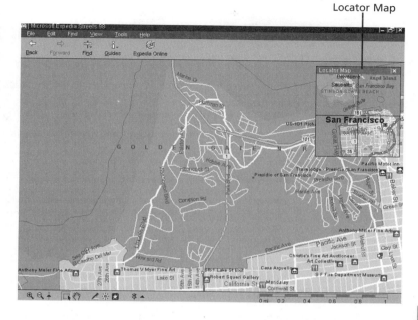

FIGURE A.9

Use the Location Sensor dialog box to gauge the latitude and longitude of the area you're viewing.

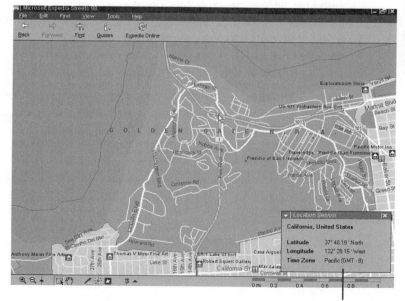

Location Sensor

A

Locating Addresses and Other Places with Streets 98

The best part of any mapping program is being able to locate exactly where you want to go. With Expedia Streets 98, you can look up all kinds of addresses, including residential and business addresses. As long as you know part of the address, Streets 98 can help you locate the place. You can also look up restaurants and hotels, or just about anywhere you need to go.

Although Expedia Street's database of addresses is fairly exhaustive, you won't find every address on the map. For example, you won't find streets for new housing editions. However, Streets 98 comes pretty close, and tries to match the address you enter as best it can.

Finding an Address

Need a map to your newest client's office? Need to find the location of the nearest license branch? You can easily look up addresses for any city or town across the U.S. When it comes to locating addresses, you can be as specific or vague as you want to be, and Streets 98 finds the closest possible match. For example, if you know the street address, but not the city, state, or zip code, Streets 98 finds any matches and presents them to you as a list. You can then examine each one individually.

Use the Find Address dialog box, as shown in Figure A.10, to enter the information you want to look up. You don't have to fill in each field, but if you enter as much information as you can, Streets 98 will be more likely to find a match.

To Do: Looking Up an Address

1. Click the Find button ▣ on the navigation toolbar, and select An Address, or choose Find | An Address. This opens the Find Address dialog box, as shown in Figure A.10.

FIGURE A.10

Use the Find Address dialog box to locate an address anywhere.

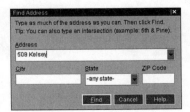

▼ 2. Click inside the Address text box and enter as much of the address as you can. You can use abbreviations, such as St for street or Ave for avenue.

3. Click inside the City text box and enter the name of the city.

4. Use the State drop-down list to select the state.

5. Enter a zip code in the ZIP Code text box.

6. Click Find. If there is more than one such address, Streets 98 presents a Found Addresses dialog box, as shown in Figure A.11.

7. Select the address that most closely matches the location you want to look up, and the map automatically zeroes in on the address (see Figure A.11).

Select the address

FIGURE A.11

Select the address that matches the one you want to find and Streets 98 identifies it on the map.

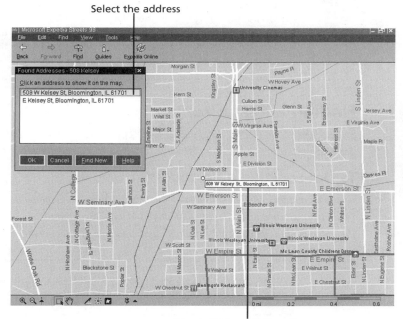

Streets 98 locates it on the map

▲ 8. Click OK to close the dialog box and mark the address with a pushpin.

After you find an address on the map, you can mark it with a pushpin so you can easily find it again. Learn all about pushpins in the section "Working with Pushpins" later in this appendix.

A

Use the Find a Place command to locate points of interest on the map. First make sure your map displays the type of place you're looking for. Choose View I Show Points of Interest. This opens the Show Points of Interest dialog box. Select the category that best matches the type of place you're looking up and click OK. Choose Find I A Place. In the Place text box, enter the name, and then use the State drop-down list to choose a state. Click Find and Streets 98 tries to locate a match.

If you have an Internet account and Internet Explorer installed, you can tap into Streets 98's Web features for more information. Click the Expedia Online button ▦ on the navigation toolbar; then select a Web link from the list. This opens the Internet Explorer window and a connection box for logging onto your Internet account. Make the connection, and then use the Expedia Web site to learn more about the link or city you selected.

Finding a Restaurant

Streets 98 comes with a database of over 16,000 restaurants rated by ZAGATSURVEY, a popular restaurant guide, plus several hundred thousand unrated restaurants.

To Do: Locating a Restaurant

To Do

1. To use the ZAGATSURVEY database, click the Guides button ▦ on the navigation toolbar and choose ZAGATSURVEY Restaurants. This opens the ZAGAT-SURVEY Restaurant Guide dialog box, shown in Figure A.12.

You can also choose Find I ZAGATSURVEY Restaurants to open the dialog box in Figure A.12, or press Ctrl+R on the keyboard.

2. Fill out the fields according to the type of restaurant you're looking for, including location, type of cuisine, and even price range.

3. Click the Find button. A Found ZAGATSURVEY Restaurant Guide dialog box opens (if it found a match) listing the closest matches (see Figure A.13).

4. Choose a restaurant from the list and click the Information button to display another dialog box with details about the restaurant.

▼ **Figure A.12**

Use the ZAGATSURVEY Restaurant Guide dialog box to look up interesting restaurants.

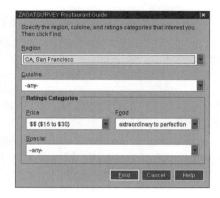

5. To locate the restaurant on the map, click the Locate button.
6. Click the Close (X) button to exit any open dialog boxes.

Click here to open a dialog box with a review of the restaurant

Figure A.13

ZAGATSURVEY pulls up the closest matches to your requests.

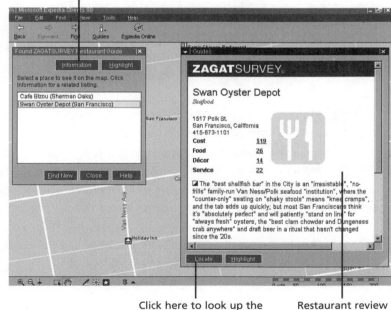

Click here to look up the restaurant on the map

Restaurant review

Finding Lodging

Use the Expedia Hotel Guide to look for lodging anywhere on the map. You can specify the type of amenities you're looking for, price range, and general location. The database contains listings for more than 13,500 hotel accommodations across the country. If you have an Internet connection, you can even go online and book your reservations.

To Do: Locating Lodging

1. Click the Guides button 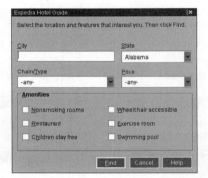 on the navigation toolbar and then select Expedia Hotel Directory (or choose Find | Expedia Hotel Directory). This opens the Expedia Hotel Guide dialog box, as shown in Figure A.14.

FIGURE A.14

Use the Expedia Hotel Guide dialog box to look up lodging.

2. Fill in each field as necessary, and use the Amenities check boxes to select the amenities you're looking for; then click Find.

3. Streets 98 produces a list of matching hotels. Select the one you want; then click the Information button to open another dialog box offering details about the hotel.

4. Click the Locate button to find it on the map, or click the Online Reservations button to go online with your Internet connection and make reservations.

5. The first time you click the Online Reservations feature, the Web Link dialog box appears, as shown in Figure A.15. Click OK and you can log onto your Internet account and the Internet Explorer window opens.

To use Streets 98's Online Reservations feature, you must have a modem or direct connection to the Internet, an account with an Internet service provider, and a browser (such as Internet Explorer). If you installed the

Internet Explorer browser that comes with Works Suite 99, you can learn all about viewing Web pages and setting up an Internet account in Part III of this book.

Figure A.15

Streets 98 tells you that you're about to connect to the Internet and lets you know how to find your way back to the program.

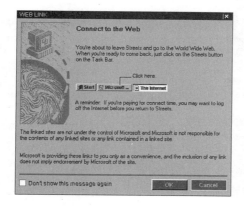

If you prefer not to see the Web Link dialog box each time you use the Online Reservations feature, select the Don't Show This Message Again check box and you won't have to view it again.

A

6. Streets 98 sends you to the Expedia Web site, which uses the Hotel Wizard to walk you through the process of booking reservations. Depending on the hotel you selected, the Internet Explorer window opens Web page with information about the hotel and a form to fill out to make your reservations. Figure A.16 shows an example of a hotel Web page.

7. After you finish, click the program window's Close (X) button to return to Expedia Streets 98.

If you're planning a trip along with the lodging, you can use Streets 98's Points of Interest feature to look up surrounding places of interest you might want to check out during your stay. Click the Points of Interest button on the toolbar; then click the area of the map that interests you. Streets 98 searches its database and displays a list of categories. Select the ones you're interested in and Streets 98 displays them on the map. To learn more about a place, select it and click the Information button.

▼ **FIGURE A.16**

Internet Explorer displays a hotel page from which you can make online reservations.

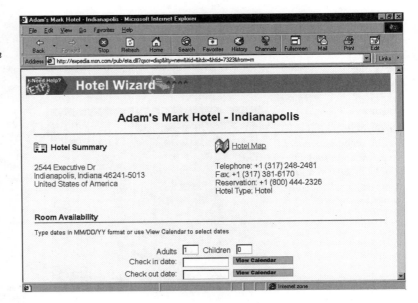

▲

Planning a Route with Streets 98

Streets 98 can help you plan a route to take, whether it's a trip across town or a trip across the country. The route you plot out on the map is highlighted, and you can easily print it out to take it with you. You can even save the route and use it again.

To Do: Drawing a Route

1. Start by selecting the Route Highlighter tool ![ ] on the toolbar, or choose Tools | Route Highlighter. This opens the Route Highlighter dialog box, as shown in Figure A.17.

2. Use the Zoom tools to display both the starting point and destination point of the route you plan to take. (If it's a particularly detailed route, you can use the direction arrows to scroll the map as you go.)

3. Click the Highlighter tool at the beginning of the route; then begin clicking at every turn or bend to highlight the route. Figure A.18 shows a highlighted route in progress.

If you make a mistake while drawing a portion of your route, click the Back button ![ ] to remove the last line drawn. To clear the route completely from the screen, choose Edit | Clear Highlights | Last Route.

▼

Use these options to
change the route color
and line weight

Measure the route
distance here

FIGURE A.17

*Use the Route
Highlighter to trace a
route on the map.*

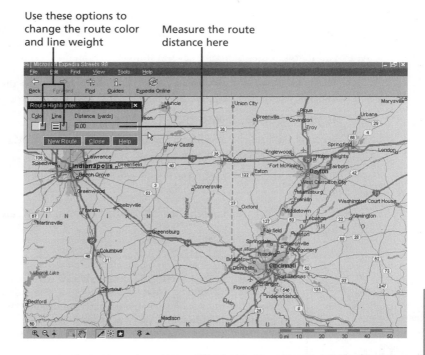

FIGURE A.18

*The route appears
highlighted with color
as you trace its path.*

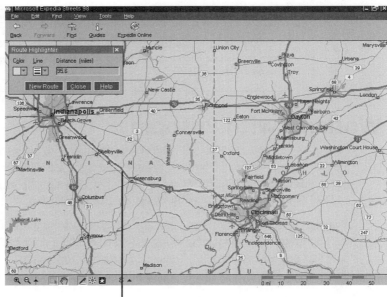

Highlighted route

A

4. When you reach the final destination of the route, press Esc. The mouse pointer changes back to a regular pointer and the route appears highlighted on the map.

After you map a route, there are several things you can do with it:

- To save the route to use again, choose File I Save Map. This opens the Save As dialog box where you can give the route a name and save it as a file.

- To print the route, choose File I Print I Map.

- To copy the route to another program, choose Edit I Copy I Map to place the route in the Windows Clipboard (then open the receiving file and select Edit I Paste).

- To open a saved route, choose File I Open Map; then select the route you want to open.

- To start another route, click the New Route button in the Route Highlighter dialog box.

A quick way to measure the distance between two points is to use the Measuring tool. Choose Tools I Measuring Tool. The mouse pointer becomes a ruler. Click the starting point; then click the destination point. The ruler displays the measurement. You can keep clicking points along the path to add to the distance. Press Esc or select another tool to close the Measuring tool.

If you prefer to see the map distances measured in kilometers instead of miles, choose Tools I Options, and then select the Kilometers option. Click OK and it's changed.

Working with Pushpins

Streets 98 lets you mark places you find on the map with pushpins, electronic versions of the real-life tacks used on bulletin boards. When you learned how to find an address earlier in this appendix, Streets 98 marked the spot with a pushpin and a note about the address (which happened to be the location's street address).

You can mark a spot with a pushpin any time by clicking the Pushpin button [🎲 ▲] on the bottom toolbar, and then clicking the map. To add a note, click inside the pushpin note text box and start typing. You can enter a title for the pushpin, and note text about the pushpin. Figure A.19 shows a pushpin marking a spot on the map.

To quickly add a pushpin, double-click the map.

Note box

FIGURE A.19

*A pushpin marks a spot
and highlights a specific
area on the map.*

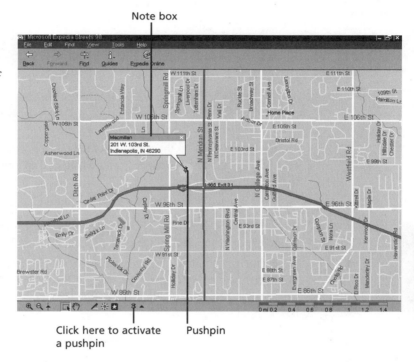

Click here to activate
a pushpin

Pushpin

A

You can organize your pushpins into sets. By default, Streets 98 organizes pushpins
found with the Find Address command into a folder called *Found Addresses*.

To Do: Organizing Your Pushpins

▲ To Do

1. To organize your pushpin sets, choose Tools | Pushpin Explorer. This opens the
   Pushpin Explorer dialog box, shown in Figure A.20.

2. Double-click the folder containing the pushpins you want to see. The left pane,
   called Sets, lists the pushpin folders available. The right pane lists the pushpins in
   a selected folder. As you can see in Figure A.20, you can do a variety of things
   with pushpins from the Pushpin Explorer dialog box:

   - To move a pushpin from one folder to another, select the pushpin, and then
     drag the pushpin to the left pane and drop it on the folder where you want to
     store it.

▼

▼ FIGURE A.20

*Use Pushpin Explorer
to move, rename,
delete, or edit your
pushpins.*

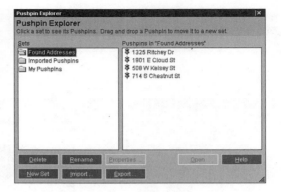

- To find the pushpin on the map, select the pushpin from the list box; then click the Open button. This closes the Pushpin Explorer box and whisks you to the map location.
- To create a new folder, click the New Set button and give the folder a name.
- To rename a pushpin, select the pushpin, and then click the Rename button.
- To delete a pushpin, select the pushpin and click the Delete button.
- To change a pushpin's label or type, select the pushpin and click the Properties button. This opens the Pushpin Properties dialog box where you can change the pushpin icon style, assign it to a new pushpin set, or rename the pushpin title.

You can share your pushpin sets with others if they, too, use Expedia Streets 98. To give a set to another user, select the pushpin set in the Pushpin Explorer dialog box that you want to export, and then click the Export button and give the file a name. To import a set from someone else, open the Pushpin Explorer dialog box and click the Import button, and then locate the file. You can also perform both these commands via the File menu.

▲

APPENDIX B

Using Expedia Trip Planner 98

Trip Planner 98 is an exhaustive trip-planning program you can use to help you plan vacations and any other trips across North America. Trip Planner 98 details more than a million roads across the United States, Canada, and Mexico. You can use the program to plan routes, locate points of interest, look up campgrounds, research articles about favorite travel sites throughout North America, and more. Planning out your traveling routes with Trip Planner is easy, fast, and informative.

In this second bonus hour, you'll learn how to use Trip Planner 98 to do any of the following:

- Plan a detailed trip anywhere in the U.S., Canada, or Mexico.
- Find invaluable information about the place you want to visit with the Travel Guide, including articles, Web links, and interesting attractions to see.
- Print detailed driving instructions to guide you every step of the way to your final destination.
- Keep a record of sightseeing stops you don't want to miss.

If you learned how to use Expedia Streets in the previous Appendix, you'll be happy to know both Streets 98 and Trip Planner 98 share many common features. After you learn how to navigate one, the knowledge applies to the other. Trip Planner 98 can help you find the best route to anywhere you want to go.

Starting and Exiting Trip Planner

If you just finished learning how to use Expedia Streets 98, opening Trip Planner 98 gives you an overwhelming sense of déjà vu. The program looks and feels a lot like Streets 98. However, the goal of Trip Planner is focused on one thing—helping you plan the best possible trip, whether it's a family vacation, a weekend getaway, or a business trip. Trip Planner 98 has tools to help you get the most out of your time on the road.

To open Trip Planner, pop the Trip Planner 98 CD into your CD-ROM drive. If the Auto Insert Notification feature is turned on, the Trip Planner 98 program starts immediately when you insert the CD. If not, you'll need to start the program using the Start button; click the Start button on the Windows taskbar, and then select Programs | Microsoft Expedia | Trip Planner 98.

There are far too many maps on the Trip Planner 98 CD to install them onto your computer's hard drive. The information would take up too much space. When you install Trip Planner 98, only the crucial files for running the program are loaded onto your hard drive; the maps and graphics remain stored on the CD. That's why you always need to insert the CD.

When you open Trip Planner 98, a map appears and the Start Screen dialog box appears, as shown in Figure B.1. You can use the Start Screen to begin planning a route, finding a place, or using the Travel Guide.

Click the Close button to exit the dialog box. After you exit, you can return to the Start Screen at any time by opening the Help menu and choosing Start Screen.

If you don't like the Start Screen and prefer to jump right into using Trip Planner, consider turning off the Start Screen. Click the Don't Show This Screen Again check box option.

Table B.1 explains each of the Start Screen options. To select an option, move your mouse pointer over the appropriate button and click. Each of these options on the Start Screen is also available through tools and menus in the program window.

FIGURE B.1

The Trip Planner Start Screen offers a jumping off point for using the program.

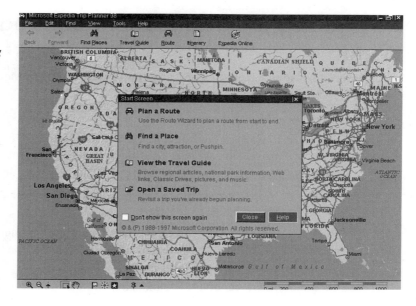

TABLE B.1   START SCREEN OPTIONS

Option	Description
Plan a Route	This option lets you immediately begin planning a route on the map.
Find a Place	Use this option to look up a place you want to visit.
View the Travel Guide	Select this option to peruse Expedia's Travel Guide, a source for vacation spots, parks, Web sites, and more.
Open a Saved Trip	To reopen a trip you previously routed and saved, use this option.

To exit the program at any time, use any of these methods:

- Click the program window's Close button.
- Choose File | Exit.
- Press Alt+F4 on the keyboard.

Use Trip Planner's help features any time you need additional help with the program. Choose Help | Contents to look up help with specific parts of the program, or use the Trip Planner Online command to log onto the Internet to find help.

B

Navigating the Trip Planner 98 Program Window

The default map shows the 48 states, plus portions of Canada and Mexico (see Figure B.2). Here's what you're looking at onscreen:

- Title bar   This bar displays the name of the program.
- Menu bar   Use the menu bar to access the Trip Planner 98 commands. To display a menu, click its name; to select a command, click the command name.
- Navigation toolbar   The buttons on this toolbar help you navigate the map.
- Map area   The middle portion of the program window shows the map, which you can zoom in and out for more or less detail.
- Toolbar   The buttons on this toolbar are shortcuts to common Trip Planner 98 commands or features. To activate a command, click the icon button. (This toolbar is almost the same as the toolbar in Streets 98.)
- Program window controls   Use these buttons to minimize, maximize, or close the program window.

Working with the Trip Planner Toolbars

Trip Planner 98 has two toolbars you can use. The navigation toolbar, located at the top of the program window (see Figure B.2) has seven buttons for navigating the map and program features. These buttons duplicate many of commands found in the menus. See Table B.2 to learn what each toolbar button does.

TABLE B.2   NAVIGATION TOOLBAR BUTTONS

Button	Description
Back	Click this button to move back to the previous view or undo an action you just did.
Forward	Click this button to move forward to the next view (but only if you used the Back button to move back) or redo your most recent action.
Find Places	Opens the Find Place dialog box you can use to locate a particular place on the map.
Travel Guide	Opens the Travel Guide dialog box where you can find articles about travel locations, links to the Web, and points of interest.
Route	Opens the Route Wizard to help you plan a route and calculate driving time, number of days, and number of stops along the way.
Itinerary	Opens a horizontal Itinerary pane at the top of the map. (Click again to close the pane.)
Expedia Online	Opens the Travel Guide dialog box with links to the Internet.

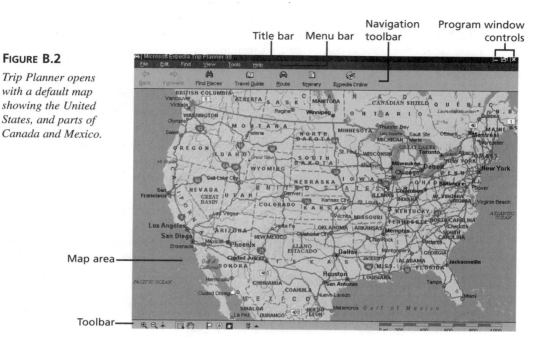

FIGURE B.2

*Trip Planner opens
with a default map
showing the United
States, and parts of
Canada and Mexico.*

The toolbar at the bottom of the window contains useful shortcut keys to commonly used commands. Most of these commands work the same way that they do in Streets 98. Table B.3 defines each toolbar button.

TABLE B.3   TOOLBAR BUTTONS

Button	Description
	Click this button to zoom the map view out.
	Click this button to zoom in.
	Use the Zoom Slider button to open a slider control for zooming your view in and out.
	Use this tool to zoom in on a particular area of the map.
	Use this button to drag your view of the map in any direction.
	Click this button to display a pop-up menu of Map Flagging tools. Use the tools to mark the start and end points of your route.
	Click this button to mark a spot on the map with a highlighted circle.
	Click this button, and then click on the map to locate points of interest.
	Click this button to mark a spot on the map with an electronic pushpin. Click the drop-down arrow to display a palette of symbols you can use.

Moving and Zooming the Map

There are several ways to move round the map display and change the way you look at the map. Here are a couple of ways to move around the map:

- Move the mouse pointer to any edge or corner of the map area and the pointer takes the shape of a large arrow icon. Click to shift the map in the appropriate direction.
- Hold down the left mouse button over any edge or corner to scroll around the map.
- Click the Hand tool on the bottom toolbar; then drag on the map to move the map view.

> Trip Planner has two display modes for viewing the map: Road Map and Terrain Map. You can switch between them using the View menu. Choose View | Map Style, and choose the map display you want to view.

To zoom your view of the map in or out, try any of these methods:

- To zoom in closer, click the Zoom In button 🔍.
- To zoom out, click the Zoom Out button 🔍.
- Click the Zoom Slider tool 🔼 to display a slider gauge you can use to zoom in or out. Drag the arrow up or down the gauge, or click the up or down arrow buttons.
- Click the Selector tool ▣, and then draw an outline on the map around the area you want to look at more closely. Next, click inside the outline and your view is zoomed.
- Right-click the map and select Zoom; then choose which zoom direction from the submenu.
- Choose View | Zoom; then choose a zoom direction from the submenu.

> Trip Planner 98 uses the same map tools as Streets 98, and you'll find them on the Tools menu. For example, you can use the Measuring tool to quickly measure distance between two points, view the Map Legend, or use the Locator Map. To learn more about these features, turn to the section "Changing the Map Display" in Appendix A.

Finding Places

To quickly look up a place on the map, use the Find Place feature.

To Do: Finding Places on a Map

1. Click the Find Places button , or choose Find | Places. This opens the Find Place dialog box, as shown in Figure B.3.

FIGURE B.3

Use the Find Place dialog box to look up a place on the map.

2. Type as much of the place name as you can (the more specific you are, the faster Trip Planner can find the location).

3. Click the Find button and Trip Planner presents a list of matches, as shown in Figure B.4.

FIGURE B.4

Choose a place that best matches the location you're trying to find.

4. Select a place in the list and the Trip Planner map immediately locates the place, as shown in Figure B.5. To look up information about the place, click the Article button to view an article in the Travel Guide dialog box.

> To add the place to your Trip Digest, click the Link to Trip button in the Select a Place dialog box. To learn more about using the Trip Digest, see "Keeping a Trip Digest" later in this appendix.

5. Click OK to close the Select a Place dialog box. After you locate a place on the map, you can look up nearby attractions using the Points of Interest button ⭐ on the bottom toolbar.

▼

▼ **FIGURE B.5**

Trip Planner locates the place on the map.

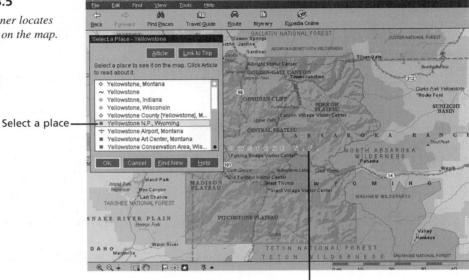

Select a place ────

The map shows you the location

Like Streets 98, you can mark places you find on the Trip Planner map with pushpins. For example, when you look up a place with the Find a Place dialog box, it's immediately marked with a pushpin.

You can mark a spot with a pushpin any time by clicking the Pushpin button ⓢ ▲ on the bottom toolbar, and then clicking the map. To add a note to the pushpin, click inside the Pushpin Note text box and start typing. To learn more about working with pushpins, see the section "Working with Pushpins" in Appendix A.

6. Click the button to open the Find Attractions dialog box, as shown in Figure B.6. Use the slider to set the distance you're willing to go to find nearby attractions (0–50 miles) and Trip Planner lists the nearby points of interest.

7. Select an attraction, and then click the one you want to locate and Trip Planner looks it up on the map.

8. Click the Article button to look up information in the Travel Guide to find out more about the selected attraction. (Learn more about using the Travel Guide in the next section.)

▼ 9. Click the Close button to exit the dialog box.

FIGURE B.6

You can easily locate nearby points of interest such as hotels, camping facilities, museums, and more.

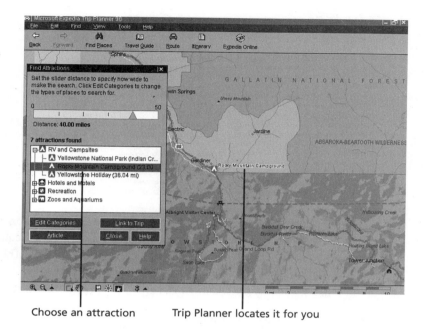

Choose an attraction   Trip Planner locates it for you

Trip Planner 98 uses the same restaurant and hotel guides as Streets 98. You'll find the ZAGATSURVEY Restaurant Guide and the Expedia Hotel Directory on the Find menu. In addition, you can look up campgrounds using Woodall's RV and Campsites Guide.

B

Using the Travel Guide

One of the best features of Trip Planner is its Travel Guide, an exhaustive collection of articles and other information about travel destinations all over the United States, Mexico, and Canada. You can access the Travel Guide from numerous places throughout the Trip Planner program.

To Do: Reading Information with the Travel Guide

1. Click the Travel Guide button [Travel Guide] on the navigation toolbar to access it directly. This opens the Travel Guide dialog box.
2. Start by clicking the drop-down list to select a country, state, or province you want to look up. In Figure B.7, information about Florida is displayed.

FIGURE B.7

Use the Travel Guide to look up articles about vacation destinations, find links to the Internet, and more.

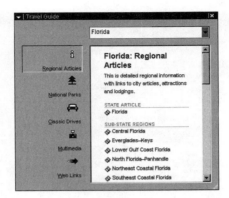

3. You have several options to pursue in the Travel Guide dialog box, and the following sections explain how to use each. As you explore each feature, you can always return to the Travel Guide's opening screen by clicking the Travel Guide button on the navigation toolbar.

4. Click the dialog box's Close (X) button to close the Travel Guide at any time.

To Do: Reading Articles

1. To read articles about a travel destination, click the Regional Articles button in the Travel Guide dialog box.

2. Select the region, city, or other topic you want to research.

3. To read an article in the list, click it. This opens the article and links to related articles, as shown in Figure B.8.

4. To follow a link, click it.

5. To locate the place discussed in the article, click the Locate button at the bottom of the dialog box.

> To add the place to your Trip Digest, click the Link to Trip button in the Select a Place dialog box. To learn more about using the Trip Digest, see "Keeping a Trip Digest" later in this appendix.

To Do: Finding Parks

1. To learn more about NationalParks in the area, click the National Parks button. The Travel Guide displays a list of national parks you can read more about.

2. Choose one from the list to open an article detailing information such as when the park is open, fees to get in, camping facilities, phone numbers, and more.

FIGURE B.8

Not only can you read articles, but each article also has links to related articles.

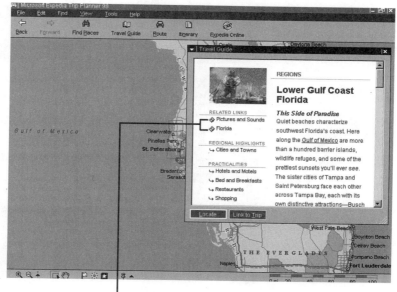

Links to other articles

Many of the articles you select include pictures or multimedia presentations. Learn more about this in the later section "Using Multimedia."

A unique feature of Trip Planner is Classic Drives, a collection of more than 100 self-guided historic or scenic road trips you can take, ranging from hour-long jaunts to week-long adventures. Classic Drives lets you look up articles, maps, and plan the route to take.

To Do: Finding Classic Drives

1. To use the feature, click the Classic Drives button in the Travel Guide dialog box. Trip Planner displays a list of Classic Drives for the state or province you selected when you first opened the Travel Guide.
2. Click a drive from the list to view an article.
3. To see the map and itinerary for the Classic Drive, click the Open Route button. The itinerary and the map detailing the drive appear behind the Travel Guide dialog box, as shown in Figure B.9.
4. To print the itinerary, choose File | Print | Route.
5. To return to the Travel Guide, click the Travel Guide button on the navigation toolbar.

Many of the articles found in the Travel Guide include pictures and multimedia sounds or photographs.

To Do

B

FIGURE B.9

*The Classic Drives fea-
ture lets you plan a trip
with a preset itinerary.*

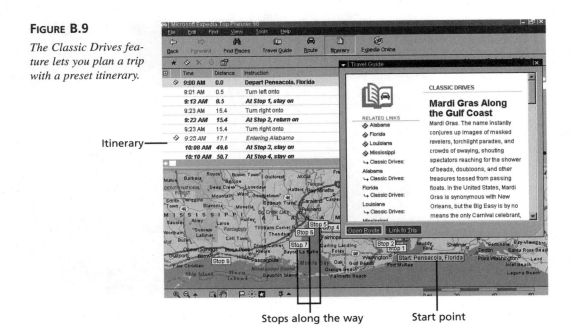

Itinerary——

Stops along the way   Start point

To Do: Using Multimedia

1. To look up multimedia resources about the region or state you selected, click the
   Multimedia button in the Travel Guide dialog box. This displays a list of pictures,
   sounds, and panoramic images you can view.

2. To view a multimedia item, select it from the list. The image opens in a full screen
   display in your Trip Planner window, as shown in Figure B.10.

3. Use the buttons at the bottom of the screen to view the picture, play a sound clip,
   return to the map, or return to the Travel Guide.

4. To return to the Travel Guide, click the Back button 🔙 on the navigation toolbar.
   This returns you to the point in the Travel Guide where you left off.

To Do: Finding Web Links

1. To look up more information about a travel destination on the Internet, click the
   Web Links button in the Travel Guide dialog box. This display a Web Links dialog
   box warning you you're about to connect to the Internet.

2. Click OK and connect to your Internet account. Internet Explorer opens to the
   Expedia Web site with the related Web page displayed, as shown in Figure B.11.

▼

FIGURE B.10

Use the Travel Guide's multimedia features to see pictures and hear sound clips about the location.

Click here to return to the Travel Guide

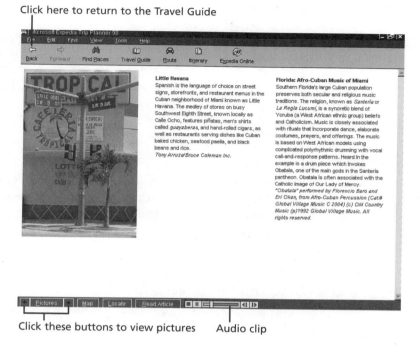

Click these buttons to view pictures   Audio clip

FIGURE B.11

You can connect to the Internet through the Travel Guide dialog box and find more information about a trip destination.

▼

B

▼
▲

3. From the Web page, you can explore more links and read more articles about the region, place, or city. To exit, close the Internet Explorer window and log off your Internet account.

> To use the Travel Guide's Web links, you must have an Internet account and Internet Explorer installed.

Planning a Trip

After you investigate the areas you want to visit using the Travel Guide, you're ready to plan your route. There are two ways to plan a route with Trip Planner. You can let the Route Wizard map out the route for you, or do it yourself directly on the map. Regardless of which method you use, the route is plotted on the map with a green line. After marking the route, Trip Planner calculates the distance, traveling time, and cost of fuel. You can then save the route and print it.

To Do: Using the Route Wizard

1. To open the Route Wizard, click the Route button ⭐ on the navigation toolbar. This opens the Route Wizard dialog box, as shown in Figure B.12.

2. Use the Route Wizard dialog box to enter the starting and ending points of your trip, and then click Next to continue. If you weren't specific enough in the names of the starting and ending points, a Select a Place box appears where you can narrow down the exact start or end location. (For example, you might need to enter the name of the state or province.)

FIGURE B.12

Use the Route Wizard to help you plot out your trip.

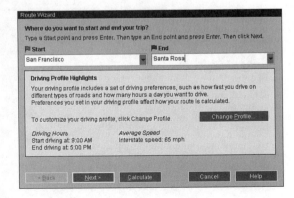

To change the details of your driving profile, such as the speed you like to travel, fuel costs, or driving hours, click the Change Profile button in the Route Wizard dialog box. Use the three tabs to change the settings that effect your trip, and then click OK.

3. In the next Route Wizard box, shown in Figure B.13, specify any stops you want to make along the route. By default, the Route Wizard assumes you're driving straight through unless you indicate what stops you want to make.

4. Enter a name, and then press Enter.

5. As with the Start and Stop locations, a Select a Place box might appear for you to confirm the exact location. Select it from the list and click OK. The stop is added to the list box.

6. Continue entering the stops you want to make; use the Move up or Move down buttons to change the order in which the stops are made.

7. To let Route Wizard determine the order, click the Best Order button.

FIGURE B.13

Enter any stops you want to make during the course of the trip.

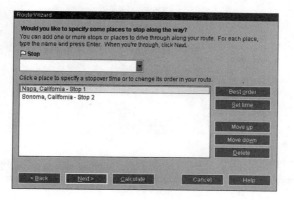

Use the Set time button in the Route Wizard dialog box to record a specific amount of time for each stop along the route you plan.

After arranging all the stops you want for the trip, click the Calculate button to recalculate all the stops and assigned times and adjust your schedule accordingly.

▼   8. The next Route Wizard dialog box, shown in Figure B.14, asks you to specify the
        kind of route to take. This determines the type of calculation Route Wizard per-
        forms. You can choose from the following:

        • Quickest Route   Select this option to have Route Wizard calculate the least
          amount of time needed to complete the trip.

        • Shortest Route   Select this option if you want Route Wizard to calculate the
          shortest distance between the Start and End points.

        • Use Preferred Roads   This option calculates a route that matches your
          Preferred Road settings. To change the settings, click the Preferred Roads
          button and make adjustments.

        • Set Route Segments Individually   Use this option to plan travel details for
          each segment in the trip. If you select this option, you must click Next and
          choose routing methods for each point in the journey.

FIGURE B.14

*Determine the kind
of route you want to
calculate.*

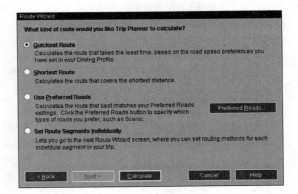

    9. Finally, click the Calculate button and Route Wizard calculates the route, including
       the departure time, arrival time, distance, fuel cost, and driving time. Figure B.15
       shows an example of the results.

   10. Click OK to exit the Route Wizard and view the trip itinerary and route on the
       map, as shown in Figure B.16.

   11. To return to the Route Wizard and make changes to the data you entered, click the
       Route button ⭐ and use the Next and Back buttons to change the details in each
       Route Wizard box.

   12. To print the route, choose File I Print I Route.

   13. To save the route, choose File I Save Trip and assign a name to the route.

   14. To retrieve it again later, choose File I Open Trip, and then locate and open the
▼   route file again.

FIGURE B.15

Route Wizard calculates the route details.

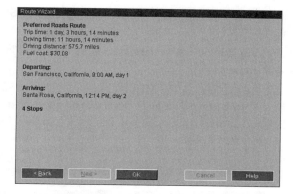

▼

FIGURE B.16

The Itinerary shows each stop along the route, and the map displays the route itself highlighted in green.

Itinerary——

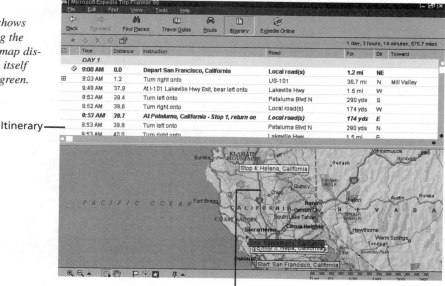

The highlighted route

▲ 15. To edit the route, choose Edit | Route, and then change the various settings using the Route Wizard dialog boxes.

Planning a Route Directly on the Map

Another way to plan a trip is to do so directly on the Trip Planner map.

To Do: Planning a Route on the Map

1. Start by selecting the Map Flags button 🏴 and select Set Start of Route.
2. Click the starting point of your trip, to mark it with a green icon on the map.

3. To add a stop, click the Map Flags button and select Add a Stop; then click the first stop on the trip.

4. Continue clicking stop points on the route, using the Map Flags button, until you reach the end destination.

5. At the end of the route, click the Map Flags button, choose Set End of Route, and click the final destination on the map. Figure B.17 shows a trip up and down the Napa Valley in California. Although you can't see it in this figure, the marked points are highlighted in color.

FIGURE B.17

Here's an example of a planned trip through the famous Napa Valley area of California.

Stops along the way

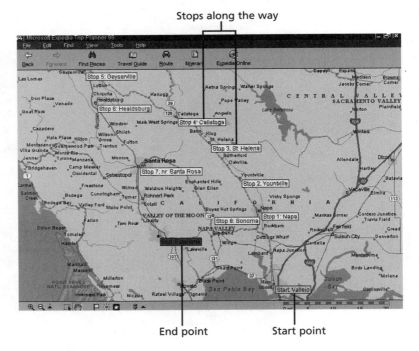

End point   Start point

6. When you're ready to have Trip Planner calculate the route, click the Map Flags button one last time and select Calculate Route. Trip Planner calculates the trip, displays the itinerary with all the details, and highlights the route on the map, as shown in Figure B.18.

7. To print the route, choose File | Print | Route.

8. To save the route, choose File | Save Trip and assign a name to the route.

9. To retrieve it again later, choose File | Open Trip, and then locate and open the route file again.

FIGURE B.18

Trip Planner's itinerary gives exact directions for reaching each stop point along the journey.

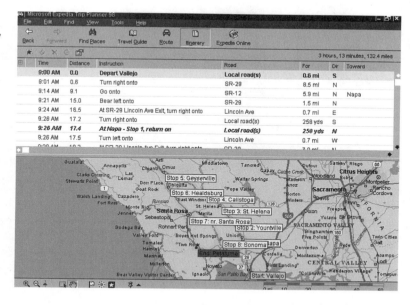

As you can see in Figure B.18, the Itinerary pane has its own toolbar and several fields showing the calculated results of the route.

To Do: Working with the Itinerary

1. Click any line on the Itinerary pane and the map below zooms in on the spot. Table B.4 explains how to use each Itinerary toolbar button.

TABLE B.4   ITINERARY TOOLBAR BUTTONS

Option	Description
★	Click this button to view attractions located near the route.
◇	Click this button to view related Travel Guide articles about the location.
✕	Click this button to delete the selected Itinerary item.
⊘	Use this button to change the amount of time spent at the place.
🖼	Click this button to customize the fields displayed in the Itinerary.

2. To customize the Itinerary, click the Customize button 🖼 to open the Itinerary Options dialog box, as shown in Figure B.19. Here you can change the font size used, and specify which columns appear on the Itinerary pane.

3. Click OK after making any changes.

FIGURE B.19

Use this dialog box to change which columns are displayed in the Itinerary pane.

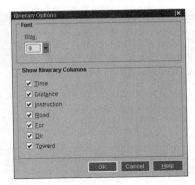

To customize the Trip Planner window, choose Tools | Options. This opens the Options dialog box where you can change the display of toolbars, fly-out menus, and whether distances are measured in miles or kilometers.

Keeping a Trip Digest

Another unique feature Trip Planner offers to help you plan your trip is the Trip Digest where you keep a log of all the places you want to stop and visit during the trip. Use this feature to record sightseeing stops you don't want to miss, articles you want to keep with the trip information, and plans for overnight stays. You can record any point along the route in the Trip Digest.

To Do: Working with the Trip Digest

1. Any time you find an article or point of interest to add to the Trip Digest, click the Link to Trip button. The items you add to the digest are kept at the bottom of the Itinerary pane. (You have to scroll down the Itinerary to see them.) Figure B.20 shows an example of Trip Digest entries.

2. When you've recorded everything you want to include, print the Trip Digest to take along with you; choose File | Print | Trip Digest. When you print the Trip Digest, all the listed places and articles you linked to the digest print, too.

You can remove a link you no longer want in the Trip Digest; select it and click the Delete button ☒ on the Itinerary toolbar.

FIGURE B.20

The Trip Digest has links to places you'd like to stop along the route.

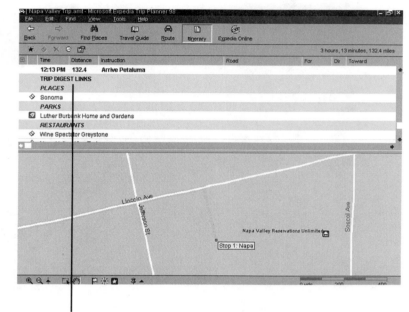

The Trip Digest starts here

B

APPENDIX C

Installing Works Suite 99

If you just purchased a new computer, it may have come to you with the latest version of Works Suite already installed. If so, you can stop reading this appendix and go to another part of the book to start learning about using the software.

On the other hand, if you're installing Works Suite for the first time, updating to the new version, or installing or removing a particular component of Works Suite, this appendix offers some useful information. Specifically, it covers how to

- Start the Setup program.
- Install one or more of the Works Suite applications.
- Remove a Works Suite application from your system.

Starting the Setup Process

The Works Suite software (which includes Works 4.5a, Word 97, Money 99, Works Calendar, Microsoft Graphics Studio Greetings 99, Encarta Encyclopedia 99, and Internet Explorer 4.01) comes on four CD-ROM discs, labeled Disc 1–Disc 4. Depending on which version you have (U.S. or Canadian), your set may include an additional disc for Microsoft Expedia Streets 98 or Trip Planner 98. These programs are installed separately from the Works Suite group.

To start the overall setup process, insert Disc 1 into your computer's CD-ROM drive. The Setup program should start automatically and display the Microsoft Works Suite initial Setup window, shown in Figure C.1.

If the Setup program doesn't start on its own, you can start it manually. Choose Start | Run. In the Open text box of the Run dialog box, type `d:\setup.exe`. (Replace the `d:` with the drive letter for your CD-ROM drive, if needed.) Click OK to start the Setup program.

FIGURE C.1

You can choose a Typical or Custom installation from this Microsoft Works Suite setup window.

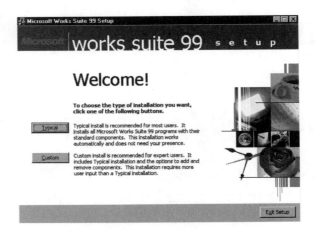

When installing, you can choose to install every component, called a Typical install, or just the ones you want, called a Custom install. Regardless of which installation type you choose, the setup program walks you through the steps necessary to install each program. You may be prompted from time to time to insert different discs into your CD-ROM drive; just follow the prompts as needed.

If you're using Windows 98 on your system, it should already have Internet Explorer 4.0 and its companion, Outlook Express, installed. You don't need to install them again from the Works Suite CD-ROMs.

Performing a Typical Install

If you plan to install all the Works Suite 99 programs, the Typical install is the best way to go. Click the Typical button on the Welcome window. This opens a window for entering your CD KEY. You'll find this 11-digit number on the back of your CD case. Enter the number, and then click Continue.

The next window you see lists all the programs to be installed, as shown in Figure C.2. If there's a program you don't want installed, deselect its check box; otherwise, click Continue. The setup program begins installing each Works Suite component. When the installation is complete, another window appears telling you the installation was a success. Click Finish. Now you're ready to use the programs.

FIGURE C.2

The window appears when you perform a Typical install.

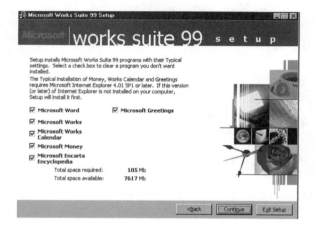

Performing a Custom Install

If you know you only want to install certain components of Works Suite, you can perform a Custom install. Click the Custom button in the Welcome window. This opens the window shown in Figure C.3. Here you can run separate setup utilities for each program. For example, to install Microsoft Greetings, click the Greetings button and follow the onscreen directions. With a custom installation, you can decide exactly which program elements to install. After each installation, you're returned to the window shown in Figure C.3, where you can choose to install another program.

C

FIGURE C.3

Use this window to perform a Custom install.

Microsoft's Expedia Streets 98 (U.S.) and Trip Planner 98 (Canada) programs are separate from the Works Suite programs. To install either of these programs, simply insert the disc and follow the onscreen prompts as directed. Like Works Suite 99, the setup program will walk you through the steps for installing the necessary files.

Removing a Works Suite Application

Even though hard disks have many times more storage space than they used to, there's still no use in having disk space filled with an application you're not using. For example, you may find that the Word Processor tool in Works can handle all your documents, so you don't need the more advanced features offered by Microsoft Word. You can remove the Word application—or any other Works Suite application—from your system using the Maintenance Mode window, as shown in Figure C.4.

You can also choose to add programs you didn't install the first time around, or reinstall program files you're having trouble with. Although the specifics for each of these tasks vary slightly, follow these steps to get yourself started:

To Do: Starting the Maintenance Mode

▼ To Do

1. Insert Works Suite Disc 1 in your computer's CD-ROM drive. The Setup program should start automatically and display the Microsoft Works Suite initial Setup window. If the Setup program doesn't start on its own, choose Start I Run. In the Open text box of the Run dialog box, type d:\setup.exe. (Replace the d: with the drive letter for your CD-ROM drive, if needed.) Click OK to start the Setup program.

FIGURE C.4

Use this window to make changes to your program's installations.

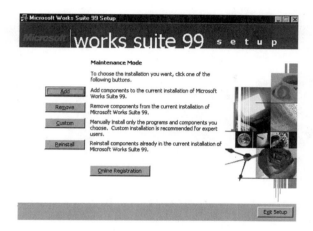

2. To remove a program, click the Remove button, and then click the button representing the program you want to remove. Follow the onscreen prompts as needed.

3. To add a program, click the Add button and select the program you want to add.

4. To reinstall a component, click the Reinstall button and choose which program you want to install again. This lets you copy files to your computer and overwrite any bad files with which you might be experiencing trouble.

5. You can even register your copy of Works Suite 99 from this window; click the Online Registration button and follow the prompts.

6. After adding, removing, or reinstalling, you may be returned to the Maintenance Mode window. Click the Exit Setup button to close the Microsoft Works Suite Maintenance Mode window.

There's an alternative way to start the process for removing an application. This method is simpler for some of the applications, such as Greetings Workshop. Choose Start | Settings | Control Panel. Double-click the Add/Remove Programs icon in the Control Panel window. Scroll through the list of applications on the Install/Uninstall tab of the Add/Remove Programs Properties dialog box, and click the application you want to remove. Then click the Add/Remove button to display the screen or dialog box that provides the button for uninstalling the application.

C

INDEX